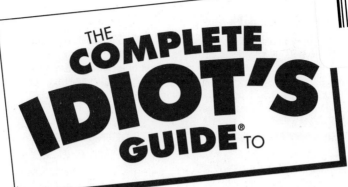
THE
COMPLETE
IDIOT'S
GUIDE® TO

Christianity

by Jeffrey B. Webb, Ph.D.

ALPHA

A member of Penguin Group (USA) Inc.

International Standard Book Number: 1-59257-176-X
Library of Congress Catalog Card Number: 2003115224

06   05   04   8   7   6   5   4   3   2   1

Interpretation of the printing code: The rightmost number of the first series of numbers is the year of the book's printing; the rightmost number of the second series of numbers is the number of the book's printing. For example, a printing code of 04-1 shows that the first printing occurred in 2004.

Printed in the United States of America

Most Alpha books are available at special quantity discounts for bulk purchases for sales promotions, premiums, fund-raising, or educational use. Special books, or book excerpts, can also be created to fit specific needs.

For details, write: Special Markets, Alpha Books, 375 Hudson Street, New York, NY 10014.

Publisher: *Marie Butler-Knight*
Product Manager: *Phil Kitchel*
Senior Managing Editor: *Jennifer Chisholm*
Senior Acquisitions Editor: *Randy Ladenheim-Gil*
Development Editor: *Suzanne LeVert*
Senior Production Editor: *Billy Fields*
Copy Editor: *Amy Borrelli*
Illustrator: *Richard King*
Cover/Book Designer: *Trina Wurst*
Indexer: *Heather McNeil*
Layout/Proofreading: *Ayanna Lacey, John Etchison*

Contents at a Glance

Contents

Foreword

A woman kissing icons of Christ and St. Nicholas; teenagers dancing ecstatically—but in church; a man stammering with excitement in what seems to be a foreign language but what is understood to be the Holy Spirit speaking through him; dark-robed men chanting the psalms; suburbanites rising before dawn to study and pray; professionals filling the trays of hungry neighbors in a basement soup kitchen; people maintaining vegetarian diets; pilgrims fingering beads of the rosary at a shrine where the Virgin appeared; adults being immersed three times; citizens protesting the American military action in Iraq, visiting AIDS patients with meals, both applauding and condemning the consecration of an openly gay man as a bishop; an enthusiastic congregation shouting approval to an even more enthusiastic preacher whose sermon grows and bursts into song; young and old alike seeking healing through anointing and the laying on of hands …

What could these and numerous others have in common? They do not agree on the organization of their communities of faith, on the veneration of the Virgin Mary and the saints, on the role of bishops or the pope, on the place of women in leadership positions, but they share communion bread and wine in great ceremonial splendor as well as in simplicity and silence. Who are they? Jeffrey Webb knows who they are and introduces them to us—the amazingly diverse, colorful, sometimes disappointing and sometimes encouraging people called the Christians.

Given its title, in the now well-known series of books for "idiots," one might think such a guide was intended only for outsiders, those without any personal or formal knowledge of the Christian faith, tradition, and its history and many expressions here in America. However, when you have worked through this lucid, witty, and insightful overview, you will have become an insider. You will have not only an accurate idea of what Christianity teaches, how Christians organize themselves and worship, even how they both agree and disagree with each other—in both the simplicity and complexity of all these—but you will also have the perspective of someone within the Christian tradition. An insider himself, Professor Webb, who teaches at Huntington College, is a member of the Presbyterian Church in the United States, serving as an ordained elder in his home congregation.

I suppose I am myself an insider, too, as a scholar, a professor at a large public college, a priest in the Orthodox Church, and yes, a baptized, believing, and I think practicing Christian. As an "insider," more often than not I find that even academic specialists don't always get it right when it comes to the precise feel, touch, taste, even smell of lived Christianity. This is especially true regarding my own part of the Christian churches, the Eastern Orthodox. Webb not only gets Orthodox Christianity right, he gets all the other many expressions exactly right as well, from the Roman Catholics to the Protestant "mainline" (the Lutherans, Episcopalians, Methodists, among others, and his own Reformed churches) to the radical Reformation churches (Mennonites, Hutterites, Brethren) as well as the many varieties of Baptist, Evangelical, and Holiness churches. Why is it that these churches, located along the once prestigious "mainline" of the old Pennsylvania Railroad, have fallen prey to the passage of time, just as this great line has? Why is it that the U.S. is home to so many religious groups, "American originals" such as the Mormons, Christian Scientists, Unitarians, Jehovah's Witnesses, and the Seventh-day Adventists? Another home-grown and powerful group, the Pentecostals, appear to be the coming form of Christianity both here and in the booming Christian communities of Africa and Asia.

This guide, no pun intended, will be a revelation to readers who know these groups only as labels. It will make readers insiders themselves to the surprising people here and worldwide who differ in many things but are held together by the person of Jesus Christ. It informs but more importantly welcomes you into the communities, the worship and work, the beliefs and stories of the Christians. One early Christian named Philip, when asked if anything good could come from Nazareth, Jesus' hometown, said, "Come and see." (Gospel of John 1:45–46) The reader is similarly invited here. You will experience Christianity as you never have before.

—Rev. Michael Plekon, Ph.D.

Rev. Michael Plekon, Ph.D., has taught courses on the history of Christianity, the sociology and history of religion in America, and others for twenty years at Baruch College of the City University of New York. He specializes in several aspects of contemporary Christianity, including the Danish theologian Søren Kierkegaard and twentieth-century Russian émigré theologians such as Paul Evdokimov, Mother Maria Skobtsova, Alexander Schmemann, and Nicolas Afanasiev. A priest in the Orthodox Church, he has also served in the ordained ministry for over twenty years.

Introduction

You can be excused if you're baffled about the Christian faith. Sometimes it confuses me, too. I can't count the number of times I had to grab an encyclopedia or hand-book, or scroll through a website, to find a short description of Eastern Orthodoxy, Quakerism, or Lutheranism. In fact, when he learned I was working on this book, one of my Ph.D.-holding colleagues asked what a Methodist believes.

This book tries to answer two questions: (1) Why are there so many different groups under the umbrella of Christianity? and (2) How do they differ from one to the next? The answers are not easy to state in simple terms. If they were, you wouldn't find so many long books that attempt to describe the various factors at work. Maybe we shouldn't be so surprised. Christianity is the chief means by which a billion people find answers to the most important questions of life: How did we get here? What's the purpose of life? Why is there so much suffering in the world? Where are we headed? Questions so deep and powerful result in a very complicated set of beliefs and practices.

So in your hands you have a snapshot of Christianity, not only of its different parts, but also how the different parts come together to make a larger whole. Keep in mind that Christianity is a complex faith and snapshots tend to flatten out the picture. And keep in mind that Christianity is a moving target that changes with each passing month and year. Needless to say, snapshots have to be satisfied with a picture frozen in time. But enough hemming and hawing. We're ready to tackle the big stuff here, starting with the question, How does it all fit together?

Think of how a language works. Languages have a common root and numerous branches. The roots of the English language lie in ancient times, with Latin, and then later with the Germanic tongues spoken by tribes that came into contact with the Roman Empire. English evolved from Anglo-Saxon to Middle English after con-tact with the French, but then morphed into the Shakespearean dialect we know from *Hamlet* and *Midsummer Night's Dream*. Today's English differs in shape and content from the English spoken and written in the past. That's to say nothing of the many dialects and accents that you'll discover as you move from London to Manchester, and from New York to Melbourne. Or even from Boston to Brooklyn, and from Wheeling to San Francisco, for that matter.

With languages, you'll find experts who write dictionaries and grammatical guides to explain the proper mode of expression, or to bracket the acceptable range of mean-ings. You'll also find purists who complain about the dialects and accents that distort the form of language they've come to see as correct. But try as they might, they can't contain the changes to language as it moves through time and meets new environments.

In the same way, Christianity has an overall unity, but dialects and accents give it a diverse appearance. The beginnings of Christianity are actually more clear than the beginnings of language. Jesus Christ started the church 2,000 years ago and left in place a group of apostles to spread the faith. But soon enough, Christianity left its home in Galilee and Judea and found new destinations in Asia Minor, Greece, North Africa, and Europe. These new settings did the same thing to Christianity as new settings do to language. Lots of adjustments made Christianity look a little different in Rome than it did in Antioch or Jerusalem, just as English sounds a bit different in Boston, Brooklyn, New Orleans, and Minneapolis.

This book explains why Christianity has branches, like Eastern Orthodoxy, Roman Catholicism, Lutheranism, Episcopalianism, Methodism, and Pentecostalism. It also details what makes these branches different from each other. But keep in mind that if you speak English, you can still understand what most people are saying in London, Manchester, New York, and Melbourne, despite their dialect. That's true for Christianity as well. You can find some pretty sizeable differences out there on the denominational landscape, but you'll also recognize many common features as you move from Catholic cathedral to Baptist church to Quaker meetinghouse.

So who gets to say which version is proper and correct? Many have come forward, like so many grammar teachers who try to set their pupils straight on the English language. Christianity has a few "dictionaries," like the Apostle's Creed and even the Bible itself. But there's no correct and proper form of Christianity, just like there's no correct and proper dialect in which English is spoken. There are older forms, and there are dominant forms. But to speak of a correct form is to replay the quest of Don Quixote. Perhaps the basic unity that you can find amid the great diversity of denominations is enough.

Here's What You'll Find Inside

This book is divided into six parts.

Part 1, "A World of Christians," begins the search for answers to why there are so many different versions of Christianity. You'll be surprised to learn that the word "denomination" applied only to Christian groups in the United States for a long period of history. That is, until other nations decided to finally legalize religious diversity.

Part 2, "The Universal Church," goes to the Holy Lands and to Rome to discover the roots of the Christian faith. But it doesn't stop there; it describes how the most ancient versions of Christianity adapted to the New World. Here you'll get acquainted with Eastern Orthodoxy, which is perhaps the most traditional of all the denominations in the United States. And be ready for some surprises as we answer the question, What's American about American Catholicism?

Part 3, "Liturgical Protestantism," starts the Protestant ball rolling with a discussion of the Episcopal, Lutheran, and Reformed churches. All the classic Protestant beliefs are here: biblical authority, justification by grace through faith, and the priesthood of all believers. I'll even try to explain how Protestants can invite change and still be tradition-minded, with their formal liturgies (forms of worship) and their written confessions of faith.

Part 4, "The Pietist Churches," explores the denominations that bear the imprint of Pietism, a religious movement that taught the importance of a conversion (or born-again) experience, a deeply personal relationship with Jesus, and a higher standard of personal morality. This is where you'll find coverage of the Mennonite, Amish, Brethren, Baptist, Methodist, and Quaker churches. It's also the place in the book where you'll begin to see lots of African American Christians.

Part 5, "Homegrown Denominations," moves on to the denominations that started in the United States, like the Adventists, Jehovah's Witnesses, Mormons, and Christian Scientists. These believers trace their histories back to one or another inspired leader who caught a vision and started a movement. You'll learn that visions are gender-neutral; for every Joseph Smith Jr., William Miller, and William Seymour, and there's a Mother Ann Lee, a Mary Baker Eddy, and an Aimee Semple McPherson.

Part 6, "Christianity Outside the Lines," takes the measure of several broad movements that span the denominational landscape. You'll find out why some Christians aren't satisfied to describe themselves as Baptist, Methodist, or Episcopalian—they want to add fundamentalist, evangelical, or charismatic to the name. Want to know the difference between a Methodist and an *evangelical* Methodist, or a Catholic and a Catholic *charismatic*? You'll find out here.

Extras ...

My goal is to make your learning experience as fun and inviting as possible. So along the way, you'll find lots of sidebars that contain a wealth of information. These self-contained boxes, located in the margins alongside the text, include such things as ...

Steeple Talk

This sidebar contains definitions of words that Christians across the denominations will use from time to time, but may be unfamiliar to you.

Edifications

This sidebar adds tidbits of information about different subjects to the mix, which should add some color and texture to the parade of individuals and movements that you'll encounter in the text.

Everybody Said Amen

This sidebar gives you some handy ways of remembering movements and denominations, and reveals insights that will help you get to the bottom of complicated and highly technical matters.

Lo and Behold

This sidebar gives me the opportunity to address myths, misconceptions, distortions, and errors associated with different Christian groups, and to help you avoid common pitfalls in dealing with various topics in Christianity.

Acknowledgments

Lots of people helped me to research and write this book, so I'd like to take the time to thank them by name. This is my first *Complete Idiot's Guide*, and I could not have seen it through to completion without the patience and good advice of my agent, Jessica Faust, and my first editors, Randy Ladenheim-Gil and Suzanne LeVert. The editorial staff at Alpha Books, a division of Pearson Education, went to great lengths to transform my rough drafts into a readable book, and they deserve much more credit than I for making it happen.

My friends at Huntington College helped me work out some thorny problems and even struggled through some early drafts. In no particular order, they are Jake Sikora, Morris Davis, Robert Leach, John Sanders, Tom Bergler, Todd Martin, David Woodruff, Paul Michelson, Brett Bailey, and Kevin Miller. Thanks to Dwight Brautigam for making research funds available, and to several students who helped me more than they can ever know: Danielle Villafana, Joni Michaud, Dwight Simon, and Tara Enck. I would also like to thank Sister Lucy Marie Vega, Eric Shoening, and Randy Neumann for their kind assistance in locating suitable images. Special thanks to my children, Christian and Aaron, for enduring my long absences, and to my wife, Jill, for proving a cheerful partner. They remain, as ever, my greatest blessing.

Trademarks

All terms mentioned in this book that are known to be or are suspected of being trademarks or service marks have been appropriately capitalized. Alpha Books and Penguin Group (USA) Inc. cannot attest to the accuracy of this information. Use of a term in this book should not be regarded as affecting the validity of any trademark or service mark.

Part 1

A World of Christians

Before we try to figure out why there are so many different kinds of Christians, we'll first have to find out what a Christian is. Surprisingly, this is not an easy thing to do. But don't lose heart. The vast majority of Christians share a common worldview that explains the nature of God and God's relationship to humankind through the person of Jesus Christ.

In the following chapters, you'll come to terms with the major factors that lead to branching of the Christian faith. Much of the diversity of Christianity is the result of Christians coming into contact with new people with different ideas for how to practice the faith. All the factors that produce diversity are magnified in the United States, perhaps the world's most permissive environment for the creation of new denominations. And that leads naturally to the question: Is the United States a Christian nation?

Defining Christianity

In This Chapter

- ◆ Consider why it is worth learning more about Christianity
- ◆ Hear a little about the background of the word "Christian"
- ◆ Learn the different ways that Christianity is defined
- ◆ Discover what unifies Christians across denominations

Christianity is the world's largest religion, no matter how you measure it. Nearly a third of the world's population can be labeled Christian, and Christians can be found in every one of the countries listed by the United Nations. In the last generation, Christianity grew by almost 800 million people. However, this largest of the world's religions is also incredibly complex, with thousands and thousands of subdivisions of the larger Christian community. Although Christians often use the label Christian to identify themselves, they freely use other labels as well, such as Catholic, Orthodox, Lutheran, and Baptist. And new subdivisions surface every day, because Christianity keeps changing in the face of new circumstances, new environments, and new problems.

This welter of groups may bring you to the point of despair if your goal is to understand the world's largest and most dynamic religion. With this in mind, the question becomes: What makes all of these groups Christian?

In other words, what—if anything—is the "essence" of the Christian faith? Believe it or not, this question gives the experts a collective headache. For 2,000 years, scholars, theologians, religious officials, and others have been arguing over how to decide which groups merit the label. My purpose in this chapter is to give you a sense of how the experts define Christianity so that we can then focus on similarities and differences among the major Christian groups later in the book.

Why Care?

It's inevitable. Today, tomorrow, or someday soon you will come across a reference to a Christian group you've never heard of in a newspaper, magazine, or television program. The group may sound vaguely familiar to you, or it may feel like someone is playing a trick by randomly arranging religious-sounding words. A recent *Newsweek* article on religion and the U.S. presidency (March 10, 2003) mentions four different Christian denominations, and uses terms like "ultrafundamentalist," "Calvinistic," "nondenominational," and "evangelical" as if the reader knows their meanings. I assume that you have heard of Roman Catholics and Baptists, and may even know a little about their main beliefs and practices, but I'm guessing that you don't know how Catholics differ from Greek Orthodox, or how Baptists differ from Methodists.

It's natural if you're deeply confused about the wide array of groups within Christianity, or if you don't know the difference between a fundamentalist and an evangelical. The Christian faith keeps growing and growing, and it keeps splintering as well. According to David Barrett's *World Christian Encyclopedia*, more than 22,000 denominations vie for the allegiance of the world's 2 billion Christians. Each year, 270 new denominations appear on the scene worldwide, some as a result of the planned segmentation of existing denominations, still others the product of visionary prophets and ministers. When confronted with these realities, the mind goes numb. Then again, what does it matter anyway? A Christian is a Christian, right?

> **Edifications**
>
> Five new Christian denominations are created each week throughout the world. The vast majority can be found in regions of the world where Christianity is a relative newcomer, such as sub-Saharan Africa; Oceania; and central, south, east, and southeast Asia.

Christianity and World Politics

It matters if you want to understand how politics and religion shape the world. If you read the *Newsweek* article mentioned above, you can get a general sense of how Christianity shapes the outlook of American presidents, but you miss out on quite a lot if you fail to see the significance of the fact that George H. W. Bush is an Episcopalian, and his son George W. Bush is an evangelical Methodist. (Speaking of Episcopalians, would it enrich your experience of the Mel Gibson film *Signs* to know that his character was not only an ex-minister, but also an ex-minister in the Episcopal Church? It might if you knew a little about Episcopalians.)

The most talked about book on Christianity in the last several years is Philip Jenkins's *The Next Christendom: The Coming of Global Christianity* (New York: Oxford University Press, 2002). Jenkins believes that worldwide shifts in religion, especially Christianity's explosive growth in Latin America, Africa, and Asia, "are the most significant, and even the most revolutionary" changes in the contemporary world. He cites the outbreak of conflict between Muslims and Christians in Indonesia, Nigeria, and the Philippines—and the interest of the United States in these conflicts—as evidence of the importance of religion in early twenty-first-century geopolitics.

Jenkins's book highlights the differences between the Christianity practiced in Europe and North America, and the Christianity practiced in other parts of the world. In very general terms, Christians in the industrialized West seek political influence, economic success, and creature comforts, while their spiritual brothers and sisters in the southern hemisphere live out a faith with a stronger sense of God's presence in everyday life. For example, belief in miracles, demonic possession, and prophetic visions is stronger among African and Latin American Christians than among Christians in Europe and even North America. Since Christians are more conservative and even anti-modern in these respects, the fear is that religious differences will merge with resentments over economic disparities, planting seeds for a new generation of international conflicts.

I'll give you one more example of how the differences among Christians can matter quite a bit. The *Left Behind* series of books by Tim LaHaye regularly trounces its competition on *The New York Times* bestseller lists. These books, including the recent titles *The Remnant* and *Armageddon: Cosmic Battle of the Ages* (Carol Stream, Illinois: Tyndale House Publishers, 2003), dramatize the events foretold in the books of Daniel and Revelation in the Bible. Remarkably, LaHaye purports to represent a Christian view of the end times, and yet his version would not be accepted by all Christian denominations.

A Christian Nation?

The truth is, it's essential to know something about Christian denominations in today's world. In the United States, Christianity touches on nearly every aspect of public life. It's hard to watch a whole football game on television without seeing a running back or wide receiver kneeling in prayer after a touchdown. Allusions to the Bible abound in films and popular music, and biblical phrases are emblazoned on billboards and T-shirts. As the constitutional debates on the separation of church and state continue to rage, American culture nevertheless remains infused with Christian themes and images.

Even if you yourself do not consider yourself a Christian, you can't deny the importance of Christianity. In fact, Christianity is likely to become even more important in the future. The relationship between the United States. and the Middle East, east Asia, and south Asia continues to intensify, and most of the people living in these regions believe that the United States is a "Christian nation." Although this may not be completely accurate, such perceptions are hard to shake, especially when they're reinforced by polling data: Eight-six percent of Americans identify themselves as Christian. Furthermore, every U.S. president in the twentieth century professed Christian belief or maintained membership in a Christian church.

If you know more about the shape of Christianity in the United States, and the relationship between Christianity and other world religions, it is less likely that you will be misled by catchy concepts like "clash of civilizations" that pretend to explain the complex and evolving relationship between the West and other regions of the world, particularly the Middle East. You might even get a better take on the question of whether the United States is, in fact, a Christian nation. In short, being an educated person means knowing more about Christianity today.

Lo and Behold

Be careful when you encounter numbers that claim to describe religious affiliation, religious devotion, or religious practice. Although 93 percent of American have a Bible in their home, only 54 percent read it more than once a month, according to a 1996 Gallup poll. Lots of families have a Bible around, but this doesn't necessarily translate into actual reading hours. Millions of Bibles are actually family heirlooms that are passed from generation to generation.

The Invisible Church

So if you're ready to learn more about Christianity, you've got your work cut out for you. Simply giving Christianity a definitive (ahem) definition has proved to be an insurmountable task that has frustrated countless experts. At first blush, the task seems easy enough; Christianity is a set of beliefs and practices that Jesus taught his followers, as recorded in the Bible. For more than 2,000 years, however, Jesus' followers have squabbled over how to interpret his teachings, how to apply his teachings to everyday life, how to tell the difference between a genuine Christian and a poser, how to promote the Christian faith among nonbelievers, and a host of other issues. Today, if you look up Christianity in a half-dozen dictionaries and encyclopedias, you're likely to read a half-dozen different accounts. The description of Christianity given by a Roman Catholic priest will be different from the description given by a Baptist minister or a scholar of religion.

For the time being, we should set aside the idea of defining Christianity as a whole, and instead focus on the more narrow issue of what (or who) is a Christian. Sometime during the first century, people who followed Jesus were called Christians. The Book of Acts in the New Testament actually says, "The disciples were called Christians first at Antioch." (Acts 11:26) The Acts of the Apostles is really a history of the early church. At this point, Christianity began to enlist non-Jewish converts. Before this time, there was no need to distinguish Jesus' followers from Jews who followed other Jewish prophets. Once Jesus' teaching skipped outside of Judaism, however, a new label was needed.

The label Christian contains the word "Christ," and the use of this word to identify the non-Jewish followers of Jesus says quite a lot. Christ is the Greek word for "messiah," which is the Hebrew word for "anointed." Jesus' early Jewish followers (like, say, Peter, Paul, and John) believed that Jesus was anointed by God to be the deliverer promised in the prophetic books of the Old Testament, especially the Book of Isaiah. Greek followers of Jesus at Antioch and elsewhere picked up this line of thinking and the designation Christian stuck. Throughout the first three centuries, the label Christian was applied to those people who followed Jesus' teachings and considered him to be the Son of God.

The Christian label worked for a while, but then, in 380 C.E., things got a lot more complicated. In this year, Christianity became the official religion of the Roman Empire. Now *everyone* under Roman dominion was required to profess Christianity, including those who were not all that impressed either with Jesus' teachings or his claims to be the messiah. As a consequence, the label Christian lost much of its original meaning. No longer did it identify a group of people set apart from the rest of society by their commitment to Jesus. People with no desire to be Christians professed Christianity anyway in order to enjoy the benefits of the Roman Empire, or to avoid its rather severe penalties.

Church officials and theologians responded to this mess by using two terms that have survived to the present day, namely …

♦ The visible church.

♦ The *invisible church*.

Under the term "the visible church," religious leaders lumped together all those who live in a country where Christianity is the official religion, those who are included in lists of church members, or those who perform deeds in the name of the Christian faith. But these leaders went on to say that some of these Christians in the physical sense may not be truly Christian in the spiritual sense. They may claim to be Christians, but never enjoy the earthly blessings of Jesus in this life or earn the reward of heavenly blessings in the hereafter.

All those who are Christians in the spiritual sense are included in the "invisible church." Today, the concept of an invisible church can be a useful caution to those who wish to make hard and fast judgments about who is and who is not a Christian. In this way, we might be gently reminded that such a determination is best left to God.

In Search of Christian Essentials

Not all Christians like to use the visible/invisible distinction. Some think it violates Jesus' teachings and the apostles' writings, which stress the unity of the spiritual and physical realms. They also object that the idea of an invisible church ignores the fact that the church was meant to be a physical institution with real people doing real things. Now we are back at square one, trying to decide what groups of people who call themselves Christian really merit the label Christian.

Maybe Jesus' own teachings can rescue us. During his time on earth, Jesus roamed through Galilee and Judea telling others what it would take—spiritually and physically—to follow his teachings, as recorded in the Gospels of Matthew, Mark, Luke, and John. Throughout history, Christian churches have considered these Gospels to be the authoritative record of Jesus' teachings and have used them to sort out differences of opinion about matters of Christian faith and practice.

In Jesus' many sermons, parables, and conversations, he stressed the importance of belief. In John 3:16, Jesus said, "God so loved the world that he gave his one and only Son, that whoever believes in him shall not perish, but have eternal life." By the way, this is the very same verse that you see written on poster boards and displayed at football games. In Matthew 10:32, Jesus said that if you acknowledge your belief in him before others, he would acknowledge you before his Father in heaven.

But Jesus also wanted his followers to adhere to the commandments and to deny themselves certain earthly pleasures. In one conversation, a rich young man asked Jesus what good thing he must do to have eternal life. Jesus told him he must obey the commandments of the Old Testament. (Matthew 19:16) The man replied that he had already done this, and wanted to know what he still lacked. Jesus answered that, in order to be perfect, he needed to sell his possessions, give all his money to the poor, and follow him. This was a tough message to hear. Jesus required a radical commitment. He wanted some evidence that the young man had made Jesus his Lord.

Yet it wasn't just a matter of doing good deeds. Jesus bitterly attacked the religious leaders of the age who wanted public recognition of their spirituality. He called them hypocrites for putting up a show of being religious despite harboring evil within their hearts, especially the Pharisees, a group of teachers who fiercely defended Jewish law and tradition. According to Jesus, the Pharisees made it a point to practice their faith in public so as to win the admiration of the common people. Jesus taught that purity of the heart was more important in the cosmic scheme of things than fulfilling the letter of the Jewish law.

Such a lesson was the general idea behind the Sermon on the Mount, probably Jesus' most well-known set of teachings. (Matthew 5–7) He told the gathered crowd to follow the commandments, but to do it with purity of heart. For example, we are told not to commit adultery *and* to avoid secretly lusting after someone else's spouse. Both the act of adultery and the secret lust can result in exclusion from the kingdom of heaven. Near the end of the sermon, Jesus claims that only those who do the will of his Father deserve eternal blessings.

Jesus wanted his followers not only to believe in him, but also to experience an inner transformation. He asked them to believe that he was who he said he was, namely the Son of God. Going further, they were to demonstrate inner purity, to be humble, unselfish, patient, kind, and so on. Having said all of this, those who believe in Jesus and experience an inner transformation could still be denied membership in a number of today's churches. That's because some churches ask their members to accept certain doctrines or perform certain religious obligations beyond what Jesus actually taught.

Is There a Litmus Test?

There's a short and a long answer to the question, "Is there a litmus test?" The short answer is no, at least not in the present day. The long answer is more interesting. The long answer points us toward the larger purposes of this book, which involve trying to understand the reasons why there are so many Christian denominations.

The long answer begins by recognizing that Christianity requires fellowship, and fellowship requires the formation of a community. Communities have general norms, values, symbols, and so on that enable their members to share a common experience. When Christianity was more or less universal (say, during the late Roman Empire or medieval Europe), the terms of unity were established. Even then, however, the universal church could not claim in good faith to serve as an umbrella for all Christians. Since the Reformation, clearly, no denomination can pretend that it has the correct recipe for the Christian faith or for setting the terms of inclusion.

The Seoul Anglican Cathedral in Seoul, South Korea, is part of the Anglican Communion, a worldwide alliance of nation-based denominations with historic ties to the Church of England.

(Photo courtesy of Seoul Anglican Cathedral)

In the face of this diversity, the vast majority of Christians have come to accept the existence of different expressions of the Christian faith. Most denominations teach that their procedures for church membership so not confer eternal life in heaven, and that failure to accept them results in eternal damnation in hell. The issues that do have eternal bearing are thought to be matters best left to individual Christians in their relation to God.

Nevertheless, inclusion within a particular church, as opposed to within the universal church of all Christians, requires acceptance of certain rules, symbols, doctrines, and maybe lots of other things as well. After all, Jesus taught that the church has both spiritual *and* physical aspects. After Jesus' time on earth, religious officials began to use the term "universal church" to identify the spiritual aspects of the church, and the term "particular church" to describe its physical aspects. The particular church extends the blessings of fellowship and Christian nurture, but with a catch. The believer must submit to the discipline of a group and support the physical and doctrinal elements that the group has determined to be helpful in guiding believers on their spiritual journey.

So the long answer comes down to this: Each denomination creates its own litmus test, which is a phenomenon that I will describe in the remainder of the book. However, it is important to remember throughout that these tests are tests for inclusion in the particular church, not the universal, spiritual church. It can't be said often enough that inclusion in the universal church is a matter that lies beyond human determination.

Mere Christianity

Most practicing Christians belong to the particular church in the sense that they actively participate in the everyday life of a congregation. They regularly worship, pray, fellowship, and take the sacraments with other Christians. It might be said that the vast majority of Christians subscribe to a comprehensive worldview as well. A worldview is an outlook on life that does a number of things: It provides explanations for the origins of the universe, gives life a sense of meaning and purpose, helps to make life-changing decisions, and answers the deep questions of human existence. The following sketch presents an example of how the Christian worldview is commonly formulated.

St. Augustine wrote The City of God *from 413 to 426 C.E., which is the first and clearest description of the Christian worldview. This image of Augustine the teacher is a detail from Benozzo Gozzoli's cycle at the Church of Saint Augustine in San Gimignano, Italy (1465 C.E.).*

(Photo courtesy of James J. O'Donnell)

To start with, Christians believe they are part of a cosmic struggle between good and evil. This struggle began after God created the universe and called it good. In the heavens, God gave his angels the ability to make their own decisions, which brought one of them, Satan, to act on his ambition to become as powerful as God. Satan thus introduced evil into creation. In response, God expelled Satan from the heavens, thus bringing evil to earth. Most Christians believe that this occurrence explains the origins of the universe and the presence of evil.

In time, God created men and women with the same ability to make their own decisions. God put them in paradise and gave them a few simple rules to obey, but when tempted by Satan, they succumbed to their desire for godlike knowledge. As a consequence God banished them from paradise and required them to work for a living. In addition, they were made to experience suffering, and eventually die; now men and women would not live forever on earth, but would die a physical death and enter the spiritual realm. Once there, they would remain separated from God for all eternity. Humankind offended God, and nothing people could do on their own would make up for it. These consequences are severe, but God is merciful. God provided a means by which people's sins can be eliminated.

Edifications

The phrase "mere Christianity" is taken from the title of a book by C. S. Lewis (1898–1963), a member of the Church of England and a professor at Cambridge University. Lewis's book updates Augustine's effort to explain the Christian worldview in response to modern criticism.

The second person in the trinity, Jesus, took the form of a man and offered himself as a once-and-for-all sacrifice (the other two persons being God the Father and God the Holy Spirit). Jesus' suffering, death, and resurrection enabled people to escape the prospect of an eternal spiritual death. Simply by acknowledging Jesus' sacrifice, they become reconciled to a just and merciful God and secure the blessings of eternal life.

However, the cosmic struggle between good and evil did not end with Jesus' death and resurrection. The Christian worldview holds that the church is God's ongoing means of showing the world how Jesus saves humankind from sin and spiritual death. Before he left the earth, Jesus instructed the church to explain God's plan and to help people become reconciled to God. Yet, in time the church will no longer be necessary. That is because Jesus will return one day to wage a final battle with evil. Once his victory is complete, he will establish the kingdom of heaven on earth.

This example of how the Christian worldview is commonly formulated brings together the enormous variety of Jesus' followers, while ironically fueling further disagreement and division. Christians may agree that God created the heavens and the earth, but may disagree on whether it took six 24-hour days or millions of years.

Christians may agree that humans can make their own decisions, but may disagree on whether human decision making is trumped by God's knowledge of the past, present, and future. Christians may agree that Jesus will return, but may disagree on the timing and circumstances. These disagreements and their consequences will occupy our attention for the remainder of the book.

The Least You Need to Know

- ◆ Christianity is the largest religion in the world, but its many divisions confuse and disorient those who wish to understand it.

- ◆ The word "Christian" was first used at Antioch in Syria to identify non-Jewish followers of Jesus.

- ◆ Jesus taught that those who follow him should be committed to him and his teachings in both thought and action.

- ◆ The label Christian may identify a universal fellowship of souls, a group of people who profess faith in Jesus Christ, people who actually join a church, or people who follow the teachings of Jesus.

- ◆ Nearly all Christians ascribe to a worldview with a comprehensive interpretation of history, depicting a cosmic struggle between good and evil with Jesus as the central figure.

2

The Varieties of Christians

In This Chapter

- ◆ Learn why Christians start new denominations
- ◆ Find out what Christians mean when they use the word "orthodoxy"
- ◆ Understand how Christianity resists, yet also encourages, innovation
- ◆ Consider the family resemblances among the different Christian groups

In my small college town, there are at least 41 churches representing at least 22 different denominations, serving a population of less than 16,000. And this number includes only those churches that maintain an active phone line. The major denominations are all here: Roman Catholic, Methodist, Presbyterian, and Baptist. There are also some interesting new startups, like a church that describes itself as "charismatic Anglican" and a group that meets on Sunday mornings in a local coffee shop. This seems like a lot of different churches for such a small town, and yet this is typical of towns and cities across the United States. A recent study showed that more than 75 percent of the 3,141 counties in the United States have at least eight different Christian denominations.

It may be hard to understand why 41 small-town congregations maintain 41 different facilities, staffs, programs, and the like, all calling themselves Christian. But there are perfectly sound explanations for the wide diversity of Christian churches in the United States and abroad. Social, political, geographical, and cultural factors splintered Christianity as it moved away from its birthplace in the Middle East, extended across the European continent, and took root in the New World. Today, the splintering of Christianity continues unabated. Some Christians lament this lack of unity, but most concede that it helps to meet the needs of a diverse population while reflecting the strength and vitality of the Christian religion in the present age.

A Bewildering Array of Sects

Way back in the 1830s, the array of Christian groups in the United States bewildered French tourist Alexis de Tocqueville. "There is an innumerable multitude of sects in the United States," he remarked, also noting that they all seemed to value democracy. This was more than 170 years ago. The number of denominations has multiplied in the years since that time, and new Christian denominations appear each week. Put simply, Christianity is a world religion, and the diversity of Christian sects in the United States and elsewhere mirrors America's and the world's diversity. But this alone can't account for all the sects, since denominational boundaries don't neatly follow the lines of race, language, culture, or region in the United States or in the world at large.

In fact, religion has a dual quality: It brings together both what we believe *and* how we relate to others. Given the inventiveness of the human mind, perhaps we should expect to find an even broader array of denominations in Christianity. Christianity is a religion that channels inventiveness through existing organizations, namely its denominations. Occasionally, these denominations resist innovation, which results in disagreements, schisms, and ultimately new denominations.

But don't assume that all theological disagreements inevitably result in schisms and new denominations. Churches can and do reform themselves when challenged by new ideas and precepts. And individual members often stay committed to their churches despite disagreeing with their theologies. Recently I read a newspaper article about an Episcopalian priest who disagrees with her own denomination's doctrine of heaven and hell. She believes that people move into the eternal realm at different levels and continue their progression toward God. And she is far from the only example of a church member or even a minister who remains committed despite taking issue with some of his or her church's official beliefs.

Nevertheless, differences of opinion on theological, doctrinal, and ethical issues continue to splinter the Christian faith. As the old saying goes, simply changing the color of the sanctuary's carpet can send a dozen church members packing. Of course, disputes over the church carpet often conceal deeper divisions, having more to do with personality or generational conflicts, worship-style preferences, or perhaps even theology and doctrine. Whatever the case, denominational diversity is the norm in Christianity. Today, more than 80 denominations in the United States claim to have more than 100,000 members each, and millions more belong to churches without any denominational affiliation.

Orthodoxy and Innovation

But theological, organizational, and ethical disputes aren't the only source of energy driving denominationalism. Christianity actually encourages innovation, if unintentionally. Although it tries to channel innovation into pre-cut channels, often innovation produces new movements in the existing denominations, and of course new denominations altogether.

Every Sunday morning I recite the Apostles' Creed, along with the other people who attend church with me. Our liturgist—the person who directs the worship service—reminds us that throughout the world and throughout history, Christians have joined together as one body by reciting this creed. Toward the end of it I get to the line, "I believe in the holy catholic church." When I first recited the creed years ago I was confused. I'm Presbyterian, not Roman Catholic. Then I realized that our denomination takes catholic to mean universal and orthodox, not the specific denomination we know as the Roman Catholic Church.

This image celebrates the Council of Nicaea and the Nicene Creed, which tried to resolve a dispute over the doctrine of the trinity, and which enjoyed the support of the Emperor Constantine (center).

(Photo courtesy of Peter Cade)

What in the world is orthodoxy? To answer this question we need to go back to the first couple of centuries C.E., when the Apostles' Creed and other creeds came into fashion. The Christian church at Rome used an early version of the Apostles' Creed as a test. Yes, a litmus test: One had to affirm the creed before he or she could proceed to baptism. As it reads now, following some revisions by the Council of Trent (1545–1563), the creed goes

> I believe in God the Father Almighty, Creator of Heaven and earth, and in Jesus Christ, His only Son, our Lord, who was conceived by the Holy Ghost, born of the Virgin Mary, suffered under Pontius Pilate, was crucified, died, and buried; He descended into hell; the third day He rose again from the dead; He ascended into Heaven, sitteth at the right hand of God the Father Almighty; From thence He shall come to judge the living and the dead. I believe in the Holy Ghost, the Holy Catholic Church, the communion of saints, the forgiveness of sins, the resurrection of the body, and life everlasting.

Roman church leaders fretted over a teacher known as Marcion. Marcion gave them fits since he and his large following believed that Jesus was actually a kind of apparition. This led people to doubt that Jesus was fully human. To address this claim, Roman church officials insisted that prospective members affirm the creed, or what was then known as the Roman Symbol. The creed, developed by church leaders and affirmed by councils of bishops, states clearly that Jesus is God's son, but nevertheless was birthed by a human mother and later to die a human death.

The earliest creeds were designed to be authorized expressions of Christian teachings about Jesus. They intended to narrow the range of theological possibilities by establishing a set of approved beliefs. We refer to this effort to create an authorized set of doctrines as orthodoxy. But the Roman Symbol didn't make the Marcionites go away. And the Council of Trent version of the Apostles' Creed didn't make Protestants like Martin Luther and John Calvin go away, either. They simply defined these people as heterodox, meaning outside the boundary of beliefs approved by the Christian church at Rome.

In an odd way, you can't have orthodoxy without also having heterodoxy. Orthodoxy doesn't mean unity. It means that there exists a set of beliefs that some define as authoritative *in light of* the existence of other, unauthorized beliefs. Initial differences of opinion about aspects of the Christian faith become formalized as orthodox and heterodox positions once they enter the terrain of everyday church life. As a result, orthodoxy and heterodoxy are locked in an eternal embrace.

Throughout Christian history, churches created orthodoxies in an effort to standardize beliefs. In reaction, however, sects developed in opposition to those orthodoxies.

Churches viewed the sects that developed as heretical and divisive, while sects viewed the churches as tyrannical and oppressive. This general pattern still exists in the Christian church today. Conversation about church teachings generates disagreement, which in turn triggers the creation of orthodoxy. When dissenters challenge the orthodoxy, church leaders face a dilemma: Force the dissenters to submit, or send them on their way to form new sects.

Creole Christians

New sects are often the by-product of a church's effort to impose orthodoxy. This is but one factor that generates new denominations; another is the spread of Christianity to new regions. Christianity adapts and changes when it plants itself on new soil. Consider Cajun food as an illustration. French Canadians who moved to Louisiana in the eighteenth and nineteenth centuries brought their food traditions along with them, but then adapted them to their new surroundings. Cajun food, which uses flavors from Africa and the Caribbean along with France, is a unique blend of foreign tastes and local food practices.

Understanding the word "creole"—which generically means a pidgin language that develops into the official language of a community—is helpful here. Creole was first used to identify people of European descent born in the New World in the sixteenth century, and soon came to signify the blending of African, European, Caribbean, and Native American cultures. Especially in places like Louisiana, Creoles remembered and celebrated the traditions of their parents and grandparents, and yet learned to carry out these traditions in new and creative ways. In a similar manner, Christianity became a creole faith as it spread from the Jews of Palestine to the Jewish and Greek settlements in Asia Minor and North Africa, and then to Rome. The Roman Empire spread the church to the people of northern Europe and the British Isles. Later, the Spanish, Portuguese, French, and British Empires transported the church to the Western Hemisphere, Africa, and Asia.

The Bible itself tells the story of how Jesus' teachings found new listeners. The first Christians were Jewish, but then Christianity soon spread to Gentile communities in Palestine and Asia Minor. As the person most responsible for this expansion, Saint Paul frequently pointed out his Hebrew background and his training as a Pharisee, and yet used the Greek language and Hellenistic philosophical concepts to explain the teachings of Jesus. He believed that Jesus' teachings were not restricted to certain races, genders, or social classes: "There is neither Jew nor Greek, there is neither slave nor free, there is neither male nor female; for you are all one in Christ Jesus." (Galatians 3:28) And it was Jesus himself who once commanded his followers to "make disciples of all nations, baptizing them in the name of the Father, and of the Son, and of the Holy Spirit." (Matthew 28:19)

Many church buildings in the Southwest are examples of the creolization of Christianity. This church-yard is built with dimensions and materials that reflect its surroundings.

(Photo courtesy of Denver Public Library)

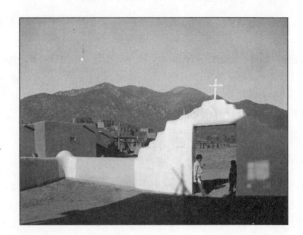

Jesus' message of salvation is universal, but the way it gets expressed differs from place to place. Everything from the design of church buildings to the music used in worshipping God reflects the culture in which Christianity is practiced. As you can imagine, cultural differences can result in boundary lines among different Christian denominations. The division between Roman Catholicism and Eastern Orthodoxy persisted, in part, because of the differences between Latin and Byzantine cultures in Rome and Constantinople, while Protestantism splintered in the seventeenth century as its leaders wrestled with church reform in different national settings in the German states, Switzerland, the Netherlands, Scotland, and so on.

The United States provided, and continues to provide, a fertile ground for the creation of new Christian denominations. Independence from England prompted one or two Christian churches to sever ties with parent churches in Great Britain and Europe and set up their own organizations. Thus the Church of England became the Episcopal Church in the United States. Religious freedom and democratic values encouraged religious leaders like Mother Ann Lee of the Shakers and Joseph Smith Jr. of the Mormons to build their movements. Many Christian denominations in the United States have a strong racial and ethnic quality, since race and ethnicity continue to play an important role in the U.S. economy, politics, society, and culture.

Edifications

Dozens of new denominations arose in the period between the American Revolution and the Civil War. As political leaders were building new civic institutions across the United States, religious leaders were starting new institutions as well. Unitarians, the United Brethren in Christ, the Cumberland Presbyterian Church, the Seventh-Day Adventists, and a host of other denominations sprang into being, often under the leadership of a visionary inspired by the political and social energy present in the new United States.

Race and Religion in America

Take race, for instance. Once the institution of slavery became identified with the African and African American race in the seventeenth century, racial boundaries hardened and carried over into religion. Initial reluctance to convert slaves to Christianity gave way to evangelical efforts by Baptists and Methodists to bring slaves and free blacks into the church in the decades leading up to the Civil War. African American Christians organized separate denominations in a climate of slavery and racial segregation, such as the African Methodist Episcopal Church founded in 1814. Ethnicity plays an important role as well. In the nineteenth century, Lutherans tended to be either German or Scandinavian by heritage, while Reformed Christians tended to be British or Dutch. Orthodox churches such as the Greek Orthodox Church and the Orthodox Church in America have Greek and Slavic roots.

The wide variety of denominations in the United States owes its origin to ancient schisms in the church, but this variety was more intense in the United States because of this country's more permissive environment. In fact, rather than complain about the "innumerable multitude" of Christian sects in the United States, Thomas Jefferson considered it a benefit: "Difference of opinion is advantageous in religion. The several sects perform the office of a *censor morum* [regulator of morals] over each other." Making a virtue of necessity is, of course, characteristically American. And perhaps it's not surprising that one of the Founding Fathers could see in the many Christian denominations a religious version of checks and balances. In short, the abundance of denominations in the United States is an example of how Christianity adapts to a particular setting.

Religious Entrepreneurialism

While we're on the subject of Founding Fathers, Jefferson and Adams wrote one another frequently after they left public life. Some of their correspondence dealt with matters of Christian belief. In a letter to Jefferson, Adams remarked, "The Ten Commandments and the Sermon on the Mount contain my religion." It is tempting to dismiss Adams's comment as typical for the period. Lots of educated men and women were challenging the established beliefs and practices of the Christian faith. But Adams touched on something more fundamental about Christianity, an aspect of the faith that should be counted among the factors that lead to new denominations.

Jesus protested against the externals of religion, such as the showy rituals, the ceremonial dress, the public displays of devotion. Of the leaders of first-century Judaism, Jesus said: "Woe to you, scribes and Pharisees, hypocrites! for you are like whitewashed tombs, which outwardly appear beautiful, but within they are full of dead men's bones and all uncleanness. So you also outwardly appear righteous to men, but within you are full of hypocrisy and iniquity." (Matthew 23:27–28) Jesus believed that the Pharisees got it all wrong when it came to religion. To Jesus, all the religious observances in the world mattered little if a person is corrupt within. He thought you shouldn't pray aloud in the public square if you harbor deceit, bitterness, or jealously in your heart.

So Adams could consider himself in the spirit of Jesus' teachings by wanting to get rid of the trappings of religion and practice something close to a pure, unadorned faith. As religions pass through time, they change. Sometimes new customs develop, or new traditions emerge. Throughout history, numerous believers have found cause to criticize their Christian brothers and sisters for permitting rituals, ceremonies, icons, and so forth to crowd out the radical message of Jesus. Those who founded the earliest monastic communities in order to escape a luxurious and corrupt society carried forward Jesus' message. So did dissenting groups like the Waldensees and Albigenses of the Middle Ages, who believed that true faith could be practiced outside of the formal routines of the Roman Catholic Church. Protestants of the sixteenth century had this idea, too, as did the revivalists of the eighteenth and nineteenth centuries.

Steeple Talk

Scholars of Christianity in the United States use the word **primitivism** to describe the impulse of reformers to turn back the clock on centuries of history in order to restore the church to its original condition at the time of Christ. Usually, this results in protests against fancy church decorations, elaborate worship ceremonies, hymn singing, and sophisticated statements of doctrine or theology.

Today, many U.S. denominations trace their roots to a particular moment when a group of Christians came to believe that the church in their time was burdened with too many externals of religion, and sought to restore "*primitive* Christianity" as taught by Jesus and lived by the apostles. As a church in a nearby town advertises in the yellow pages, "Experience a relationship, not a religion."

Again, the United States provided a fertile ground for religious entrepreneurs to start primitivist Christian movements. The Constitution forbade the establishment of an official version of Christianity for the nation, and so no group enjoyed the special privileges of state sponsorship. Without a monopoly in place, denominations were thrown together in a free marketplace for religion. In time, U.S. Christians suffered no penalty for leaving one church and joining another, and so competition among denominations ruled the day. New denominations like the Disciples of Christ, which later gave birth to the Christian Churches and the Churches of Christ, found converts in the early nineteenth century among a rapidly expanding frontier population. They did so by positioning themselves as primitive churches, in contrast to the time-worn Eastern churches with their creeds and confessions and formalized church hierarchies.

Today, most Christians in the United States choose denominations based on family tradition, but are free to leave and try others. Switching denominations is common, due to interfaith marriage, change of location, personal conviction, or a variety of other reasons. A recent survey reported that 33 million U.S. residents have switched religious affiliation at least once in their lifetime. Americans value personal choice and self-determination, and these values are reflected in the free marketplace of religion.

> **Lo and Behold**
>
> Be aware that polls that track change of religious status sometimes don't distinguish people who change affiliation from one denomination to another from people who drop out of formal denominational affiliation altogether. It can be hard to know whether people in the latter group still consider themselves Christians or have become atheists.

Religious entrepreneurs like John Wimber of the Vineyard Association of Churches are free to create churches designed to appeal to new groups of potential converts, whether they are recent immigrants, religious switchers, or young adults forming new families.

This climate of religious freedom and organization-building contributes to the pattern of innovation in Christianity in the United States. By constantly appealing to new sorts of immigrants or rising generations of Americans, often through calls to restore primitive Christianity, new denominations take their place among the established groups, all equal in the eyes of the Constitution. On the one hand, Christianity in the United States maintains its vitality and its appeal through the work of primitivists and entrepreneurs. The focus remains Jesus Christ and his message. On the other hand, the innovators breed contention and division. They also feel less committed to inherited traditions that may have real value. In the end, one's opinion on the subject may depend largely on one's location on the denominational spectrum.

Unfortunately, the innovators and traditionalists have gone round and round for centuries, and the argument between them leads to inevitable stalemate. In fact, they sound rather like squabbling brothers and sisters or frustrated parents with strong-willed children. So maybe we should think of the different Christian denominations as being part of one big family. They trace their ancestry to a common source, and retain strong family resemblances. In such a family the members are linked together by strong ties of kinship, but over time, develop subtle variations that result in differences in doctrine, church organization, worship style, and so on. In other words, Christianity today is essentially a family of faith communities.

A Family of Faith Communities

Grandpa Sooy, or Pudge as we in our family called him, had orange-red hair. As he reached into his 70s, his hair stayed virtually the same in color, texture, and thickness. But as children, grandchildren, and great-grandchildren appeared, he was disappointed to find that nobody inherited his beautiful head of hair. Then out popped my niece Hailey with hair the same shade of orange-red (well, maybe a little more strawberry, but you get the idea). Baby after baby appeared in the Sooy family without a nod to Grandpa Pudge's fiery crown, but when Hailey appeared, the generational link was confirmed.

Grandpa Pudge's search for red-haired descendants illustrates a point about Christian denominations: They're bound together by family resemblances, even if there are no clones, or even identical twins. If you have a keen eye, the family resemblances show themselves. Maybe the grandchildren don't have red hair, but have Grandpa's gentle spirit, or maybe Grandma's quick wit. Likewise, Christian denominations resemble one another in lots of ways, and more often than not, the similarities are more striking than the differences.

To be sure, Christian denominations differ in age, shape, size, and temperament, just like members of any family. As new denominations take shape, they create separate identities with the customary growing pains. When they strike out on their own, their parent denominations experience the trauma of separation and feelings of abandonment. Like any long-lived family, successive generations have a multiplier effect. With more denominations, you get more possibilities for subdivision; increase in the number of denominations is a natural consequence of the initial divisions of the Christian faith. Nevertheless, the family resemblances are plain to see.

Across the denominational landscape, Christians pray to God, read the Bible, participate in worship services, and support their churches financially. They consider the church to be an important way to spread the faith and to promote justice and goodwill throughout the world. They find meaning in the sacraments of communion and baptism, and ask clergy to lead their marriage ceremonies and funeral services. They see images of the cross and understand its significance. And to them, hope lies in a life beyond this life. You can find other similarities as well. These generations share a common heritage, and they share a common destiny.

Fellowshipping Together

Christian denominations have family resemblances, since they trace their roots to other denominations, and often use the Bible and ancient creeds to work out their beliefs and practices. Furthermore, dozens of denominations in the United States got started when two factions in a pre-existing denomination disagreed on a point or two, and one decided to leave to start its own. You'll find the new denomination very similar to the old with the exception of the original point of contention. The similarities between these kindred denominations generate repeated movements for reunion or affiliation. Examples abound; my own denomination is the result of a reunion in 1983 between strands of the Presbyterian Church that were originally separated by revivalism and slavery in the decades leading up to the Civil War.

Christians who try to discover points in common and to build greater understanding among the denominations practice what is called *ecumenism*. This is not to be confused with reunion efforts of churches that were previously divided. It refers instead to the ecumenists' efforts to promote respect and toleration among the family of churches and to build programs that harness the resources of multiple denominations. Some Christians see this as a valuable way to encourage reconciliation, while others see it as a compromise of principle.

Steeple Talk

Ecumenism is the practice of seeking greater understanding and cooperation among people of faith. Among Christians, the ecumenical movement produced the National Council of Churches in 1950, with a current membership of 36 Protestant, Anglican, and Orthodox denominations—more than 50 million believers.

The ecumenical movement has a long history, and efforts in the United States predate our independence from Great Britain. Jefferson expressed confidence that Christians would find points of convergence on important theological topics, but turned out to be a lousy prognosticator: "I trust that there is not a young man now living in the United States who will not die a Unitarian." The Disciples of Christ began as an effort by early-nineteenth-century revivalists Alexander Stone and the father—son team of Thomas and Alexander Campbell on the early American frontier to eliminate denominations and divisive doctrinal formulas, even if they ultimately produced yet another denomination.

Reaching Across Boundaries

In recent years, Christians have attempted to reach across denominational boundaries to form mutual understandings. In 1994, a group calling itself Evangelicals and Catholics Together produced a report of their two-year long consultation. The group didn't represent denominations, and their report was not meant to be binding. But the list of names included in these conversations is impressive. Prominent Catholics like J. Francis Cardinal Stafford of the Pontifical Council for the Laity at the Vatican and Francis Eugene Cardinal George, O.M.I., archbishop of Chicago, were involved, as were Evangelicals like writer and lecturer Charles Colson and former National Association of Evangelicals president John White.

Pope John Paul II greets the Rev. Joe Hale (right) during a worship service at the Saint Paul Outside the Walls Basilica in Rome during the Week of Prayer for Christian Unity in January 2001. Hale served as staff executive of the World Methodist Council.

(Photo courtesy of the United Methodist News Service)

They disagreed about some things, such as whether the church is a visible communion or an invisible fellowship of true believers, and whether the sacraments are symbols of grace or means of grace. But they found lots of things to agree about as well. They affirmed that Jesus is Lord, that the Bible is the infallible Word of God, that the Holy Spirit leads believers to a deeper faith, and that the Apostles' Creed is an accurate statement of Scriptural truth. Furthermore, they agreed that the main goal of the church is to proclaim the Gospel and "sustain the community of faith, worship, and discipleship that is gathered by this Gospel." Toward the end, they went on to state a set of shared political positions on abortion, school choice, separation of church and state, pornography, welfare reform, and foreign policy.

This consultation represents just one example of how Christians try to find common ground in the United States. It shows how one set of church leaders discovered the family resemblances among their denominations, while nevertheless acknowledging the boundaries that continue to divide them. Still, many Christians belong to churches that reject calls for unity and enforce denominational boundaries. For instance, shortly after the terror attacks of September 11, 2001, a group of Protestant, Catholic, Muslim, Jewish, and Hindu leaders gathered in Yankee Stadium for an event called Prayer for America. One of the Protestant ministers was suspended by his denomination for violations that included "unionism," or worshipping with clergy who are not of his denomination. Such actions serve as reminders that the family resemblances that link Christian denominations exist in an environment where millions of Christians still care deeply about the unique features of their own denominations.

The Least You Need to Know

♦ Christians in the United States are free to switch denominations, but they often stay put even if they disagree with their denominations' doctrines or practices.

♦ The factors that produce new denominations include theological, organizational, and ethical disagreement; the creation of orthodoxy by established churches; the transfer of Christianity to new settings; and environments like the United States that promote division and innovation.

♦ One of the main reasons why there are so many denominations in the United States is because of an ongoing desire among U.S. Christians to restore the church to its original condition.

♦ Christian denominations are like a multigenerational family, with numerous family resemblances that extend downward through the generations.

♦ A key feature of Christianity in recent years is the practice of ecumenism, or the celebration of points of agreement among different denominations.

Roots of Denominationalism

In This Chapter

- ◆ Discover the key turning points in the history of Christianity
- ◆ Find out why early Christianity separated into two large factions, Roman Catholicism and Eastern Orthodoxy
- ◆ Grasp the central ideas behind Protestantism, and understand its three main branches
- ◆ Discover the importance of religious freedom in making new denominations in the United States

The story of church history is a long and complicated one; I have a history of Christianity book that runs more than 1,500 pages. And that's with very tiny print, too. It will be easier to tell the story of church history if we focus only on the major events that helped to splinter the church into thousands of denominations. Unfortunately, this means that we'll have to set aside many of the biographical details of church leaders, skip lots of interesting historical sidelights, and gloss over a number of complex issues. But we stand to gain in the process because focusing on those major events will help us understand how the Christian denominations came into being in particular places at particular times.

At risk of generalizing too much, Christianity as we know it is the result of a string of developments set in motion when believers first gathered to worship in the name of Jesus 2,000 years ago. These early Christians made choices and started traditions that guided the way their successors expressed and practiced the faith. But these successors also made choices and started new traditions, as did their successors, and their successors' successors, and so on, all the way down to the present day.

The Early Church

It isn't hard to find examples of factions and divisions in the first-century church. In the Book of Acts in the New Testament, Jewish and Greek converts to Christianity argued over how much of the old Jewish law still applied, while Paul chastised factions of the church at Corinth for identifying with different disciples, rather than with Jesus. Teachers who blended Christianity with *Gnosticism* or paganism worried Paul as well, and he singled out men like Hymenaeus and Philetus for distorting the apostles' message. (II Timothy 2:17)

> **Steeple Talk**
>
> First-century Christian leaders considered **Gnosticism** to be a threat to the faith, and Christian churches continue to guard against a resurgence of Gnostic ideas. Gnostics believed that sin is a physical entity located in actual objects. They developed severe restrictions concerning such things as food, beverages, clothing, and furnishings. Today, Christians who oppose rule making denounce such action as being in the spirit of Gnosticism.

Jesus appointed apostles to guide the early church through its infancy, and the church could stray only so far from their memory of Jesus' teachings as long as they were alive. The church also gained unity through the sacrifice early leaders made through persecution. Early leaders like Stephen, Peter, and Paul were killed for preaching about Jesus, and Roman emperors like Valerian and Diocletian confiscated church leaders' property, destroyed their meetinghouses, and ultimately killed tens of thousands in ghastly spectacles. Apostolic leadership and unity through persecution helped the church manage its early factionalism. Nevertheless, Gnostic Christians pulled some believers away from the mainstream with different ideas about the nature of sin, while the Marcionites denied that Christ ever became a real human being. Though these factions eventually died out, permanent divisions began to appear in the third and fourth centuries over the nature of the Trinity. The basic problem was how to maintain one's belief in monotheism and still believe that Jesus—a human being—was actually God as well. This dilemma was complicated by Jesus' promise to send the Holy Spirit to be among his followers once he returned to be with the Father. (John 16:7-10) How do three—God the Father, Jesus Christ, and the Holy Spirit—become one?

The doctrine of the Trinity provided an early point of disagreement among Christians. Here, the Trinity of God—the Father, Jesus Christ, and the Holy Spirit—are represented together.

(Permission for use from the Museo del Prado, Madrid)

Arius, a priest from Alexandria, argued that if Jesus was God's Son, he must therefore have had a beginning point. His followers, called the Arians, reasoned that Jesus couldn't be part of God because God has no beginning. Another faction, led by Alexander and Athanasius, two leaders from Antioch, identified this as a denial of Jesus' divinity and argued by contrast that God and Jesus were one and eternal. Emperor Constantine called for a meeting of the bishops to resolve the matter, which convened at Nicaea in 325 C.E.

> **Everybody Said Amen**
>
> Keep in mind that Constantine did not make Christianity the official religion of the Roman Empire. That was the work of Emperor Theodosius in 379 C.E.

This council produced the Nicene Creed, which quickly assumed its place as the most important statement of Christian doctrine concerning the Trinity. The Nicene Creed differed from the Apostles' Creed in detailing exactly how the persons of the Trinity relate to each other, and adding that all are of the same substance. The result was a defeat for the Arians, and Arius was banished from the church, his books burned, and his ideas condemned.

An important principle emerged from the actions taken by Constantine and Theodosius. Religion and politics got mixed together. Anxious rulers of a weakening Roman Empire came to see factions in the church as a problem to be solved in order to maintain imperial unity. Argumentative bishops, lacking a chain of command, came to rely on Roman emperors to help resolve their disputes. The principle of religious and political unity—Christendom—was established, if imperfectly obtained.

Two Christianities?

Theological controversies and political adjustments in the Roman Empire in the first four centuries after Christ planted the seeds for the eventual division of Christianity into two large factions: the Roman Catholic Church and the Eastern Orthodox Church.

Roman Catholicism and Eastern Orthodoxy had already begun to move down separate paths well before the Great Schism. Racial, ethnic, and linguistic differences played a role. The churches to the east, centered in Asia Minor and Greece (Byzantium), spoke and wrote in Greek. The churches of the west, on the other hand, were under the influence of Rome and used Latin. In the centuries between the Council of Nicaea and the Great Schism, Byzantine Christianity spread to the Slavic people in Bulgaria, Serbia, and Russia. Meanwhile, Latin Christianity spread to the northwestern parts of Europe and to Britain.

> **CAUTION**
>
> ### Lo and Behold
>
> One confusing point about Christian history is that two major events are both called the Great Schism. One refers to the division of Christianity into Roman Catholicism and Eastern Orthodoxy in 1054; the other refers to the division within the Roman Catholic Church between 1378 and 1417 when as many as three different popes claimed to be the one true pope. This problem was resolved at the Council of Constance with the selection of Pope Martin V.

Edifications

Eastern Orthodox Christians and Roman Catholics disagreed about a clause that Roman Catholics added to the Nicene Creed. It states that the Holy Spirit proceedeth from both God the Father and the Son Jesus Christ. Orthodox Christians believed, and still believe, that the Holy Spirit proceedeth only from the Father. This is known today as the "filioque" clause, and is one the main reasons why Roman Catholicism and Eastern Orthodoxy are still separated.

Eastern churches grew to resent the influence of the pope at Rome, and the eventual claims made on his behalf for papal supremacy. They conceded that the pope took precedence over the bishops of the other major centers of Christianity: Constantinople, Alexandria, Antioch, and Jerusalem. They reasoned that Rome was first among equals because the Apostle Peter founded the church there, and Jesus himself identified Peter as the rock upon which he would build the church. Also, the city played host to Peter and Paul's martyrdoms and served as the traditional hub of the Roman Empire, so it was logical to give it priority. But the eastern bishops rejected the pope's claim to supreme authority in church affairs.

After 1054, they went their separate ways. Pope Leo IX excommunicated Patriarch of Constantinople Michael Cerularius (the highest church official after the pope) for using the Nicene Creed differently, while Cerularius was upset with Leo IX for insisting on a certain kind of bread in the Eucharist. These don't appear to be insurmountable differences, but other differences had their effect, having more to do with geography, ethnic background, and politics.

Reformation at a Glance

The Great Schism of 1054 created two separate entities within Christianity. The Reformation of the sixteenth century pulled millions of Christians out of the Roman Catholic Church, and they formed dozens of new Christian organizations that together we call Protestantism.

Why did the Protestants leave? Well, in some ways the Roman Catholic Church was a victim of its own success. It entered the second millennium after Christ as the most important institution left standing in the ashes of the Roman Empire. Rome's demise in the seventh century created a power vacuum in Europe that the church tried to fill. It took over many of the jobs that once belonged to Roman officials and eventually became king maker in the politics of Medieval Europe.

The Roman Catholic Church's teachings and its rituals gave life meaning when nothing else in society seemed to be working. Barbarians invaded at will; famine and disease ravaged the countryside; Roman roads crumbled away and markets shriveled. In this climate, the church offered hope. It stood guard over the ancient creeds, or what people understood as truth itself. Its sacraments and the Mass connected a desperate people with a better world beyond the one they knew. But in the minds of some, church officials had erred, building up the wealth and political influence of the church at the expense of religious devotion. A few notorious popes seemed to care little about the faith and instead pursued their own political, economic, and social ambitions.

Begging Indulgences

By 1520, the church seemed to be broken in the eyes of many observers. Abuses were barely hidden; wealthy banker and merchant Lorenzo de Medici got one of his younger sons, Giovanni, elevated to cardinal at age 17 and then pope at 38. Giovanni, as Pope Leo X, drained Vatican treasuries to pay for the work of Raphael and Michelangelo and to finish Saint Peter's Cathedral in Rome. Like other popes, Leo generated revenue through annates, or appointment fees paid to the pope by new bishops or archbishops (usually a year's salary). Pope Leo appointed Albert of Brandenburg to

Steeple Talk

An **indulgence** is a priest's declaration waiving a sinner's punishment for sinning. An indulgence decreases the penalties that sinners may receive on earth or in purgatory for their sins, but does not alter the penalty for those who are to be eternally damned.. The practice of selling indulgences developed alongside the practices of confession and penance in the Roman Catholic Church as a way of assuring repentant sinners of God's grace and forgiveness.

Edifications

In Latin, the three principles of Protestantism are expressed as *sola fide, sola gratia,* and *sola scriptura.* They translate as "faith alone," "grace alone," and "word alone," and Protestants refer to them as the "Solas of the Reformation."

be archbishop of Mainz, the highest church office in the German states; Albert in turn expected to pay his costly annate with money raised through selling *indulgences,* or declarations by a priest that punishment for sins had been waived. And the matter of indulgences is the issue upon which the Protestant Reformation turned.

The selling of indulgences raised the ire of many Christians in the Middle Ages, as did other policies of the Roman Catholic Church. Early reformers like John Wyclif (1324–1384), who anticipated many of the ideas of Martin Luther and John Calvin 200 years later, taught that all Christians are priests and do not need intermediaries between them and God. He believed in the doctrine of predestination— that God has elected those who will be saved. Indulgences, though they often followed true contrition and penance, were sometimes simply purchased by sinners looking for a way to clear their consciences or restore their privileges in society.

Going further, Wyclif rejected the sacraments, saints, relics, and pilgrimages as unnecessary to salvation. He was joined by other teachers and priests like John Hus in Bohemia, John Pupper of Goch in the Netherlands, John Wesel of Maintz, and Girolamo Savonarola of Florence, all of whom sought greater purity in the Roman Catholic Church and in society. Wyclif, Hus, and Erasmus produced new translations of the Bible and other ancient texts, signaling the importance of the original sources of the Christian faith. They believed the Bible should be used to determine what is necessary and unnecessary to the faith, and that parish priests and even common people should be able to read it for themselves. This is where Martin Luther comes into the story.

Luther was a monk with a doctoral degree who began to doubt that his prayers, fasting, confessions, and penance had removed the eternal penalties that await the sinner in the hereafter. In 1519, Luther challenged his fellow theologians in the German town of Wittenberg to debate the use of indulgences. In this debate and the debates that followed, along with Luther's widely circulated writings, three positions emerged that became central principles of Protestantism:

1. Christians receive justification from God—or spiritual cleansing—through faith, not the rituals of the church like confession, penance, and indulgences

2. Christians are saved from sin and death by God's grace, not their own good deeds or admirable personal qualities

3. Christian beliefs should be based on the Bible, not papal edicts or church traditions

Every Man His Own Church

To Luther, Christians are saved by grace through faith grounded in Scripture. These ideas, when linked together, worked in concert to create a radical new vision for the Christian faith. When followed to its logical conclusion, the result is the idea of the priesthood of all believers, that all Christians are competent to follow their own lights in matters of religion.

It is hard to find an idea in the history of mankind with more far-reaching consequences. People began to question the need for priests, sacraments, church buildings, images, candles, and altars. They began to question the whole church hierarchy with its bishops, archbishops, cardinals, and popes. They wondered openly if the creeds they had learned as children helped or hurt their understanding of the faith. Individualism was born.

The priesthood of all believers put a radical spin on the Christian idea of individual moral responsibility. What's the point of church if everyone is his or her own priest? But Luther didn't want to destroy the Roman Catholic Church, only reform it. He decided it could keep its crucifixes, candles, images, and altars. He also kept church services, ministers, hymn singing, and two of the sacraments (baptism and communion). But the pope and the cardinals who ran the Vatican were left out, as were many parts of the Latin mass. Indulgences, confession, and other aspects of the priest's job were eliminated. In trying to devise an example of how to reform Catholicism, Luther ended up creating Lutheranism.

CAUTION
Lo and Behold

Martin Luther began the Reformation as a movement to reform the Roman Catholic Church, not to start a new Christian denomination. After being excommunicated, he started his odyssey of building a separate organization. His fear of separating from the church was so great that he condemned others who began to do the very same thing in other German states, including all of the so-called Anabaptist sects that rejected infant baptism.

Lutheranism became the state church in his home kingdom, Saxony, and in a few dozen other German states, while Catholicism remained the state church in others. Soon, Denmark instituted Lutheranism as its official version of Christianity, followed by Norway, Sweden, Iceland, and Finland. To some people, however, official versions of Christianity seemed to be at odds with the spirit of the emerging Reformation. In this way, Luther's protest created another great separation in the church, but perhaps more importantly made separation over matters of principle seem to be a moral necessity for Christians who opposed church teachings. Denominationalism had found its theological voice.

Three Streams of Protestantism

Luther's break with the Roman Catholic Church unleashed a lot of pent-up frustrations. Some of the people who followed Luther's teachings raided churches, destroyed images, and toppled altars. In 1524, oppressed peasants in Germany used the occasion of protesting authority to attack their landlords. Once the dust settled on the Peasant's Revolt, tens of thousands had been killed. Luther was appalled. During the crisis, he told local German officials that they should kill the rebels, and then worked closely with the officials to ensure order in both political and religious affairs. Amid the chaos of rebellion and war, reforming Christians took a dozen different shapes.

Looking back from our own time, we can group these movements into three major streams: Lutheran, Anabaptist, and Reformed. Lutherans and Anabaptists disagreed over the issue of who should be considered part of the church. Luther believed that no human institution could perfectly replicate the invisible church. Amid chaos and disorder, however, Luther believed that the church should nevertheless exist and represent all the people living in a specific territory under a sovereign government. Everyone would be baptized as infants into the version of Christianity that a majority professed, whether Lutheran or Catholic. Anabaptists rejected Luther's understanding of the church and the compromises with the state that Lutheranism required. They believed that the church should be composed of only those who had faith in Christ. The visible group of churchgoers, Anabaptists thought, should copy as closely as possible the invisible church of the saints. Baptism was to be a sign of personal commitment and faith in

> **CAUTION**
>
> ### Lo and Behold
>
> The word "Protestant" comes from protestor, referring to the group of Lutheran princes who in 1529 protested the Diet of Speyer's reversal of an earlier act that allowed German princes to decide for themselves whether Catholicism or Protestantism would be the state religion in their territories. They used the word "protest" in their message and the label stuck. Today, many people wrongly use "Protestant" to refer to all non-Catholic Christians.

Christ, which of course meant that infant baptism had to go. Only people of age could make such a commitment to Christ.

The Anabaptists arrived at the "gathered church" idea. True believers in Christ would gather themselves together, away from the wicked and unredeemed. Anabaptists like Conrad Grebel (c. 1498–1526) not only rejected compulsory churches and infant baptism, but a host of other practices not found in the Bible. In a very un-Lutheran spirit, they wanted nothing to do with government and refused military service. Gathered churches appeared throughout Germany, Switzerland, and Hungary, and especially in the Netherlands, where Menno Simons (1496–1561) organized the largest group of Anabaptist churches in Europe (eventually known as Mennonites).

The third major stream, Reformed Protestantism, grew out of a disagreement between Luther and another reformer, Ulrich Zwingli (1484–1531), over the sacrament of the Eucharist. Luther rejected the Catholic doctrine of transubstantiation, where bread and wine actually become the body and blood of Christ, but thought Christ was nevertheless present in the elements. Zwingli, a priest in Zurich, believed the ceremony was intended only to be commemorative. Zwingli and another Swiss clergyman and theologian, John Calvin, carried on the Reformation in Switzerland. Calvin's *Institutes of the Christian Religion* stressed God's control over all creation and thus de-emphasized the role of human action in salvation. Human beings were not in control of their own destinies—they were *predestined* for salvation or damnation.

To Calvin, both church and state exist to carry out God's plan on earth. So rather than either cooperation (Luther's approach) or withdrawal (the Anabaptists' approach), Reformed Christians believed that government should be founded on Biblical principles and pursue the will of God. Starting in Zurich and Geneva, Reformed Protestantism spread from Switzerland to parts of Germany and France, and ultimately became the state church in the Netherlands and Scotland.

Four major versions of Christianity struggled for survival in sixteenth-century Europe. An important question then arose by 1540: How would the states with official churches deal with religious dissenters within their borders? How would Catholic monarchs deal with Protestants? How would Lutheran princes deal with Reformed churches? How would governments that established the Reformed Church handle the Anabaptists? The answer to this question helps explain the beginnings of religious toleration, an essential ingredient in denominationalism.

Making Sectarianism Legal

Initially, the state churches were not too happy about nonconformists. Catholics feared the onset of disunity and schism; Lutherans and Reformed Protestants feared the collapse of the Reformation. All three groups feared the Anabaptists with their tendency to withdraw. In these circumstances, groups of religious nonconformists came to be seen by the authorities as sleeper cells of rebels who would gladly seize the opportunity to bring down their own governments with a favorable shift in the political winds.

In 1555, German princes finally agreed to let Lutherans practice their faith in Catholic states and vice versa, but Reformed and Anabaptist Christians were left out. Even so, their agreement established an important precedent of legal *toleration* of religious dissent that would mature later in Europe. When people of different religious persuasions came together under one political umbrella and practiced their faith without legal penalties, the conditions were ripe for a multiplication of religious groups. Full toleration for sectarians, especially the Anabaptists, would take another hundred years or more in many European countries. Perhaps the relation between legal toleration and denominationalism is best explained by reference to the English Reformation, since it was the beginning point of so many Christian groups in the United States today.

> **Steeple Talk**
>
> Officially, **toleration** refers to the extension of religious freedom to citizens of a sovereign state. It is sometimes confused with disestablishment, which means the removal of special government privileges for a particular religion or religious organization.

The English Reformation

Englishmen like John Wyclif, the Lollards, William Tyndale, and others struggled to restore religious vitality and purify the Roman Catholic Church prior to Martin Luther's break with Rome in the 1520s. But there was nothing inevitable about the formal separation of the English church with Rome. It happened when Henry VIII (1491–1547) asked the pope to annul his marriage to Catherine, daughter of Ferdinand and Isabella of Spain. Henry had secretly married Anne Boleyn, who was pregnant with his child at the time, and wanted his children by Anne to be legitimate heirs to the throne. The pope refused and excommunicated him, which prompted Henry in 1534 to sever ties between the English church and Rome. Parliament made this official by declaring the English king to be the supreme head of the church in England.

Now the work that began as early as John Wyclif and the Lollards could proceed, since the Church of England was free and clear of papal control. This triggered a hundred-year-long struggle between English monarchs and church reformers. Some English kings moved along with the reformers toward greater purity; others were more interested in compromise or even turning back to Catholicism. English priests and theologians who sought drastic purification of Catholic elements of the church—Puritans—were often branded as fanatics and either exiled or executed. Many Puritans went to Calvin's Geneva or the Calvinist Netherlands and became even more committed to radicalism; others went to the English colonies in America, like Plymouth or Massachusetts Bay, to create the pure church on earth.

The struggle for reform reached a fever pitch in the 1640s when it intersected with a struggle between King Charles I and Parliament for control of the English government. Puritans took over Parliament, built an army, fought and won a civil war against the king, and beheaded him on charges of treason in 1649. Political upheaval brought to the surface some of history's most radical schemes for reforming the church. Diggers advocated confiscation and redistribution of property; Ranters stripped bare to protest the corrupt "externals" of religion; Quakers believed that God spoke directly to them through the Inner Light and let women speak in their meetings. In 1660, Parliament restored the monarchy and soon after outlawed sectarians like the Quakers, Baptists, and some Puritan groups who wished to create independent churches.

> **Everybody Said Amen**
>
> The Puritan movement in England is very complicated and hard to understand. You'll have an easier time learning about them if you keep in mind that they were deeply influenced by John Calvin and writers who tried to advance Calvinist theology in the British Isles.

Christians disagree on the issue of whether women should be allowed to preach. Quakers encouraged women to speak in their meetings, as did the A.M.E. Church in the United States much later.

(Permission for use from the Library of Congress, Washington, D.C.)

The Plot Thickens

It was when King James II, a Roman Catholic, signaled his intention to hand the crown to a Catholic heir that Parliament took decisive action. They invited a Protestant prince from the Netherlands, William of Orange, to be their king, chased

James II from England, and in 1689, extended legal toleration to Protestant dissenters. Because of James II's plots to return to England, and because of England's nettlesome problems with Catholic Ireland, toleration for Catholics had to wait another generation. However, the tide of history had shifted in the direction of religious freedom, and the English government could do little to stop the further splintering of Christianity.

American Patterns

The English colonies brought over many of the religious quarrels that wracked Great Britain and the European continent. By 1750, numerous versions of Christianity already existed in the British colonies, including English Baptists, Quakers, German and Swedish Lutherans, English Puritans of the Presbyterian and Independent varieties, and the Church of England itself. You could also find Scottish Presbyterians; Dutch Calvinists; German Anabaptist sects like the Dunkers, Schwenkfelders, and Mennonites; and, of course, Roman Catholics. It's hard to imagine that anyone in 1776 might have thought that creating a national church was a workable or even desirable idea.

Still, several colonies did have government-sponsored churches, including Massachusetts Bay's Congregational Church and the Church of England in Virginia. Religious revivals in the 1730s and 1740s made people think harder about government-sponsored churches, and movements to abolish official supports for particular denominations took root. Baptists in Massachusetts Bay and Virginia led the way in pressuring the governments to end preferential treatment for these churches. Virginia disestablished the Church of England by law in 1786, while the state of Massachusetts took a little longer, eliminating the last government support of the Congregational Church in 1833.

These circumstances virtually guaranteed that the federal constitution of 1789 would deny Congress the power to make any version of Christianity the official U.S. religion, or the power to prevent people from worshipping God in their own way. In contrast to the state churches of the German-speaking region in Europe, Denmark, Sweden, Great Britain, and of course the Catholic kingdoms in France, Spain, Portugal, Italy, and so forth, the United States had nothing of the sort. The Founding Fathers set up a free marketplace for religion.

Denomination: A Working Definition

The choices made by people like Arius and Constantine, Pope Leo IX and Patriarch Michael Cerularius, and Martin Luther and Menno Simons ultimately produced the hundreds of species of Christianity that exist in the United States today. The common word for the various "schools" of Christians is "denominations." In a technical sense, U.S. Christian organizations are called denominations because of the nation's peculiar relationship between its religions and the government.

Years ago, scholars developed two broad categories to identify European Christian organizations: church and sect. Churches are organizations like the Roman Catholic Church, the Lutheran Church, the Church of England, and the Reformed Churches that idealized the close relationship between church and state in the Roman Empire and Medieval Europe. They worked together with political authorities and insisted on a civil function for religious institutions. The ideal arrangement was for the state to officially sponsor the organization and assist in its work through tax dollars, moral legislation, the court system, and so forth. They considered all people living in the state's jurisdiction as included in the church and baptized everyone into membership. Most organizations of the "church" type practiced a formal style of worship and won favor with politically influential members of the upper classes.

Edifications

Church and sect were the yin and yang of Christianity during the period when governments established official versions of Christianity for their people, and punished religious dissidents. If you didn't belong to the church, you were considered a sectarian and bore the full brunt of the law. In 1656, for example, an English Quaker named James Naylor had his tongue bored through with a hot poker and his forehead branded for expressing his faith in a way that displeased the Puritan authorities of Bristol.

Sects had a different purpose. Sectarians thought they had a mission to purify the church by separating from society and admitting only those who made a personal commitment to Christ. They wanted to copy the church described in the New Testament, not the Roman Empire. They wanted fellowships of believers who possessed a zeal for Christ and lived as if their citizenship lay in heaven, not earth. Of course this disallowed any involvement with politics because of the inevitable moral tradeoffs. Most believers of the "sect" wanted to abolish formalities and sought a genuine, even primitive style in worship. Sects like the Mennonites, Brethren, Quakers, and Baptists appealed to political and social outsiders with little ambition for power and status.

Church and sect were two parts of a whole in the period between 1520 and 1800. In this way, they served as an organizational counterpart to the doctrinal division between orthodoxy and heterodoxy described in Chapter 2. But in the United States,

Steeple Talk

A **denomination** is an association of Christian churches that exists in a society with multiple associations, none of which enjoys the support of the state. Denominations usually have more than a few individual congregations in their association, but do not claim to represent all Christian churches. Denominations exist in societies marked by religious pluralism.

official versions of Christianity in the states didn't survive very long after the colonial period, and never took root at the national level. That's why, technically speaking, "church" and "sect" don't really apply to religious organizations in the United States. Instead, we needed a new term, and scholars came up with *denomination*.

The word "denomination" itself has its own meaning. The state is officially neutral toward religious organizations. In theory, no single version of Christianity enjoys the favor of the national government in a free market for religion. Religious organizations are *denominated*, one after another, in no particular order of priority. Each is free to practice its version of Christianity of so long as it doesn't violate the same freedom extended to other denominations. So a denomination is an association of Christian churches that exists in a society with multiple associations, each equal in the eyes of the state, enjoying no favor or enduring no penalty for their expressions and practices of faith.

The Least You Need to Know

♦ Disagreements among Christians are as old as the faith itself, and factions developed despite the unity imposed by the Roman Empire.

♦ The Roman Catholic Church and the Eastern Orthodox Church officially separated in 1054, producing two major blocks of Christians in Europe, Asia, and the Near East.

♦ The Protestant Reformation further splintered Christianity in the sixteenth century and justified disunity in the name of principle.

♦ Religious freedom in Europe, Great Britain, and the United States is one of the key ingredients to the proliferation of denominations.

♦ Denominations are associations of churches that develop in countries where no one religion is given official status or special advantage.

4

U.S.A.: Christian Nation?

In This Chapter

- ◆ Learn what the Constitution actually says about religion
- ◆ Find out where the phrase "separation of church and state" comes from
- ◆ Discover how Christianity influenced civil society in different periods
- ◆ Understand the importance of religious pluralism to the United States

Is the United States really a "Christian nation"? No, or at least not officially. Religion comes up in the U.S. Constitution only twice: once to prohibit any religious tests for officeholders, and once to disallow Congress from either infringing on citizens' rights to freely express their faith or creating an official government-sponsored religion.

Both clauses are stated in the negative: no tests, no laws. Yet the perception of this country as a Christian nation is hard to shake. When Americans pledge allegiance to the flag, 80 percent of them identify the God of Christianity as the God mentioned in "one nation under God." Lyrics of some of the most well-known patriotic songs are starkly Christian in content. Federal buildings in Washington, D.C., are covered with religious messages. And other countries view the United States as a Christian nation regardless of what the Constitution says, as when the *People's Daily* (China) recently accused the United States of disrespecting all the world's religions except for Christianity.

Is the United States *unofficially* Christian, then? It's hard to get at an answer to this question, but we can say that Christianity is a very important ingredient in what is commonly called civil society, meaning the media, clubs, charities, businesses, schools, hospitals, restaurants, entertainment sites, and other places where people work and play together. Here, civil society is bathed in Christian images and language, as is clear to anyone reading the masthead of the *Indianapolis Star,* which cites a verse from the Bible, or listens in on a session of Congress, which opens with prayer. The religiously neutral Constitution sits atop a civil society that is nevertheless very religious and in fact quite Christian. Perhaps many of the misunderstandings about church and state in the United States stem from the tendency to confuse the Constitution with civil society.

This billboard illustrates the comfort that Americans have with the use of religious language in public places.

(Photo by the author)

What the Constitution Says

The Founding Fathers thought that creating a free market for religious denominations would produce some healthy competition and serve the purposes of Christianity in the long run. More people would be added to the faith, and no sect would grow so dominant that it would begin to infringe on people's religious freedoms through votes in Congress. During the debates over the ratification of the U.S. Constitution in Virginia (1788), James Madison said that the protection of religious rights lies in a "multiplicity of sects" that check and balance one another, and not just in Constitutional safeguards like the First Amendment.

The Constitution's religion clauses are expressed in the negative. Again, they are as follows:

- ◆ "No religious test" for any office (Article VI)

- ◆ Congress can make "no law respecting the establishment of religion, or prohibiting the free exercise thereof" (Amendment I)

So tests, prohibitions, and establishments are quite literally a no-no for the U.S. national government. These negatives perform two basic tasks: They prevent the national government from interfering with the states' support for certain denominations, or from supporting one itself; and they keep the government from persecuting people for their religious beliefs. The founders also intended these clauses to benefit religion, too. They argued in these debates that religion was poorer for having been too political in earlier times. Government limits on religion seemed mutually beneficial to church and state.

Another issue besides what the Constitution actually says is what people *think* the Constitution says. Most people think that the Constitution says there should be separation of church and state. However, nowhere is such a principle stated in the document. Instead, it comes from a letter from Thomas Jefferson to a group of Baptists who asked him for clarification. Jefferson said he believed the Constitution created a "wall of separation" between church and state.

> ### Everybody Said Amen
>
> One easy way to remember what the Constitution says about religion is to think, "no-no." No religious tests for political candidates or appointees, and no laws by Congress to favor certain religions or to restrict religious freedoms.

Note that Jefferson wasn't entirely alone among the founders in feeling this way. James Madison agreed. He thought government ought to maintain "a perfect separation between ecclesiastical and civil matters." And Madison was the person who actually drafted both the Constitution and the First Amendment clauses about religion. The phrase "separation of church and state" has passed from Jefferson and Madison down to the present day.

Lo and Behold

The Thanksgiving tradition goes back to the Pilgrims, though the evidence for the first Thanksgiving is sketchy. Two documents exist from the period, with two very different accounts. One describes a fairly traditional peasant feast with days of hunting, eating, and games between Pilgrims and Indians. The other describes a more muted affair with a stronger religious element. They have been fused together to form one, largely mythological, event.

Thanks Be ... to God

Still, despite the Constitution's double "no" about religion, and despite Jefferson's wall analogy, the founders appreciated the value of religion in making dutiful and orderly citizens. Washington proclaimed days of prayer and humiliation and even declared a day of thanksgiving to "Almighty God for His great goodness." People were not required to observe, but Washington encouraged them to do so; he also sprinkled his speeches with references to a divine being that helps people in their worldly affairs.

Later presidents followed Washington's example. Lincoln freely used religious phrases in his speeches and proclaimed national days of thanksgiving. Franklin D. Roosevelt and Congress made Thanksgiving a permanent national holiday during World War II. Today, presidential speeches include verses from the Bible, requests to God for blessings on the nation, and suggestions for citizens to pray for peace and security.

Tradition, Tradition

These examples of religiosity in government are in keeping with long-established traditions. The Supreme Court hears cases from time to time that arise when religious groups use government facilities or officials participate in religious activities. They are wary of any attempt by the government to compel religious observance or to provide preferential treatment for one sect or another. In general, however, they find religious expressions in public gatherings to be customary and therefore permissible according to the legal doctrine of *accommodation*. This doctrine means simply that the government must defer to the desires and needs of the people wherever they are located on the denominational map.

Steeple Talk

Accommodation is a principle of constitutional interpretation used by the Supreme Court. It helps the court to determine whether certain religious groups should be allowed to practice their faith without interference from the government, which is a freedom guaranteed by the First Amendment.

Accommodation permits Congress to have a chaplain open sessions with prayer. It allows the government to release conscientious objectors from military service. And it allows the government to exempt property owned by religious organizations from taxation. Today, presidents can speak in religious language while nevertheless acting in an official capacity because the Supreme Court acknowledges the religious heritage of the nation and the customs of presidential speech making, and applies the principle of accommodation in its interpretation of the First Amendment nonestablishment and free-exercise clauses.

Watershed Moments

Although the doctrine of accommodation doesn't make the United States a Christian nation, it does suggest that the Supreme Court find ways to interpret the Constitution to defer to the religious heritage and customs of the people. Usually, issues come to the Supreme Court's attention when the religious parts of the civil society start to expand. Courts are asked to deal with separation of church and state issues all the time, but even more so during intense periods of religious revival and innovation, when public places are given over to religious activity. Religious people in this country have always been busy creating new organizations and institutions. But there are a few key points in history, or watershed moments, when they multiplied.

> **Edifications**
>
> The Presbyterian and Congregational denominations cooperated in meeting the needs of the frontier, agreeing to recognize each other's doctrines and share ministers. Frontier churches that resulted from the Plan of Union of 1801 were called "presbygational."

The Great Frontier of Christianity

Christianity really took off when church leaders began to think about the frontier in the 1790s. Settlers crossed the Appalachian Mountains to start new towns in Ohio, Indiana, Kentucky, Tennessee, and elsewhere, posing a huge problem for the churches back east. How would these people maintain their Christian faith? How would they convert the Native Americans they encountered? The denominations responded by creating mission societies to organize, fund, and direct the effort. They formed the American Bible Society, the American Sunday School Union, and various denominational publishers to flood the frontier with religious literature. They organized seminaries and ministerial training schools to send new clergy out to European settlers and Native Americans. In other words, they expanded the religious part of civil society in the United States.

> **Everybody Said Amen**
>
> The United States experienced three major periods of religious revival and renewal, though only two have formal names. The First Great Awakening of the 1730s and 1740s gave us Jonathan Edwards, George Whitefield, and Gilbert Tennent. The Second Great Awakening of the 1830s to 1850s gave us Charles Finney, Lyman Beecher, and Joseph Smith. The third, which took place between 1900 and 1930, is as of yet unnamed.

All of this organization-building achieved its desired result. New converts came to the faith through the traveling ministers of the frontier who served the Baptist and Methodist denominations back east, and many other ministers that served no denomination in particular.

The Second Great Awakening

The religious energies coming from the frontier swelled in the 1830s and produced the so-called Second Great Awakening, a period of intense religious activity from the 1830s through the 1840s when the nation was concerned with religious matters like no other period in U.S. history. Dozens of new denominations appeared, many fueled by developments on the frontier, distant from the control of the denominations headquartered along the Atlantic seaboard. They gave more control to the churchgoers and less to the clergy, they made do with fewer formalities, and they insisted on less conformity to creeds and established doctrines.

Besides the creation of new denominations, reform was also in the air, and religious figures organized antislavery societies, temperance organizations, and public-school movements. On the eve of the Civil War, civil society began to look more and more Christian.

Religion in the Civil War

Probably at no time in history was civil society in the United States more Christian than during the Civil War. Churches fiercely debated the sectional issues at hand and several national denominations split in two over the war. Abolitionists like John Brown attacked slavery in the name of Christ with both the printed word and armed violence. Both North and South went to war deeply convinced that God favored their political aims. Both interpreted events as either divine rewards or divine punishments for their degree of faithfulness. Both interpreted their casualties as sacrifices for a righteous cause. Soldiers carried Bibles into battle and listened to chaplains commissioned by the U.S. and Confederate governments. Songs like the "Battle Hymn of the Republic" seemed to place the federal army at the climax of God's unfolding plan for saving mankind from sin. Black ministers freely applied passages of the Bible about deliverance to the military campaigns of McClellan, Sherman, and Grant. "In God We Trust" became the national motto.

Yet when the war ended, practical concerns took over. The South had to be rebuilt and reintegrated into the nation. Former slaves had to adjust to freedom and a competitive job market. Millions of veterans required care and resettlement. Financial problems in the 1870s occupied the attention of the wealthy and well connected.

Land out west awaited development. In these circumstances, religion didn't exactly vanish, but it didn't run white-hot either, at least not the way it did in the decades prior to the Civil War.

Everybody Said Amen

In 1865, the U.S. Mint inscribed a new motto on coins, "In God We Trust." The Mint's director was involved with a group called the National Reform Association, a group of 11 Protestant denominations whose goal was to change the Constitution to indicate that the United States is a Christian nation. The motto effort succeeded, perhaps because of its nonsectarian and nondenominational quality, but the amendment effort failed.

Religion in a New Century

But then Christianity seemed to crest again in the period between 1900 and 1930. Turn-of-the-century revivals throughout the nation gave birth to the Pentecostal movement and dozens of new denominations. Urban churches and their clergy reworked theology in light of injustices suffered by new immigrants and workers.

Conservative Protestants objected to the new theology and the Fundamentalist movement came into being, reaching national prominence in the Scopes Monkey Trial of the 1920s. Woodrow Wilson's second inaugural evoked God's providence in the midst of a horrible European war, and he once told a confidant, "My life would not be worth living if it were not for the driving power of religion, for faith, pure and simple." Aimee Semple McPherson and Billy Sunday became the first religious figures to acquire national celebrity through radio and film.

Edifications

Francis Bellamy wrote the Pledge of Allegiance in 1892 to commemorate the 400th anniversary of Columbus's arrival in the New World. Bellamy served as a Baptist minister in Boston, but after associating with communists and preaching sermons like "Jesus the Socialist," he was forced to resign.

You can find all kinds of religious activity in the 1940s and 1950s too, perhaps a byproduct of the awakening of the first part of the century. Evangelical crusades barnstormed cities and towns throughout the nation, as black ministers used their congregations to build the civil rights movement. Menaced by atheistic communism, Dwight Eisenhower lobbied Congress to add "under God" to the Pledge of Allegiance: "In this way we are reaffirming the transcendence of religious faith in America's heritage and future; in this way we shall constantly strengthen those spiritual weapons which forever will be our country's most powerful resource in peace and war." Through the 1950s, denominations maintained the high levels of church membership they had achieved in the 1930s.

The presence of Christianity in civil society has always been strong, yet more visible in some periods than others. During these times, the label Christian nation seems fitting, at least more fitting than at other times. You might be tempted to say that the United States is a Christian nation today because religion has a strong hold on civil society right now. Keep in mind that this may change, and perhaps will, since awakenings don't last forever. Then again, the periods between them don't seem to last forever, either.

A Fourth Great Awakening?

Today we're in the midst of another awakening. At least that's what observers who know something about it are saying. If so, this period would be the fourth, if you count the 1730s to the 1750s, the 1820s to the 1850s, and 1900s to the 1930s as the first three. Lots of indicators point to an expansion of religion in civil society in recent years, which may encourage people to once again describe us as a Christian nation.

Events of the 1960s energized Christianity and led to movements for renewal. In 1965, Vatican II issued far-reaching decisions that rejuvenated the faith for 50 million U.S. Catholics, leading to new movements like Charismatic Renewal. These Catholics experience baptism of the Holy Spirit, which takes the form of spontaneity in worship and speaking in tongues, among other things. They draw inspiration from the Pentecostal movement that grew out of Protestantism in the earlier part of the century. Charismatic Catholics now number some 120 million worldwide (or 11 percent of all Catholics).

Catholics felt liberated by Vatican II. In fact, liberation was in the air. On the U.S. West Coast, the Jesus Movement grew out of dissatisfaction with the drug taking, sex, and aimlessness of the youth counterculture. Some "hippie freaks" converted to Christianity and became "Jesus Freaks," seeking to recreate the simplicity and earnestness of the church of the New Testament. They lived in communes to protest the materialism of the age, as well as to demonstrate a purer commitment to God and to one another. Their music, influenced by 1960s rock, gave birth to contemporary Christian music, which is one of today's most popular musical genres.

The Jesus Movement tried to re-create the New Testament church in modern America. This spirit united them with other evangelicals of the 1970s, who wanted to go back to the Bible and live lives of total commitment to Jesus. One of their own, a self-professed born-again Christian named Jimmy Carter, was elected president, prompting *Newsweek* magazine to declare 1976 the Year of the Evangelical. They were onto something, yet there was more to come.

Angered by *Roe v. Wade*, evangelicals mobilized for political action and helped to elect Ronald Reagan, who came out against abortion rights and in favor of school prayer. Reagan was another self-professed born-again Christian, but this time more sympathetic to evangelical political concerns. Through the Moral Majority and Christian Coalition and later the candidacies of Pat Robertson and Gary Bauer, conservative Christians changed the direction of American politics through the 1980s and 1990s.

Today, conservative Christian pressure groups like the Heritage Foundation and the Family Research Council keep a high profile in political debates and campaigns. But they are just one part of a larger increase in the visibility of Christianity in public life, particularly through Christian media like cable television and radio, but also Christian presses, production companies, music labels, and so forth. And the market for popular Christian literature, music, and entertainment keeps expanding. Wal-Mart, for example, stocks inspirational literature, contemporary Christian music, and religious videos. Just as a measure of the size of the market for these products, the VeggieTales video series had sold more than 20 million copies as of the end of 2001.

Does Christianity's recent expansion into civil society translate into increased church membership, or attendance, or even profession of faith in Jesus? Curiously, the numbers don't indicate a spike in religiosity. Church membership reached a peak at 73 percent in 1946 and declined slightly to 69 percent in 1998. On another front, people who said religion is "very important" in their lives numbered 60 percent in the late 1960s, dropped to 50 percent in the mid-1980s, and returned to 60 percent in 1998. Just one more figure: Seventy-five percent of Americans polled in 1970 felt religion was *losing* its influence, a number that fell to 46 percent in 1981, but went back up to 52 percent in 1998 (The Gallup Poll).

Beneath these flat numbers, it seems clear that significant changes have altered the denominational landscape. So-called conservative churches are growing while liberal churches are shrinking, but it's not clear if they grow because of the political activism of the right, or some other factor entirely.

Is the United States a Christian nation today? It's hard to deny the increased visibility of Christianity, despite the leveling off of membership in the denominations. But then again, more of civil society is visible than ever before because of changes in technology. Trying to weigh the significance of the Christian presence against other religions on the Internet, for instance, would be a difficult, if not impossible, task. This ought to remind us that it's hard to generalize about the importance of Christianity to civil society at many different points in U.S. history.

The 43rd President of the United States, George W. Bush, is an evangelical Methodist, and has made matters of faith an important and very public aspect of his administration.

(Permission for use from Newsweek)

Pluralism Yesterday and Today

You will come across people who believe the United States is a Christian nation simply by virtue of heritage and number. Indeed, Christianity has always been an important aspect of civil society here. However, the label Christian nation carries with it certain overtones that have to be understood and addressed. So here are a few warnings about using it.

First, religions other than Christianity have roots in the colonial period, too. Jewish communities popped up in New Amsterdam (New York); Newport, Rhode Island; New Haven, Connecticut; Charleston, South Carolina; Richmond, Virginia; and Philadelphia before the Revolution. Magic, astrology, and occult practices were widespread among farmers, housewives, indentured servants, and laborers, while African spiritualism persisted within the slave quarters. Rationalism permeated the educated classes to the extent that the faith of a few key founders wouldn't be recognizable to most Christians today. Of course, colonists by the tens of thousands were unbelievers as well.

Second, religions other than Christianity offer the clearest examples of America's protection of religious liberty. Religious liberty doesn't mean liberty to be Christian. It means liberty to practice any sort of faith or nonfaith that you wish, provided you don't infringe upon someone else's liberty. This freedom encouraged some of the most unorthodox groups in world history to take root in the United States. Free-love communes, Mesmerism, divination, Swedenborgianism, and other fringe movements appeared on the scene by 1830, as did a host of prophets, spiritual advisers, would-be Messiahs, healers, and so forth. Ironically, it is the American state's blindness toward the most marginal elements of society, not Christians in the majority, which offers the clearest example of its commitment to the First Amendment.

But this commitment can waver. The post–September 11 Patriot Act permits the Immigration and Naturalization Service to register immigrants from 25 predominantly Muslim countries. These immigrants fear that the INS will use registry information gained from fingerprints, driver's licenses, library cards, and so forth to monitor their activities, even in their mosques. In another instance, Florida state authorities instructed a Muslim woman to provide a replacement photo for her driver's license, since she wore the traditional hijab, or head covering, in the original. The treatment of Muslims in these cases sends a troubling message to the minority religions in the United States about America's wavering commitment to live up to its First Amendment ideals.

> ### Everybody Said Amen
>
> The Muslim population in the United States is estimated at anywhere from 3 to 10 million people, with 5 million being a commonly cited figure. This number continues to grow, and today there are 4 cities that have a Muslim population of over 100,000: Los Angeles, New York, Detroit, and Washington.

Third, those citizens who practice religions other than Christianity remind the United States of its common heritage with other national groups, especially Jewish and Muslim groups. Jewish immigration of the early twentieth century worried many Americans who wanted to keep the United States white, British, and Protestant. In time, many Christian Americans learned to celebrate their common religious ancestry with Jewish Americans, and in fact began to use "Judeo-Christian" to describe the connections between them. This led to greater cross-cultural understanding. Likewise, Arab Muslims today are sometimes seen as fellow children of Abraham, and Muslims in general as one of the three "people of the book" (along with Jews and Christians). This cooperation offers hope of greater goodwill and mutual respect among religious groups in this country as fear, hostility, and terror threaten to poison the relationship between the United States and states in Africa, the Middle East, Asia, and Europe.

These are just a few things that you should keep in mind when you consider using the label Christian nation to describe the United States. The label may just fit if you are referring to civil society, and if you are referring to particular times in U.S. history. But you may gloss over a rich complexity of religious expression that the founders themselves believed to be a source of national strength. And you may give up the benefits to be gained by recognizing the extent of diversity in the United States today.

The Least You Need to Know

- The Constitution mentions religion twice: once to disallow religious tests for officeholders, and once to disallow Congress from restricting free exercise of religion
  or making laws respecting the establishment of religion.

- The doctrine of accommodation permits the Supreme Court to allow religious language and imagery to appear in public places and events.

- Christianity has played a large and often dominant role in U.S. civil society.

- Religious pluralism grew along with the country during its early years, and offers one of the best examples of the U.S. commitment to the First Amendment.

Part 2

The Universal Church

Roman Catholicism and Eastern Orthodoxy are the oldest Christian denominations, with unbroken traditions reaching back to the time of Jesus Christ. Because they're the oldest, they also have the most complicated histories and suffer from the greatest number of misconceptions. You'll want to read closely here, since 22 percent of the world's population belongs to these two branches of Christianity.

You'll learn about the similarities as well as the differences within these denominations. Roman Catholics have a pope, but not the Orthodox. Catholics developed in Latin Europe, while the Orthodox developed in the Hellenized (Greek-speaking) Balkans, Asia Minor, and Middle East. So when you enter their churches you'll notice the ethnic differences right away. Speaking of appearances, Orthodox beliefs and practices stem from their basic concept of the icon. Nothing like it exists in Roman Catholicism. In the end, what might be most striking are the different experiences they've had in adapting to the new American environment.

Chapter 5

Shaping of American Catholicism

In This Chapter

- ◆ Consider the early history of Catholicism in the United States
- ◆ Learn the key facts about the growth of American Catholicism
- ◆ Find out how Catholicism became accepted as a major denomination in the United States
- ◆ Discover the differences between U.S. Catholics and Catholics in other countries

The Roman Catholic Church is the largest denomination in the United States today. In surveys of religious preferences, 27 percent poll as Roman Catholics, which is 9 percent more than the next largest clump of Christians, or those who claim affiliation with one Baptist denomination or another. However the many different denominations that consider themselves Protestants make up 59 percent of the population. Despite their numbers, Catholics have had to fight against charges advanced by some Protestants that they aren't Christians (because of their rituals) and that Catholicism is un-American (because of its European-based pope). Years of hostility gradually gave way to toleration and acceptance. Millions of

Catholic immigrants became naturalized, raised their children as loyal citizens, served their country, and eventually won respect from the Protestant majority.

The Roman Catholic story in the United States offers one of the clearest examples of how Christianity adapts to new settings. Catholics practice a faith that has been centuries, even millennia, in the making. But life in the New World forced Catholics to respond to some new realities: Ethnic and racial diversity, separation of church and state, interdenominational competition, and other facts of American life offered serious challenges. As a result, Catholicism exists side by side with hundreds of other Christian denominations, and in some ways acts like a denomination itself, even though it doesn't accept the denominational principle that there is no one, true church.

The First American Christians: Saint Augustine

The first permanent Christian church in the territory that would eventually become the United States is located in St. Augustine, Florida. The date of its founding is 1565, about 70 years after Columbus first brought the Roman Catholic Church to the region, and 50 years before the Pilgrims brought Protestantism to Plymouth Colony. So Roman Catholicism is as American as any other species of Christianity.

Priests, parishes, dioceses, bishops, the mass, and other aspects of Roman Catholicism all got their start on U.S. soil through the Spanish colonies. Catholics rely on priests to administer the sacraments and to conduct the mass. They believe that priests have a special role in bringing God and human beings together, since they oversee the supernatural elements of Catholic faith and make it possible for them to fully experience the grace of God. So the Spanish government tried hard to make sure priests were available in all the cities, towns, and outposts in the Caribbean, Mexico, Central and South America, and across a swath of land that would eventually be included in the United States: Florida, Texas, Arizona, New Mexico, and California.

The most visible part of Spanish Catholicism that remains in the United States today is the missions of the Southwest and California. If you remember the Alamo, you remember an early Roman Catholic mission to the Native Americans, used later by the Mexican government as a fortress. I won't tell you the rest of the story, but ask any Texan and she or he

CAUTION

Lo and Behold

Be aware that Catholicism got a bad reputation in the United States because of the poor treatment of the Native Americans in the Spanish colonies. Catholic priests themselves struggled to make the Spanish colonial system more humane, and rightly included English Protestant abuses in their criticisms of New World slavery and exploitation.

will oblige. Santa Fe, San Diego, Los Angeles, and San Francisco all got their start as Roman Catholic missions in New Spain. These missions helped Spanish officials to lay claim to the border region between Spanish, French, and English possessions. Priests taught Native Americans the Christian faith along with other European customs, while a small unit of soldiers kept an eye out for French and English raiding parties, traders, or even settlers. The Spanish mission at the Alamo, for example, arose because of news of LaSalle's explorations in the lower Mississippi Valley on behalf of France in the 1680s.

So Catholicism in America developed in an atmosphere of bitter national rivalry between Spain, France, and England. This New World rivalry and the religious persecutions in Europe during the Reformation left a lasting legacy of hostility between Protestants and Catholics. It is hard to imagine these hatreds and suspicions developing to such a fever pitch apart from the political and economic struggles for control in Europe and the Americas. By the time the United States formed, however, Spanish Catholics were very few in number in the region.

The Church in the New World

In fact, the settlers of the English colonies were more worried about French Catholics. They were much closer in distance. If Spanish Catholics gave us San Antonio, Los Angeles, and San Diego, French Catholics gave us Detroit, Saint Louis, and New Orleans. They claimed and settled the region that is now Canada, and the regions we know as the Great Lakes and the Mississippi Valley. English Protestants in the colonies believed Catholic priests to be agents of Spanish and French kings bent on destroying England, and because of geography, they had more to fear from Catholic priests in New France.

The French Influence

English fears of Roman Catholicism stemmed from anxieties about losing their land to the French, but also about having the region brought under the pope's control. English Protestants who fled Europe because of the pope's policies toward dissenters didn't want to go back to that atmosphere. However, those fears and anxieties were misplaced because France and Spain had very different motives for colonizing. Spanish kings took over real estate and organized Native Americans into labor gangs to work the farms, ranches, and mines. French colonizers, on the other hand, wanted furs. Spain imposed a complete political, economic, and social system on the Native Americans. France told the Indians to go get furs, and exchanged them for blankets, guns, food, and spirits (not the religious but the liquid kind). As a result, Indians still lived pretty much like Indians, and French fur traders, well, they lived like the Indians, too.

French priests set up missions at trading posts in the Saint Lawrence Valley, Great Lakes, and Mississippi River systems. Most of these priests were Jesuits, a militant order of priests founded by Saint Ignatius and authorized by the pope in 1540 to do battle with Protestants in Europe. In the 1630s, the Jesuits were given the job of converting the Indians of New France, mostly Huron, Abenaki, and Algonquin. They preached, taught, translated Indian languages, distributed food and medicine, and converted thousands of Indians.

> **Edifications**
>
> Jean de Brébeuf and Sébastian Rale were perhaps the most well-known Roman Catholic martyrs in the French colonies. Brébeuf was scalded and burned to death by the Iroquois during their genocidal campaign to cleanse the Great Lakes region of the Huron Indians. As for Rale, English colonists accused him of instructing the Indians to kill Englishmen, and rumors persist to this day that they offered a bounty to the Indians who murdered him.

A Haven in Maryland

Roman Catholicism was strong in Mexico City and Havana, and surviving in Montreal and Quebec. But none of these cities were located within the colonies that formed the United States in 1776, land acquired in the Louisiana Purchase from France in 1803, or territory that the United States took from Mexico in the 1840s. So Roman Catholicism had to look somewhere else to establish its headquarters if it wanted a denomination in the United States. Maryland was the likeliest place; it was named after a Catholic queen and established as a refuge for persecuted Catholics from England. But Catholicism even in the Catholic refuge was small in number: Only about 9 percent of the population of Maryland claimed to be Catholic in 1708.

Part of the explanation for this low number might be the turn of Catholic political fortunes. Catholics and Protestants practiced their own faiths without penalty in the 1630s and 1640s, but then Puritans in Maryland took over the government in the 1650s, banning Catholic immigration as of 1654. Soon after, the Church of England became the official church. But the Revolution needed American Catholics; it needed Catholic France as well. The French-American alliance and the performance of Catholic patriots in the War of Independence helped the church to win full toleration. An openly Catholic man—Charles Carroll of Maryland—even signed the Declaration of Independence.

John Carroll was consecrated bishop of Baltimore in 1790, the first major step in the organization of the Roman Catholic Church in the United States.

(Photo courtesy of Georgetown University)

Catholics After 1776

Now the church found itself in strange territory: It had to become a denomination. A denomination assumes that it is but one among many versions of Christianity and that it can't claim to be the one universal church for all believers. Catholics weren't used to this sort of thinking. As an added problem, Catholics didn't have an organization in place at the time of the nation's founding, and this was a church that required parishes, priests, dioceses, bishops, and the rest of the Catholic government and traditions to do its job well.

In fact, the Roman Catholic Church was pretty thin as an organization in America's early days. For about 25,000 Catholics scattered throughout the 13 states in the 1780s, the church tried to make do with 25 priests. It consecrated its first bishop in 1790 and stationed him in Baltimore. By 1808, Catholicism had grown enough to support four more bishops administering their districts, or dioceses. Schools for training priests came along as well; Georgetown University was created in 1791, then came Saint Mary's Seminary later that year, followed by Mount Saint Mary's College in 1808; all were located in Maryland. Bishops, dioceses, and seminaries brought U.S. Catholics under papal supervision. Only time would tell if their traditions of church organization and government would survive the competitiveness of American's free marketplace for religion.

> **Everybody Said Amen**
>
> The first archdiocese in the United States was Baltimore, which had supervisory duties over four dioceses, or districts managed by a bishop: Bardstown (Kentucky), Boston, New York, and Philadelphia. Today there are 35 archdioceses and 165 dioceses, and more than 19,000 parishes, or neighborhoods with a Catholic church where priests administer the sacraments and conduct mass.

Immigration and Diversity

Roman Catholicism differs from Protestantism in the United States in one major way: It is a single church with an ethnically diverse membership. Protestantism splintered into dozens of subunits representing different groups from among the European, African, and New World races and ethnicities. German Lutherans, Scottish Presbyterians, Dutch Calvinists, and others each had their own independent organization. Roman Catholics in the early United States had no such luck. They worshipped cheek by jowl with a mixture of other European-Americans, even if the Latin mass gave a semblance of unity.

The Old Immigrants

In Boston, New York, Philadelphia, and Baltimore, immigrants from a dozen different European countries wedged themselves into the pews to hear mass delivered by … French priests? That's right. France threw the Jesuits out of Paris, Quebec, and Montreal in the 1760s, and many landed in Baltimore. In addition, the Society of Saint Sulpice in France adopted the U.S. church as a mission and not only sent French priests to labor in the parishes, but also gave the funds and personnel to begin Saint Mary's Seminary.

> **Edifications**
>
> The first American-born person to achieve sainthood in the Roman Catholic Church is Elizabeth Ann Seton (1774–1821). She converted to Catholicism in 1805, started a parochial school in Baltimore, and founded the first U.S. religious community for women, the Sisters of Charity (1809). She was canonized in 1975 by Pope Paul VI.

Soon ethnic tensions took over the church. First German, English, and Irish parishioners grew frustrated with their French priests, and then later, the newly ordained Irish and Irish American priests grew frustrated with their French bishops. Remarkably, over 60 percent of the Roman Catholic Church was Irish by midcentury. Later, German Catholics mounted campaigns against the Irish bishops. Church leaders could do little besides weather the storms and wait for better days to come.

The New Immigrants

After 1870, Catholicism swelled again with Italians, Hungarians, Poles, and Lithuanians, not to mention more Germans and Irish. Catholics were linked with the teeming urban ghettos of New York and Philadelphia, and now Detroit and Chicago, too. More than ever, Roman Catholicism became known as the "immigrant's church." In the 1880s, newer German immigrants asked church leaders to divide up the parishes into national groups and to give each group a priest of its own nationality. Bishops refused and encouraged new immigrants to learn English to adapt to the American setting. Eventually, immigrants clumped together anyway and many parishes got identified with certain nationalities.

The Really New Immigrants

The diversity of American Catholicism has only advanced further in our own time. Between 1990 and 2000, the U.S. Hispanic population increased from 22 million to 35 million. Of these, almost three fourths are Catholics, and two thirds attend services regularly. Today, the percentage of all U.S. Catholics who are Hispanic is just under 40 percent, at least according to the official records of the U.S. Conference of Catholic Bishops.

One of the major differences between American Catholics today and Catholics in other countries is the blending of different people together into one church. Other Catholic churches are dominated by one national group, while in the United States, Catholics originally from Ireland, Italy, Poland, Spain, Mexico, Cuba, and hundreds of other places are brought under one roof. Where the Roman Catholic Church in Ireland is a church for Irish people, and the Roman Catholic Church in Italy is a church for Italians, the Roman Catholic Church in the United States is, and must be, a church for everyone.

Hostility and Acceptance

Unfortunately, some bigoted Americans accused Catholic immigrants at the turn of the twentieth century of bringing the "un-American" ideology of socialism into the United States. When prominent Catholic Alfred E. Smith, governor of New York for four successful terms, ran for president against Herbert Hoover in 1928, anti-Catholicism reached a fever pitch. It would take the election of John F. Kennedy—the first Catholic president—to convince doubtful Americans that Catholics wouldn't turn the country over to the pope. Today, Catholics are regularly elected to high office. The Congress elected in the year 2000 contained 150 Catholics, more than twice the number of the next-largest group (Baptists). And nearly a third of the nation's governors are Catholic, by the way.

Catholicism as a Denomination

Ethnic and racial diversity not only aggravated Protestant-Catholic hostility, it also affected the way the Roman Catholic Church is governed.

Trustees

Early on, U.S. Catholics faced a serious problem in getting priests for their local parishes. They needed a bishop to consecrate and assign priests, which they got in 1790. Once in place, however, Americans began to doubt the need for bishops. Americans had been questioning how civil leaders were selected for decades, and this issue simply carried over into the Catholic Church. As a result, rank-and-file Catholics put trustees into office. Their job was to appoint and dismiss priests and to manage church finances and properties. Rome was displeased. After a long struggle, the pope allowed Catholic parishes to have their trustees to manage its funds, but reserved the powers of priestly appointment to the bishops.

The trustee controversy gained momentum because of ethnicity. For example, German-speaking Catholics didn't want French- or English-speaking priests, so they took matters in their own hands, incorporated themselves, and began appointing their own priests. In response, American bishops convened a series of councils, which met every three years in the 1830s and 1840s in Baltimore. These councils did two things: They kept the U.S. church from slitting into different ethnic groups and they kept the U.S. church in sync with the mother church in Rome.

Political Freedom

But the pope never commanded affairs in the United States to the extent that the Catholic haters sometimes claimed. The pope gave Catholics freedom to choose sides during the Civil War, for example. Catholics fought in both Union and Confederate armies; Pierre Beauregard for the Confederacy and William Rosecrans for the Union are prominent examples. More than 40 Catholic chaplains served Union soldiers, and some 30 served the Confederates. Lincoln even sent the archbishop of New York, John Hughes, as an official representative to Napoleon III to try to maintain France's neutrality. Indeed, U.S. Catholics enjoyed a high degree of freedom to participate in the American democratic process.

The U.S. government puts the Catholic Church on the same footing as other denominations, even though church officials don't identify the church as a denomination. Rome keeps control of appointments to the office of bishop, archbishop, and cardinal, and offers moral instruction to the faithful through encyclicals, or open letters. In this way the Roman Catholic Church lacks the independence of other U.S. denominations, especially the Protestant churches. The Roman Catholic Church adapted to its new surroundings, but it is not self-contained.

Plenary Councils

The Vatican removed the U.S. Roman Catholic Church from its list of missionary operations in 1908, meaning that the U.S. church now received equal status with the Roman Catholic Church in Poland, France, Spain, and other countries. The bishops in these different countries form *plenary councils* that make decisions for Catholics under their jurisdiction, but they must submit these decisions to the pope for approval. Today, the Roman Catholic Church is in the hands of the U.S. Council of Catholic Bishops, which maintains a headquarters in Washington, D.C., and operates dozens of departments and committees to oversee the different activities and programs of the church.

Steeple Talk

A **plenary council** in the Roman Catholic Church is composed of the church officials who hold the rank of bishop and are active in the ministry. They make decisions for the church in their country, subject to papal approval. Plenary councils meet infrequently; the last plenary council of U.S. bishops met in 1884 to enact the Baltimore Catechism.

Parish Councils

Since the Second Ecumenical Council in the mid-1960s, commonly called Vatican II, the national councils have gained more control over their operations. In more recent years, lay Catholics have grown frustrated with the lack of accountability among the priests, bishops, and archbishops, particularly over the handling of sex-abuse charges against parish clergy. As a result, parish councils have taken on more and more significance. These are made up of leaders in the local church who meet with the parish priest to help make important decisions that impact the congregation, evaluate the priest's performance, and implement changes in worship or church programming. These trends seem to be moving the Roman Catholic Church in the United States to act more and more like a denomination, despite its commitment to the universal church ideal and its connections to the papacy at Rome.

What's American About American Catholicism?

Catholics have made great strides in adapting to America's democratic system and its diversity of races, ethnicities, and religions. After just a hundred years here, Catholics had adapted so well that Rome got worried. Maybe they went too far, at least in the mind of Pope Leo XIII. To discover what's American about American Catholicism, we don't have to look farther than a letter he sent to the American bishops in 1899. Many of his observations about the American church still apply today.

Catholic institutions like the Gary-Alerding Settlement House (Gary, Indiana), pictured here in 1957, helped immigrants to adapt to the American environment.

(Photo courtesy of Our Lady of Victory Missionary Sisters)

Pope Leo XIII thought American Catholics were too quick to trust their own judgment and disregard the church's teachings and traditions. The pope thought that the Americans were too confident that they could discover truth on their own, without the aid of the ancient creeds, the decisions of the ecumenical councils, or the continuing instruction of the Vatican. He thought they needed "external guidance" to prevent them from falling into error.

Lo and Behold

If you are a Catholic and disagree too much with church teachings, you run the risk of being anathematized, which means to be officially removed from the church and, according to church teachings, "condemned to eternal fire with Satan and his angels and all the reprobate." This is done by means of a grave ceremony led by the pope, wearing special robes and the mitre (hat), and twelve priests bearing candles. But anathema is not final; provision is made for absolution and reconciliation.

In the letter, he told Americans he believed the church should "accommodate herself to the character and genius of the nations which she embraces," but denied that the church in America should be "different from what it is in the rest of the world." Trustees might seem perfectly natural to Americans who were used to picking their own leaders, but to the pope they showed how much the laity distrusted the clergy, and how much the American church distrusted Rome. In the pope's mind, Americans were free to make up their own minds in politics, but in cases of morality and doctrine, the leadership of the church still provided the shortest path to truth.

The U.S. Roman Catholic Church is different from the church in other countries in a few ways. The basic structure is the same, but it has a larger number of newspapers and other publications because of the freedom of the press, and it has more schools, colleges, universities, and seminaries because of the relative freedom of education from government control. These differences aside, perhaps the main difference is the independence of mind that American Catholics seem to have in relation to their own clergy, and especially in relation to the pope.

Recent polls offer a glimpse of this independence of mind. American Catholics disagree with the church's teaching on a broad range of issues. Large majorities believe that women should be ordained as priests, that priests should be allowed to marry, that divorced Catholics should be allowed to marry in the church, and that Catholics should be allowed to use artificial means of birth control. Confirming the fears of Pope Leo XIII, nearly 80 percent say they are more likely to follow their own consciences than to obey the teaching of the church or the pope. U.S. Catholics are skeptical about what they hear from Rome, and it's hard to find a more telling example of how Catholicism has adapted to its American environment and become one denomination among many.

The Least You Need to Know

♦ Catholicism had to adjust to the separation of church and state and to its new status of being one Christian church among many.

♦ Immigration played a large role in shaping American Catholicism, since it gave the church one of its defining features: ethnic and racial diversity.

♦ U.S. anti-Catholicism is the by-product of Spain's rivalry with England over control of the New World, lingering resentments over the Reformation and Wars of Religion, and anti-immigrant bias by longer-settled Americans.

♦ U.S. Catholics are more prone to think democratically than Catholics in other countries, so they sometimes disagree with their local church leaders as well as with the pope.

Chapter 6

Contemporary Catholics

In This Chapter

- ◆ Find out what Catholics believe and how they worship
- ◆ Learn how to become a Catholic
- ◆ Consider the importance of the Eucharist and the role of the priest
- ◆ Discover some recent trends in Catholic faith and practice

Now that you know a little more about how Catholicism took shape in the United States, you're ready to move on to the main questions at hand. What do Catholics believe? What do they do in their worship services? How do they differ from other kinds of U.S. Christians? This chapter describes the main points of Roman Catholic belief and outlines their form of worship. It also explains certain Catholic practices, like confessing to priests, receiving absolution, praying to God through saints, baptizing infants, observing holy days, and so on. Finally, it offers some insight into recent developments within Catholicism.

Pay attention here. There are a *lot* of misunderstandings about Roman Catholics and their faith, and it's time to clear them up. If you have an open mind, you will encounter a large number of devout Christians who appreciate the mysteries of the faith, embrace the wisdom of Christian heroes and heroines of the past, provide spiritual and physical nourishment to hundreds of millions of people, and proclaim truth in an age that desperately needs to hear it. Catholicism is the largest organization of Christians in the world and in the United States, and understanding Catholicism today is an important part of understanding Christianity as a whole.

Catholic Beliefs

Roman Catholics value their history and traditions, and yet Catholicism has changed dramatically over the last generation. Pope John XXIII convened a general council in 1965 and it met for the next three years, producing a series of new policies that revolutionized the church. This meeting and its decisions are commonly called Vatican II. If you want to understand Catholicism in the United States today, you have to see it as an institution in transition.

In this chapter, when I quote or refer to subject matter from Vatican II, I identify the documents in parentheses following the citation.

CAUTION

Lo and Behold

One misunderstanding about Catholicism is that it denies the authority of the Bible. Catholics consider the Bible to be authoritative in matters of faith and practice. But they also believe that God wants people to sit down and confer about its meaning. Church councils, starting in the Book of Acts and continuing through the councils that decided what should be included in the Bible, are thought to be authoritative in their interpretation of the Word.

Scripture and Tradition in Catholicism

For Catholics, the Bible is the starting point. As Vatican II explained, Scripture is "God's own word in an unalterable form, and they make the voice of the Holy Spirit sound again and again in the words of the prophets and apostles." To Catholics, Scripture is the supreme authority in matters of faith, but the church is the ultimate interpreter of its meaning: "The task of giving an authentic interpretation of the Word of God, whether in its written form or in the form of Tradition, has been entrusted to the living teaching office of the Church alone." (Dogmatic Constitution on Divine Revelation no. 10)

From Scripture, tradition, and the church, Catholics learn about God and creation. Catholics believe that God created everything in the physical universe, and in the spiritual world as well. God sustains creation and is present within it. This includes

God's special creation, human beings. They are made in God's image, and can use their intelligence, if properly led by the Holy Spirit, to "contemplate and savor the mystery of God's design." (Pastoral Constitution on the Church in the Modern World no. 15) But sin corrupted us. Catholic theologians disagree among themselves about the origins of sin; some think that Adam and Eve sinned first and their sins tainted all humans at once, and others think that sin grew slowly and eventually became universal. Either way, sin, especially *capital* sins that lead to other sins, deprives human beings of God's grace and results in punishment on earth and in the hereafter.

Steeple Talk

Capital sins are thought to be the sources of other sins. The seven capital sins (featured prominently in the gruesome thriller *Seven*) are vainglory or pride, avarice, gluttony, lust, sloth, envy, and anger. Saint Gregory the Great, a sixth-century pope, came up with this list; later theologians would add an eighth, vanity.

Jesus in Catholicism

Catholics believe that Jesus came to earth to fix the problem of sin once and for all. Vatican II placed Jesus squarely in the center of history and in the center of Catholic faith: "The Church … believes that the key, the center and the purpose of the whole of man's history is to be found in its Lord and Master." (Pastoral Constitution on the Church in the Modern World no. 10)

Catholics believe Jesus, or God the Son, is part of the Trinity along with God the Father and God the Holy Spirit, and is equally divine and human. He demonstrated his love by confronting sin on earth and accepting death on a cross. His whole sinless life on earth, his suffering and death, his resurrection from the dead and ascension into heaven, and his exaltation at the right hand of God are all part of Jesus' work in *redemption*. People no longer need to suffer the absence of God's grace, or the possibility of eternal damnation. God rescued them through his perfectly holy son, Jesus.

So how do you make this work for you today? Catholics believe that you have to make amends for your sins, and that everything sin has tainted must be made good. Jesus can take care of you on both accounts. His work (sinless life, suffering, death, resurrection, ascension, exaltation) will be applied to your case if you sincerely ask for God's forgiveness and you

Steeple Talk

Redemption describes the nature of salvation from sins, and has two steps: removal of the guilt of sin, and payment for the penalty of sin. People who are redeemed have taken both steps.

demonstrate your remorse through acts of contrition. This is called *redemption*. If you are redeemed, the Holy Spirit will bring grace back into your life and eliminate all of your past sins.

After Death

According to the Catholic faith, people go in one of four different directions when they die. They can go to heaven, hell, limbo, or purgatory. Heaven is reserved for those who have had their sins forgiven and their punishments carried out. Hell is for those who have committed mortal sins, without the necessary forgiveness or waiver of punishment. Limbo is defined as a state of natural happiness—neither torment in hell nor eternal glory with God in heaven. Unbaptized infants have this fate. *Purgatory* is for those whose sins have been forgiven, but who are not finished paying the price. They will go on to heaven when the punishments are carried out in full. Your friends and family can shorten your punishment through prayers and other demonstrations of Christian commitment on your behalf.

> **Steeple Talk**
>
> **Purgatory** refers to the state people enter at death if they have had their sins forgiven, but have penalties remaining. Purgatory can be shortened through the prayers of those in heaven and on earth.

Catholics and the Church

Catholics have a different view of the nature and purpose of the church than Protestant or Orthodox Christians. They believe that Christians enter into a relationship with God as a community, or as a whole people together. Believers continue to encounter God as a community, through the sacraments, through the Word of God, and through the person of the priest.

Again, Vatican II offers a very simple explanation: "The one mediator, Christ, established and ever sustains here on earth his holy Church, the community of faith, hope, and charity, as a visible organization through which he communicates truth and grace to all men." (Dogmatic Constitution of the Church no. 8) Jesus also sustains the church. He is its continued source of life and power. Christ is present in the tangible elements of the church, which is God's channel by which grace flows to Jesus' followers in the present day.

Christians who are not part of the Roman Catholic Church are thought to be AWOL. To Catholics, these Christians haven't gotten the message that *all* the different things that are necessary to salvation can be found in the Roman Catholic

Church. Catholics believe that non-Catholics may be able to find their way to salvation through other churches, but it's a lot easier if they're members of the Roman Catholic Church.

Young ladies of this First Communion Class in East Chicago prepare to receive first communion and become full members of the Catholic Church.

(Photo courtesy of Our Lady of Victory Missionary Sisters)

Everybody Said Amen

Becoming Catholic in Three Easy Steps (well, not *that* easy): (1) Get baptized. This is usually done at infancy, but exceptions will be made. (2) Receive confirmation. You'll need to finish a program of religious instruction called catechism before you do. (3) Participate in the Eucharist, or first communion. You'll need the help of a priest for all three steps, since only priests can administer the sacraments of baptism, confirmation, and the Eucharist.

The purpose of the church, according to Catholics, is to be a sign of God's presence in the world. Christ sends this sign to reveal and communicate the love of God, and to "open up for all men a free and sure path to full participation in the mystery of Christ." (Decree on the Church's Missionary Activity no. 5) God wills that grace should extend to all people and all nations, and if the church does its job, eventually the entire human race can be brought into the church.

Sacraments and the Mass

New Catholics learn very quickly that the sacraments are pretty important in the overall scheme of things. According to Vatican II, "The purpose of the sacraments is to sanctify men, to build up the Body of Christ, and, finally, to give worship to God." (The Constitution on the Sacred Liturgy no. 59) Catholics believe that Christ himself dwells in the sacraments and this is where they will encounter him, which is very different than the opinion of most Protestants that the sacraments are purely symbolic. Catholics identify seven sacraments, namely baptism, confession, the Eucharist, confirmation, marriage, holy orders (ordination to the ministry), and extreme unction (anointing of the sick).

> **Steeple Talk**
>
> **Transubstantiation** is the view concerning the Eucharist or communion that the elements of bread and wine actually transform into the body and blood of Christ.

Of these, the Eucharist is the centerpiece. As Vatican II teaches: "The mystery of the Eucharist is the true center of the sacred liturgy and indeed of the whole Christian life." (The Constitution on the Sacred Liturgy, "Instruction on the Worship of the Eucharistic Mystery," A) Catholics believe the bread and wine of the Eucharist actually become the body and blood of Christ. This view is called *transubstantiation.*

Recently, a Jesuit priest offered this description: "When we gather for liturgy as this mystical assembly, that same divine power leaps from our prayerful hands and the word spoken is Christ's own word …. Everything we touch becomes alive with Christ. We are alive with Christ! This life is ours to give, shared with Christ himself and with each other. So bread is transformed into Christ's body, blood, soul, divinity. Wine is transformed into Christ's body, blood, soul, divinity. All this transformation is because of the powerful, shimmering, vibrant and real presence of Christ really and truly present in us, the members of his body, our priest leading us in praise and thanksgiving."

Priests lead their parishioners in the celebration of the mass. The subject and tenor of the mass typically corresponds to the season, with certain themes featured more prominently in some seasons than others, as with Jesus' death and resurrection at Easter. The mass has four parts: introductory rites, liturgy of the word, liturgy of the Eucharist, and concluding rites.

Introductory Rites:

- *Entrance* (of the priests, usually with music)
- *Greeting of the Altar* (and the people by the priest)

 ◆ *Act of Penitence* (confession of the people)

 ◆ *Kyrie Eleison* (chant of acclamation of the Lord)

 ◆ *Gloria* (sung by the choir with or without the people)

 ◆ *The Collect* (prayer of preparation to be in God's presence)

The Liturgy of the Word:

 ◆ *Silence*

 ◆ *Biblical Readings* (both Old and New Testaments)

 ◆ *Responsorial Psalm* (sung by leader and people)

 ◆ *Homily* (priest's exposition of the readings or theme of the liturgical season)

 ◆ *Profession of Faith* (using a creed of the church)

 ◆ *Prayer of the Faithful* (directed by the priest with participation by the people)

The Liturgy of the Eucharist:

 ◆ *Preparation of the Gifts* (the eucharistic elements are laid on the altar)

 ◆ *Prayer over the Offerings*

 ◆ *Eucharistic Prayer* (the elements are transformed)

 ◆ *Lord's Prayer*

 ◆ *Rite of Peace* (prayer for unity in the church)

 ◆ *The Fraction* (the priest breaks bread and dips it into the wine, and the people partake)

 ◆ *Prayer of Communion Rite* (concluding the Liturgy of the Eucharist)

Concluding Rites:

 ◆ *Announcements*

 ◆ *Priest's Blessing*

 ◆ *Dismissal*

 ◆ *Kissing of the Altar* (by the priest, followed by a bow to the altar)

You can find some local variation, but most U.S. Roman Catholic Churches use this format, which is published by the U.S. Conference of Catholic Bishops (the official governing body of the U.S. Roman Catholic Church). Before Vatican II, services were conducted in Latin with the priest's back toward the people. Vatican II changes led to a "liturgical revolution" in the Catholic Church, which allowed for a more informal atmosphere in many parishes, and even a charismatic movement with spontaneous prayer, singing, and speaking by the parishioners. Today the Catholic charismatic movement claims more than 120 million Catholics worldwide.

Mary and the Saints

The most widely recognized Catholic practice is the veneration of Mary, the mother of Jesus. Go to any midsized U.S. town and you'll find dozens of images and statues of Mary decorating churches, schools, and even the front lawns of ordinary Catholics. Like the Eucharist, Mary divides U.S. Catholics and Protestants. Catholics give Mary special status as the mother of God, which triggers Protestant complaints that Catholics worship Mary as a fourth part of the trinity or even a separate goddess.

Catholics have a very high regard for Mary, mother of Jesus, and ask her to carry their petitions to God on their behalf. Statues of Mary can be found in dozens of places in most cities and towns across the United States.

(Photo by the author)

Catholics offer prayers to Mary and to other saints in the same way that Apostle Paul asked the brethren to pray to God on his behalf. (Romans 15:30; II Corinthians 1:11)

The church reasons that if their prayers on Paul's behalf worked here on earth, why shouldn't they work better in heaven? Catholics don't pray to saints to give them things or help them out of trouble. Instead, they ask them to go to God with their requests, which is called *intercession*. Saints act as a go-between and are thought to have God's ear because of their track record in getting other prayers answered.

Catholics believe that only God is worthy of adoration; the saints earn something called humble reverence. And Mary gets double reverence. Christians become saints if the church

> **Steeple Talk**
>
> **Intercession** refers to the actions taken on your behalf by others. Catholics believe that others can pray for them and bring about good effects, and this applies both to people here on earth and the saints who are in heaven. Catholics believe that the saints are no less real for being invisible than the people on earth who are visible.

believes they exhibited "heroic virtue" while on earth. All the apostles qualified, as did most of the early bishops of the church, famous martyrs, virtuous popes, and zealous missionaries. There are more than 10,000 saints and counting. Pope John Paul II has declared more saints than any other pope in history—more than 470, including batches of martyrs from Japan in the 1630s, Vietnam in the 1700s and 1800s, Korea in the 1840s and 1860s, and Spain in the 1930s. Of John Paul II's saints, only one was a U.S. citizen, Katharine Mary Drexel. She founded the Congregation of the Sisters of the Blessed Sacrament for Indians and Coloured People, and the pope sainted, or canonized, her in 2000.

Everybody Said Amen

Want to be a saint? First, get listed by the Vatican Congregation for the Causes of Saints. Next, help to get some prayers answered, and then you'll be declared a "Servant of God." Once the Vatican proves that a miracle occurred because of your intercession, you'll earn the title "Venerable." Good company: Mother Theresa is there and holding. The pope then chooses a few Venerables to reach the level of "Blessed." If you are Blessed, pray another miracle into being and, *voilà*, you're a "Saint."

Priests and Parishes

Another issue that separates Catholics from non-Catholics is their understanding of the role of priest. Catholic priests do things that ministers of other denominations do not. They supervise church services where bread and wine are thought to transform into the body and blood of Jesus Christ. They listen to other Christians confess their sins. And they are forbidden to marry. Roman Catholic priests, bishops, and other church officials are more unlike the people in their own congregations than in any other Christian denomination.

Why does Catholicism set its spiritual leaders so far apart from the people in the pews? First, bishops and priests claim to have an historical connection to the apostles themselves, and second, they administer the all-important sacraments. Catholicism teaches that Jesus made Peter the head of the church and that this office was meant to be "transmitted to his successors." Bishops now take the place of the apostles as pastors of the church, and whoever listens to them listens to Christ. (Dogmatic Constitution on the Church no. 20) The Eucharist is also the key to understanding the special role of bishops and priests in Catholicism. The Eucharist contains "the whole spiritual good of the church," and the administration of the rite lies in the hands of the priest. (Decree on the Ministry and Life of Priests no. 5)

Lo and Behold

Papal infallibility is one of the least understood concepts in the Roman Catholic Church. It's complicated, but you'll have an easier time if you know what it doesn't mean. It doesn't mean the pope is sinless, or cannot err. Instead, it means that the Holy Spirit guides the pope, along with the councils of the church, in making decisions about faith and morals. Since God will provide a correct understanding of his plan to the world, the pope cannot err in these specific areas.

Catholics consider the pope to be the supreme authority in the church and, since the Vatican I council of 1869 to 1870, to be infallible. Non-Catholics have objected on both points. Catholics reply that the pope is the successor to Peter and thus inherited Peter's apostolic authority. And the pope is considered infallible only in limited cases that pertain to the church and its teachings. The pope rules along with the Papal Curia, or the permanent officials in the Vatican, and consults with a council of bishops that meets every three years. Of course the pope appoints the bishops who actually administer church affairs throughout the world. If you belong to a denomination where bishops consecrate and assign priests, approve church policies, preside over meetings of clergy, and perform other important functions, then you are under an episcopal form of church government.

Parish priests are responsible for the care of souls. Their job is to conduct the mass, administer the sacraments, tend to the poor and the sick, proclaim the word of God, and build the community of the faithful. They complete a rigorous program of education equivalent to a Bachelor's and Master's degree, and then move through a complicated ordination process. They are expected to live blameless lives of obedience and humility, and of course to remain celibate (unmarried).

Edifications

St. Paul suggested celibacy for priests in I Corinthians 7, and by the twelfth century it was the church's official policy. Church leaders face constant pressure to end celibacy, such as when Catholic-haters produced the *Awful Disclosures of Maria Monk* (1836). The book made wild accusations of sexual abuse of nuns by local priests, with illegitimate babies killed to cover up the crimes. The hoax was discovered, but the damage had been done.

New Directions

U.S. Catholics disagree about how to view the changes of Vatican II. Tradition-minded Catholics worry that the church adapted too much to the twentieth century. They believe that the new spirit of appreciation for other religions has weakened Catholics' commitment to their own faith. They believe that efforts to include the laity in decision making have produced a lack of respect for the authority of priests and bishops.

Many observers think that Pope John Paul II is less aggressive in carrying out Vatican II policies than Pope John XXIII, and this has frustrated pro-Vatican II Catholics. They believe that tradition-minded Catholics blame Vatican II for problems it didn't cause. They see Vatican II as an opportunity to spread Christianity to new people, and they believe that the church has to permit its liturgy to adapt to new circumstances. They regret that the pope has re-asserted the authority of the Vatican over the national councils and over the laity.

Edifications

Pope John Paul II is the longest-serving pope of the last century: 25 years and counting. This long tenure has enabled him to influence the direction of the church in ways that few previous popes could hope to do, principally through his appointments to bishoprics, archbishoprics, and the Roman Curia in the Vatican.

Critics of Vatican II can point to different trends that appear to support their views. Surveys show only half of all U.S. Catholics consider their faith "strong." Divorce rates are up, as are rates of remarriage outside the church. Attendance at mass has shrunk to half of all parish members in several large cities. Fewer and fewer men are choosing to enter the priesthood: 27 percent of U.S. parishes do not have a resident priest. But Vatican II supporters see things differently. They believe they must make Catholic liturgy relevant to their parishes and dioceses in order to grow, but the current pope undermines lesser bishops' authority with new teachings that cut against Vatican II. They complain that post-Vatican II efforts to sanction women priests and reunion with other Christian denominations, for example, have met with resistance from above.

The Catholic Church continues to grow and to experience vitality, but not to the satisfaction of either traditionalists or promoters of renewal. Both lament the church's response to sex-abuse charges against hundreds of priests and other church workers. And both lament the growing distrust of the bishops by lay Catholics as the church leadership probes its way through one of its more troubling chapters in recent history.

The Least You Need to Know

- Catholics believe that the Roman Catholic Church has the final say in how the Bible should be interpreted.

- The Eucharist is vital to the union of Catholics with Christ because it contains his real presence, a view that Protestants reject.

- The mass and the sacraments are the key expressions of Catholic faith, and Vatican II in the 1960s allowed for more flexibility in how they are conducted.

- Vatican II caused a "liturgical revolution," but not all Catholics think it was a good thing.

Chapter 7

Beyond the Mass

In This Chapter

- ◆ Discover how Catholics express their faith on other days beside Sunday
- ◆ Find out what monks and nuns do in the church and in the rest of society
- ◆ Learn the different ways that Catholicism contributes to American public life

Vatican II reshaped Catholic worship styles and updated some traditions that appeared a bit old to modern Catholics. And yet most Catholics experience the church locally, through the parish and local priest, and for many Catholics their experience with the church is only one aspect of their spiritual lives. If you think the pope and Vatican II represent all of Catholicism, you're off the mark.

Catholicism values the church and its traditions even as it teaches Christians to practice their faith in daily prayers and readings, family celebrations, informal pilgrimages, fasting, and meditation, among other things. Even beyond the mass, Catholicism can be a deeply spiritual faith. And this faith must be demonstrated through good works. Catholics organize charities, schools, social service agencies, and other institutions to reduce the world's suffering, ignorance, and injustice.

Catholic Devotionalism

Catholicism teaches that spirituality isn't confined to the mass and the sacraments. It suggests a number of things that Catholics can do on their own to increase their spirituality and devotion.

The main devotions taught by the church are in the form of prayers, and the Rosary is the most well known and widely practiced. The Rosary is a series of prayers addressed to God the Father, and includes *Hail Marys* and the Lord's Prayer. Catholics also recite the Apostles' Creed and several other traditional prayers during the Rosary. This is intended to focus attention on the key points of Jesus' life and of Mary's role in bringing God into human form.

Steeple Talk

Hail Mary, a traditional Catholic prayer, reads as follows: "Hail Mary full of grace, the Lord is with thee. Blessed art thou among women and blessed is the fruit of thy womb, Jesus. Holy Mary, Mother of God, pray for us sinners now and at the hour of our death. Amen."

Lo and Behold

Catholics, Protestants, and Orthodox Christians use Bibles with different content. Catholics include all of the books commonly known as the apocrypha, or documents produced during the period between the Old and New Testaments. Most Protestant denominations exclude them altogether, while the Orthodox Church includes some, but not all.

Some Catholic prayers are meant to be used on certain occasions during the week or the year. The Three Hours' Agony is performed on Good Friday, beginning at noon and ending at 3 P.M., to remember Christ's suffering and death on the cross. The Sacred Heart focuses on the union of the divine and human elements in Jesus and includes the prayers of the Holy Hour and Communion of Reparation to be used on the first Friday of each month. Night Adoration, practiced in some Catholic homes, is an hour of prayer once a month requesting forgiveness of sins.

Lots of other prayers are written out for Catholics to use on their own or with the aid of a priest, like the Forty Hours' Adoration, the Little Office of the Blessed Virgin, and the Seven Sorrows. Prayers also work as penances and indulgences for Catholics who are instructed by their priests to make amends for sins. In that way, formal prayers go hand in hand with confession, used by Catholics to restore the broken relationship between the believer and God as a result of sin.

The church also uses another devotional aid, the Stations of the Cross. This aid is a series of meditations on the suffering and death of Jesus. The person doing the meditating passes through 14 stations, each representing one step in Jesus' progression to the tomb following his condemnation by Pontius Pilate. In most places these stations are strung along a pathway, with each station marked by a plaque or similar sign where pilgrims may stop, pray, and reflect on its meaning. Many churches, monasteries, convents, and schools maintain a path for their members or visitors.

Station XIV of the Stations of the Cross depicts Jesus as he is laid in the tomb. Christians place themselves in the footsteps of Jesus as they pass from station to station, reflecting on his life and death along the way. This is one of the most popular Catholic devotional aids.

(Photo by the author)

Catholics also pray without scripted prayers, study their Bibles, read devotional literature, and do other self-directed devotions. In fact, these practices are on the rise. Ninety percent of Catholics in a recent poll said they prayed on their own within the past 30 days (The Gallup Poll). Nearly 8 in 10 Catholics also expressed a need to grow in their spirituality and devotion, but feel more inclined to go it alone, rather than use the church's programmed devotions. Only 30 percent of Catholics in the same poll prayed the Rosary, and a very low 14 percent confessed to a priest. As with most other Christian denominations, women and elderly Catholics are more likely to pray, meditate, read the Bible, and do other devotional activities than male or younger Catholics.

Steeple Talk

Parochial school comes from the Latin word *parochia,* meaning diocese or parish. Dioceses and parishes are regional and local districts marked off for the purpose of administration.

Everybody Said Amen

The average cost of a year's tuition in Catholic elementary schools in Providence, Rhode Island, is $2,600, and slightly more in Chicago, $2,745. For high school students, costs are $6,250 and $5,510, respectively.

Catholic Education

Speaking of younger Catholics, U.S. Catholics feel strongly about religious education for their kids, and they maintain local *parochial schools* in most parishes. In 1999, the Catholic Church supported 6,721 primary schools for nearly 2 million children. High schools numbered more than 1,300, with more than 600,000 students. These numbers make the Catholic school system one of the largest systems of education in the United States—the largest, in fact, outside of the public school system. Add another 240 or so colleges and universities, and you get a sense of the importance of education to Catholics in the United States today.

Trends in Catholic Education

Catholic schools peaked in the early 1960s, and have since declined in both number and enrollment. Between 1965 and 1985, enrollment at all levels dropped from 5.5 million to under 3 million. Membership in the Catholic Church rises every year, and 94 percent of Catholics polled say they want religious education for their children. But these numbers haven't translated into support for the local parish school. The main reason is cost. Catholics have complained about the double-taxation of taxes for public schools and private school tuition since the 1880s. Most Catholics support recent efforts to create a voucher system in many states. In such a system, parents who send their kids to private religious schools would be reimbursed for part of the tax money they pay to support public schools—provided this money is used to pay for tuition or other education expenses at private schools.

Catholic Higher Education

Catholic colleges, universities, and seminaries are a fixture of Catholic education in the United States as well. Some are well known, like University of Notre Dame and Boston College, but most go about their business with little fanfare, serving the needs of their towns and regions. You might not realize that some of the universities that do get some national recognition are actually Catholic: Fordham, DePaul, Villanova,

Georgetown, University of San Diego, and University of San Francisco are some examples. Most are maintained by certain orders of priests, like Jesuits, Franciscans, and Dominicans, but are not under direct Vatican control. This independence puts them in an awkward position, since the church wants them to teach its traditions, while they and their supporters want to broaden the frontiers of knowledge. And independent accreditation boards demand that they meet certain standards, which complicates the relationship even more.

> **Edifications**
>
> Notre Dame athletic teams competed under the nickname Catholics in the nineteenth century, Ramblers in the 1920s, and finally Fightin' Irish after 1927. The current name hints at the importance of Irish immigration to the growth of Catholicism in the United States over the last 200 years.

Religious Orders

Like other aspects of Catholicism, Catholic education has its roots outside of the United States. Many church fathers in the first three centuries served in schools designed to teach theology to the next generation of church leaders. With the fall of the Roman Empire, learning retreated to the monasteries of the early Middle Ages, where monks translated the Bible and wrote commentaries and theological works. Their scholarship and their monastic schools kept the tradition of learning alive.

From Monks to Priests

Monks came in two forms in the first couple of centuries: hermits who lived in complete isolation, and seekers who formed communities separated from the rest of society. Monks of the second sort generally followed the Rule of Saint Benedict, which had a strict schedule of prayers, meditation, and work, and severe limits on material possessions. In the twelfth century, monasticism changed dramatically with the appearance of the *mendicant orders:* Dominicans, Franciscans, Carmelites, and Augustinians. These four groups of monks continued to do what earlier monks did, namely pray, meditate,

> **Steeple Talk**
>
> **Mendicant orders** appeared in the twelfth century when groups of men wanted to practice a purer kind of faith without the financial support of church lands or tithes. Mendicants like the Franciscans lived only on what they could solicit from passersby. The word "mendicant" comes from the root word for "begging" in Latin.

study, and transcribe the Bible, but they also cared for the sick, taught children, and brought new converts to the faith.

Today the Roman Catholic Church makes a distinction between priests who live in communities with other priests and those who do not. The first kind, religious priests, take vows of poverty, chastity, and obedience, and are connected to one of the established orders, like Franciscans for instance. They are usually committed to doing the work that their order was established to do, like proselytizing, caring for the sick, or teaching. The second kind of priest, diocesan priests, are ordained specifically for the local church to preach, administer the sacraments, and care for the needs of parishioners. There are about twice as many diocesan priests as religious priests.

Charities and Social Services

Men and women of the different religious orders are known for their work in education, charity, and social service. They maintain nursing homes, hospitals, homeless shelters, soup kitchens, and an astonishing array of assistance programs for immigrants, orphans, pregnant women, the poor, the disabled, and so on.

> **Everybody Said Amen**
>
> Catholics give generously to causes outside of the United States as well. Catholic Relief Services collected and disbursed more than $250 million for worldwide poverty and disaster relief in 2002.

The church traces this mission to aid the sick, the poor, the fatherless, and the aged back to the original Twelve Apostles in the Book of Acts, who selected seven men to oversee the distribution of food to widows. New religious orders formed to address illness, poverty, and homelessness during the Middle Ages, and continued to form over the last few hundred years to deal with the social problems caused by industrialization, urbanization, and globalization. Catholics today use their network of dioceses, parishes, and religious communities to administer the world's largest private system of charities and social services.

Catholics operate hundreds of hospitals throughout the country, 38 hospitals in the state of New York alone. Catholic hospitals provide care in some of the most desperately poor neighborhoods in the United States, the kind that profit-seeking health-care providers tend to avoid. The 1980s television show *St. Elsewhere* depicted a hospital called Saint Eligius that got its nickname because it served the poor and forgotten people of inner-city Boston. These hospitals share a mission with Catholic hospices that help terminally ill patients live out the end of their lives with dignity. Catholic hospices accept patients regardless of their ability to pay or whether they have health-care insurance.

Another broad area of Catholic charity and social service is support for the poor and distressed. Catholics turn out in big numbers to help victims of natural disasters, and they support soup kitchens, clothing racks, and homeless shelters. The Catholic Church has always given support to recent immigrants. The Migration and Refugee Services department of the U.S. Conference of Catholic Bishops reportedly settles one in four refugees to the United States each year. Dioceses often provide help in a more concrete way. Archbishop of Miami John Favalora started the San José Mission in 1991, which operates a clinic, an English-language program, a day care, and other programs to aid the 1,500 migrant workers in the Dover-Plant City community, just east of Tampa.

Edifications

In a survey conducted by a migration policy think-tank, two thirds of new immigrants turned out to be Christian, well below the percentage of native-born Americans who say they are Christian. But the percentage of new immigrants who profess Catholicism is nearly twice as large as the percentage of their American-born neighbors (42 versus 22 percent).

Lay Movements

A common misconception about Catholics is that the clergy organize and lead while the laity sit and watch like spectators. This isn't true. For centuries, Catholic lay people have organized themselves for spiritual growth, service to the church, and charity work. Since Vatican II, Catholics have been even more inclined to start special-purpose groups without clerical leadership, though often with clerical participation.

Locally, many Catholics take part in *home cells*, or small groups that meet outside of the church for sharing, fellowship, prayer, and Bible readings. Weekly or monthly meetings of Catholic homemakers, businessmen, professionals, divorcées, singles, senior citizens, and other groups fill out the weekly routines of many Catholics. They organize local musical, theatrical, and literary clubs, too. Home-schooling Catholics form parish organizations to support one another as they educate their children outside the public and parochial school systems.

Steeple Talk

Home cells are small groups that meet outside the church in the home of one of the church members, usually no more than can fill the average-sized living room. Typically, they involve fellowship, Bible readings, prayer, and singing.

Some lay Catholics participate in local clubs tied to national organizations, like the Knights of Columbus and the Society of Saint Vincent de Paul. The Knights of Columbus numbers 1.5 million Catholic men who promote education and perform community service. In 2002, they raised and donated more than $128.5 million for charities. The Society of Saint Vincent de Paul conducts home visitation and also collects money for charity in 130 countries, including the United States. The Internet has broadened opportunities for lay Catholics to connect. They use the web to start church renewal movements and political interest groups, and even to troll for dates.

Everybody Said Amen

Father Michael J. McGivney started the Knights of Columbus in 1882, little knowing that he'd win support for sainthood. The Archdiocese of Hartford (Connecticut) wrote up a 700-page document arguing his cause to the Vatican, which declared him a Servant of God in 1997. He'll have to earn the titles of Venerable and Blessed before he can be declared a Saint. More than 50,000 lay Catholics give time, prayer, and dollars to the Father McGivney Guild in order to help the process along.

But lay associations come with a catch. The church asks that they follow certain criteria, and that they acknowledge the primacy of the institutional church. Church officials are wary of lay organizations that violate the spirit of unity in the church. Some lay organizations like the Saint Joseph Foundation and the Voice of the Faithful protest certain church policies and procedures, especially the bishops' handling of sex-abuse charges against parish priests, even as they try to build a good working relationship with their diocesan leadership and with Rome.

Catholicism in Print

Catholics publish. Each year hundreds of Catholic books go to print, and hundreds of magazines, newspapers, newsletters, and other periodicals continue their publication runs. The numbers are astonishing: The Catholic Book Publishers Association lists 88 different member businesses and organizations that publish Catholic material. You can read Catholic news in 151 diocesan newspapers and a dozen national Catholic newspapers. For those who can't get enough from books and newspapers, you have 89 Catholic magazines and serials to choose from, at least among those listed by the Catholic Press Association.

Catholics write more than just theological books. They've given us great poetry, drama, and prose in different periods in history. One scholar I know likes to say that Catholics who wrote biographies of saints in the early Middle Ages probably saved

Western civilization. Some Catholic books are classic accounts of the Christian spiritual journey. These include Saint Augustine's *Confessions*, Teresa of Avila's *Life of St. Teresa*, Thomas à Kempis's *Imitation of Christ*, and Thomas Merton's *Seven Storey Mountain*. These and others like them have universal appeal and deserve to be read by everyone, Catholic and non-Catholic alike.

The digital revolution has affected Catholicism in lots of ways. Catholics learn, discuss, debate, and organize with web technology, and the church is trying to figure out how to maximize its benefits while limiting its harmful effects.

(Permission for use from Catholic Newspapers)

As with most kinds of print, the Internet has revolutionized Catholic publishing. Thousands of sites invite web surfers to visit, chat, or download. You can find the works of the early church fathers and the medieval scholastic philosophers in digital form, and many contemporary journals and newspapers have online versions. How the digital technology will transform the way Catholics produce and distribute information is anyone's guess. If nothing else, it shows that Catholics make up a diverse community of Christians that nevertheless believe in the unity of the church and its traditions.

Catholics in Politics

U.S. citizens must participate in the political process in order for democracy to work, which meant that Catholics in early America had to set aside centuries of teaching that told them to submit to their kings and to defer to their political authorities. In America, they had to share the duties of self-government with their non-Catholic citizens. And so Catholics found it hard to make a real impact on national politics in the nineteenth century.

Catholic opponents didn't help much. They argued that Catholics were unfit for democracy. A famous intellectual from the nineteenth century, George Bancroft, complained that Catholics simply followed the pope in his political opinions. He even accused the pope of asking millions of Catholics to vote as a block, thereby controlling U.S. politics. Bancroft's views were widespread among Americans in the nineteenth and even twentieth centuries.

Edifications _____

Gallup polls indicate that 19 percent of Catholics favor a ban on all abortions, while 57 percent say that abortions should be legal in certain circumstances. Another 23 believe abortions should be legal in all circumstances. Despite this range of opinion, U.S. bishops condemned a pro-choice organization that identified itself as Catholic in 2000.

As it turns out, the pope's role in shaping the political opinions of ordinary Catholics is more complicated. Vatican II publications asked Catholic clergy to remain nonpartisan: "In building up a community of Christians, priests can never be the servants of any human ideology or party." (Decree on the Ministry and Life of Priests no. 6) More recently, though, Pope John Paul II has said that "those who are directly involved in lawmaking bodies have a 'grave and clear obligation to oppose' any law that attacks human life." This statement indicates that the pope expects U.S. Catholic politicians to oppose abortion, stem-cell research, cloning, and so forth if they are to remain good and proper Catholics. (Doctrinal Note on Some Questions Regarding the Participation of Catholics in Political Life, 2002)

But Catholics find themselves at both ends of the American political spectrum. And this has pretty much been the case for most of the twentieth century. During the 1930s and 1940s, for example, the church counted among its number both Dorothy Day and Charles Coughlin. Day was a socialist who organized the Catholic Worker movement, which protested unfair labor practices and advocated pacifism in World War II. Coughlin, on the other hand, was a priest in Michigan who despised communists and tried to organize a U.S. fascist movement in the late 1930s.

Through the 1960s, conservative and progressive Catholics squared off in the U.S. political arena. Francis Cardinal Spellman, archbishop of New York, took conservative positions on major political issues in the 1940s and 1950s, then supported U.S. involvement in Vietnam in the 1960s. Meanwhile, Catholic progressives fought racial injustice in the South and protested the war in Vietnam. Some clergy even developed a theological basis for liberal political activism—liberation theology. Today, both the left and right draw Catholics in large numbers. Catholic magazines on the left like _Salt of the Earth_ contend with magazines on the right like _First Things_, edited by a Catholic priest.

The most recent poll of political preferences found a pretty even split among Catholics: 28 percent Republican, 36 percent Democrat, and 30 percent Independent. The contrast between Sister Helen Prejean and Supreme Court Justice Antonin Scalia is about the clearest example of Catholic political diversity that I can find. Sister Prejean (author of _Dead Man Walking_) is against the death penalty, and her Moratorium Campaign struggles against a justice system that supports it. At the top of that justice system is the Supreme Court, where you find one of capital punishment's most vocal supporters in the United States, Justice Scalia—a devout Roman Catholic.

The Least You Need to Know

- Catholic spirituality extends beyond the mass to include such things as private devotions, religious education, and small-group fellowship.

- Many religious orders of priests, monks, and nuns were started in order to supply teachers for Catholic schools.

- The Catholic Church manages and supports hundreds of philanthropic and social service organizations, making it one of the largest nongovernmental providers of charity.

- Catholics participate in the democratic process with only general guidance from Rome, not specific recommendations on candidates or policy issues.

Chapter 8

The Eastern Orthodox Churches

In This Chapter

◆ Understand the unique features of Orthodox worship and church government

◆ Discover the importance of icons and other material objects to Orthodox spirituality and worship

◆ Consider the ethnic and racial differences among Orthodox denominations

Like Roman Catholics, Orthodox Christians believe they are the true heirs of Jesus' apostles. But they differ from Roman Catholics in a lot of ways, from doctrine to worship style to their form of church government. As of the turn of the twenty-first century, Roman Catholics and Orthodox Christians have been unable to completely heal their break, which is fast approaching its thousand-year anniversary. You should keep in mind that Orthodox Christians differ from Protestants in a lot of ways, too.

Steeple Talk

What's with all the names? **Orthodoxy** has several different names, like Eastern Orthodox Church, Greek Orthodox Church, and Eastern Rite Church. It's okay to refer to Orthodoxy as the Eastern Orthodox Church, but the other two refer to specific organizations within the larger family of Orthodoxy.

Between 1880 and 1920, Greek, Russian, Armenian, and Ukranian Orthodox churches shot up all over the cities in the North and East. Americans hadn't seen these groups in large numbers before, so they and their religion seemed a bit, well, exotic. This adds to the common belief held by many Americans today that *Orthodoxy* is a strange and foreign religion. It's time to set the record straight. Orthodox Christians say they practice a purer kind of Christianity than any other denomination. They hold to the agreements of the bishops' councils of the first eight centuries, and believe that Catholics and Protestants keep adding new things to the faith.

Understanding the Trinity

Orthodox Christians share lots in common with Catholics and Protestants. They have bishops and priests, saints and sacraments, and bibles and crucifixes. They believe in the trinity; the incarnation, death, resurrection, and ascension of Jesus; and the presence of the Holy Spirit on earth. Like Catholics and most Protestants, their core beliefs are summed up in the Apostles' and Nicene Creeds.

But a few key differences keep Orthodox Christians, Roman Catholics, and Protestants from merging into one giant blob of Christians. Their differences really begin with the way believers think about the nature of the Trinity. The first seven ecumenical councils of the church between the fourth and seventh centuries thought up the doctrine of the Trinity. Between the seventh and the eighth councils, however, Orthodox Christians and Roman Catholics began to disagree about how Father, Son, and Holy Spirit come together to form one unified God.

The bishops who met at the Second Ecumenical Council (at Constantinople in 381) declared that God is one essence or substance, but three persons or aspects. They decided that the Holy Spirit proceeded from God the Father, but should be worshipped together with both the Father and the Son.

Further councils affirmed the dual nature of Jesus as both fully divine and fully human, throwing out of the church those who believed that Jesus' divinity somehow swallowed up his humanity. So far so good. But in the seventh century the bishop of Rome and the churches under his jurisdiction began to express the belief that the Holy Spirit proceeded from *both* Father and Son. Christians under the rule of the other bishops disagreed. They thought this disrespected the Holy Spirit and threw the Trinity out of whack.

The iconostasis is an unusual feature of Orthodoxy. It is a screen that separates the worshippers from the altar and the priest who administers the sacraments.

(Photo courtesy of the Epiphany Byzantine Catholic Church)

Since that time, Orthodox Christians have claimed to have a greater appreciation for the Holy Spirit than Roman Catholics. They refer constantly to the Spirit in the different parts of their worship services. And every Orthodox service begins with a petition to the Spirit: "O Heavenly King, Comforter, Spirit of Truth, everywhere present and filling all things. Treasury of blessings and Giver-of-Life: come and abide in us, cleanse us of every impurity, and save our souls, O Good One."

All About Icons

The first time you go into an Orthodox church, you'll be struck by the large number of icons, or religious images. In Orthodox churches, icons cover the *iconostasis*, or the screen separating the clergy and altar from the rest of the sanctuary. Icons are also painted on the interior walls and placed in shrines around the church. Most icons depict Jesus, Mary, the apostles, and major saints of the church. Keep this in mind, though: Orthodoxy only approves of two-dimensional icons, like paintings, frescoes, and mosaics. If it looks like a statue, it's forbidden.

Icons remind Orthodox Christians that God is present not only in the spiritual world, but in the material world as well. They also serve as a reminder that the physical world will be redeemed by God and will eventually be glorified. The Seventh Ecumenical Council in the eighth

Lo and Behold

Orthodoxy has been accused of idolatry for using images to enhance their spiritual experience. They respond to this charge by saying that the image itself is not worshipped, but is considered a means by which God is revealed to the believer.

Steeple Talk

What's different about Orthodox churches? The **iconostasis,** for starters. This is a screen filled with images that separates the congregation from the altar and the priest, who officiates over the sacraments.

century declared that icons should be given the same honor as other symbols of the faith, like the crucifix or even the Gospels. Because these councils are so important to Orthodoxy, icons play a more prominent role in this tradition than in Catholicism or Protestantism.

Orthodox theologians explain that their reverence for images takes account of the entire cycle of Jesus' incarnation, crucifixion, and resurrection. In human form Jesus was still fully God, and the events of the transfiguration and the resurrection offer proof. So if you celebrate Jesus' humanity through icons, and his divinity through special transfiguration and resurrection services, you'll look an awful lot like an Orthodox Christian.

Rites of Orthodoxy

Orthodoxy teaches that Jesus Christ and his church unite together in a physical way through the sacraments. Orthodoxy observes seven: baptism, crismation (a form of confirmation), the Eucharist, repentance, holy orders (for bishops, priests, and deacons), marriage, and anointing the sick. In that way, they're like Roman Catholics. But Orthodox teachers quickly point out that the entire church is sacramental, and that these are a special set of practices among a whole range of activities that unite believers together with God. Orthodoxy keeps coming back to the ideas of visibility and invisibility. The different elements of religion—sacraments, icons, priests, and even the people themselves—are ways that God's spiritual reality becomes visible to people on earth.

This belief leads to a very different kind of atmosphere in Orthodox worship services. Orthodox Christians adorn the church with luminous religious paintings. Their bishops and priests dress in brightly colored robes with intricate detail and place beautifully embroidered cloth and ornate crosses on the altar. They worship God through elaborate ceremonies that have a long tradition. All of these visual signs are meant to enhance Orthodox Christians' spiritual experience.

> **Everybody Said Amen**
>
> Keep in mind that the 300 million Orthodox Christians worldwide are mostly located in the northern portions of the Middle East, Greece, the Balkans, Eastern Europe, and Russia, with about 5 million in the United States.

> **Edifications**
>
> Orthodox Christians usually stand through the whole service on Sundays. Many churches provide benches or chairs only for the disabled and elderly. This practice developed because the early church had no pews or benches, and Orthodoxy is a very traditional faith.

Orthodox worship reaches the senses in other ways, too. Incense burns as a sign of prayers ascending to God. Candles glow in the shrines ringing the church interior. Mass is sung in eight-tone chants by the clergy. Meanwhile, the congregation stands (yes, stands!) throughout the service as it joins with the priest in celebrating the liturgy. The goal is to mark the unity of heaven and earth, so Orthodox Christians spare no expense in trying to capture a sense of the Holy Liturgy in heaven with their rituals in the church.

The Orthodox Church is heavy on traditional prayers, ceremonies in preparation for the Eucharist, recitation of the Nicene Creed, commemoration of special days in the year, and similar routines. More recently, Orthodox Christians have added congregational singing to the menu, but don't look for Orthodoxy to follow the trends in other Christian churches. They believe they practice a faith that closely resembles the Christianity of the first century, more so than any other kind of Christianity today.

Orthodox Church in America

Orthodoxy doesn't use the word denomination to describe itself. After all, it's trying to stay true to the faith while Catholics and Protestants keep changing all the time. But let's face it, they are a denomination or a set of related denominations because being in the United States requires it. Today, the Orthodox Church in America is the major independent Orthodox denomination in the United States and happens to be the one with the longest roots in American soil.

The first Orthodox Christians in what is now the United States came by way of Russia to the islands off the Alaskan coast in the 1790s.

(Photo courtesy of Kodiak Convention and Visitors Bureau)

Coming to America

The Orthodox Church in America is also sometimes called the Russian Orthodox Church. Here's why. Orthodoxy spread from Constantinople to the Slavic people of the Balkans starting in the ninth century. Russian rulers with names like Olga, Vladimir, and Boris picked up the faith and spread it through their realm in the tenth and eleventh centuries. Russia even took over leadership of Orthodoxy when the entire Middle East—including Constantinople—fell under Muslim control. Thus Moscow became a "third Rome," as the saying goes, and was careful to take Orthodoxy with it when it colonized North America centuries later. Eight monks started the first Orthodox Church in Kodiak, Alaska, in 1794.

> **Lo and Behold**
>
> The Russian Orthodox Church suffered under communism in the Soviet Union, and its plight affected Russian Orthodox immigrants in the United States. Even today, the Orthodox Church in America struggles to unify factions that developed over the question of whether to collaborate with the Soviet regime, or resist.

But the tides of Slavic immigration to the United States shifted in the nineteenth century. By 1905, most Russian Orthodox Christians lived in New York, not Kodiak. The patriarch of Moscow, who administered church affairs in the United States, moved the headquarters from Alaska to New York, naturally. The majority of Americans at the time—overwhelmingly Protestant—then made the easy association between the Orthodoxy and the new immigrants from Eastern Europe, Ukraine, and Russia swelling the tenements of New York and other cities on the East Coast.

An Autocephalous Church

Orthodoxy suffered under the suspicion that it was un-American and that its members could never adjust to American ways. Familiar story. The same was said about German Anabaptists and Irish Catholics years before. But Slavic people eventually assimilated to American culture. They sent their children to American public schools and learned to speak the English language. The change in denominational names from the Russian Orthodox Church to the Orthodox Church in America in 1970 is telling, since the people signaled that they no longer looked backward to the motherland, and were now determined to make a home in the United States.

A little biography makes the point clear. Metropolitan Theodosius led the Orthodox Church in America from 1977 to 2002. As a kid, he worshipped alongside other Polish immigrants in Canonsburg, Pennsylvania, then got a Bachelor's degree at Washington and Jefferson College. After his ministerial training, he was appointed bishop of Alaska, then led the 1970 delegation of Orthodox bishops to Moscow to try to win independence for the Russian Orthodox Church in the United States (that's when the name changed and the organization became an autocephalous church). So Theodosius is as American as anyone else born in the states.

Autocephalous means independent. The Orthodox Church in America is nearly identical in doctrine and worship style to the other Orthodox Churches in the United States— except its heritage is Slavic, of course—but more importantly, it's completely independent of the church organizations in other countries. This isn't the case with other major groups that are part of the Orthodox tradition, like the Greek Orthodox Archdiocese of America.

> **Steeple Talk**
>
> **Autocephalous** refers to churches that are self-governing, but still in communion with the ecumenical patriarch. The term is usually used in contrast with autonomous Orthodox churches, which have some self-government, but not full independence. These are the Orthodox churches in Finland, China, Japan, and the Ukraine. Another category, autogenic, are self-starting churches that are not recognized by the main body of Orthodox churches.

Greek Orthodox Archdiocese of America

The Orthodox Church in America isn't the largest of the U.S. Orthodox churches. That would be the Greek Archdiocese of America. There are one-and-a-half Greek Orthodox Christians for every one member of the Orthodox Church in America. Beside the numbers, the main differences are (1) They are Greek in heritage, and (2) They are under a bishop in another country, the ecumenical patriarch himself.

Like the Russian Orthodox Church, the U.S. Greek Orthodox community started somewhere other than New York, but eventually moved its operations there when immigration crested in the period of 1900 to 1920. The first Greek Orthodox Church was actually started by some Greek merchants in New Orleans during the U.S. Civil War, which also served the small Serbian, Russian, and Syrian population in the area. That church is still operating today, with about 400 families keeping the tradition alive in bayou country.

> **Everybody Said Amen**
>
> Yes, most of the New Testament was originally written in a form of Greek called *koine*. Since Greek Orthodox Churches used the Greek language in their liturgy, they could claim to be closer to the original church than any other version of Christianity.

Greek rites mirror those of other Orthodox churches. Orthodox churches never used a standard liturgical language as did Roman Catholicism (which used Latin), but instead used and continues to use the language of the people. Today, most services in the Greek Orthodox Archdiocese of America are in Greek or English, just as Orthodox Church in America's services are in one of several Slavic languages or English. The Greek Orthodox Archdiocese can boast that the use of Greek in their services connects them directly to the first-century church, which of course used Greek to compose the New Testament.

The Greek Orthodox Arch-diocese of America, like hundreds of other national religious organizations, keeps a website for members and for others who wish to read its story.

(Permission for use from the Greek Orthodox Archdiocese of America)

Greek Orthodox Christians say morning and evening prayers (matins and vespers) and celebrate religious holidays in the home. Really devout Orthodox Christians will perform the daily service of the Hours, or four prayer sessions at dawn, 9 A.M., noon, and 3 P.M. (The Lord's Prayer followed by appropriate psalms or prayers for the hour), then follow up with the Compline Service, a bedtime prayer of thanksgiving and petition for forgiveness of sins. There are weekly devotions, and, of course, special observances for the liturgical year with Easter at the peak.

Orthodoxy teaches that God's presence is felt most clearly in worship with other Christians. God is present in the people, in the sacramental elements, in the icons, and in the other material aspects of collective worship. So the Divine Liturgy lies at the center of Orthodox faith and practice. The liturgy is another name for the celebration of the Eucharist. Greek Orthodox Christians use one of several standard formats to celebrate the Divine Liturgy, the most popular being the Liturgy of Saint John Chrysostom, named for a famous bishop of Constantinople in the fourth century who apparently could speak well, since his name translates into English as John Golden-mouth.

> ### Edifications
>
> Orthodoxy identifies saints of the church by popular acclaim, with approval by the ecumenical patriarch. This practice is vastly different from Roman Catholicism with its highly systematized method for canonizing heroes of the faith. Roman Catholics and Orthodox Christians share in common all saints canonized before 1054, the date of the Great Schism. This means that famous Roman Catholic saints like Joan of Arc and Francis of Assisi aren't officially recognized as saints in Eastern Orthodoxy, but are by the Catholic Church and its followers.

Some differences between Orthodoxy and Catholicism become clear in reference to Greek Orthodox Christians. The Orthodox tradition doesn't have a pope, for instance, so there's no centralized system for declaring saints. Catholics confirm children between ages of 10 and 14, while the Orthodox administer the crismation at baptism (usually at infancy). Catholics typically sprinkle the baptismal water, while the Orthodox immerse three times. Catholics use unleavened bread, Orthodox leavened.

These differences go along with differences in beliefs about the Trinity, the use of icons, and the doctrine of papal supremacy. And yet the Greek Orthodox Archdiocese in America, along with the ecumenical patriarch, search for unity with other Christian groups and are active in ecumenical organizations like the National Council of Churches and the World Council of Churches. Their official position today is one of tolerance and acceptance for other Christian churches, and so they have made peace with denominationalism and the religious pluralism in the contemporary United States.

Armenian Church in America

Orthodoxy's divisions go back to the first thousand years of church history, and have a lot to do with ethnicity and race. But there are a few theological differences, too. The Armenian Church in America is part of a set of Orthodox churches described as Oriental Orthodox churches, which together rejected the decisions of the Fourth Ecumenical Council (at Chalcedon in 451).

The non-Chalcedon churches include not only the Armenian Church but also the Coptic Church in Egypt, the Ethiopian Church, the Eritrean Church, the Syrian Church of Antioch, and the Syrian Indian Church of South India. These Oriental Orthodox churches didn't follow the bishops in 451 who decided that Jesus was one person with two complete natures, human and divine. They tended to believe that Jesus' divine nature transformed his human nature so that the whole became divine.

Churches in this family are called Oriental Orthodox to distinguish them from the Greek and Slavic churches, commonly called Eastern Orthodox. The Armenian Church has its own system of administration and isn't part of the family of auto-cephalous churches that make up the Orthodox Church. Armenians are under the spiritual leadership of the catholicos (universal bishop) of all Armenians and supreme patriarch, who lives in the holy site of Etchmiadzin, Armenia. This church also acknowledges the leadership of the catholicos of Cilicia, in Antelias, Lebanon, and the patriarchs of Jerusalem and Constantinople.

Steeple Talk

The Orthodox Church has sometimes been accused of **caesaropapism,** or putting secular kings at the head of the church. This accusation started early on with Constantine, who presided over the Council of Nicaea, and picked up steam with the conversion of King Tiritades of Armenia. Peter I of Russia (1672–1725) made the Orthodox Church a department of state, which is a pretty solid instance of caesaropapism.

In terms of worship and spirituality, the Armenian Church in America tracks alongside the Orthodox Church in America and the Greek Orthodox Archdiocese in America. Like other Orthodox Christians, they believe that the Bible is inspired by the Holy Spirit, that there are seven sacraments, and that priests can marry while bishops cannot. They observe the liturgical calendar and pray to the saints. But they have a special reverence for Saint Gregory the Illuminator, who converted King Tiritades III of Armenia in 301, enabling Armenia to stake a claim as the first country to have Christianity as the official state religion.

The catholicos oversees a church that extends to more than 30 countries, but the largest Armenian population outside of Armenia is in the United States. About 750,000 U.S. Armenians are organized into two dioceses and 108 parishes, mostly in the Northeast and California. Turkish and Soviet dominance scarred Armenia, and these political troubles found their way to North America. For example, the Armenian Church in America annually remembers the 1915 massacre of as many as 1.5 million Armenians at the hands of Ottoman Turks. On another front, the Armenian Revolutionary Federation assassinated the archbishop of New York in 1933 because the Armenian Church cooperated with the Soviets. Even today, some believe the church is divided into revolutionary and collaborationist factions.

Other Orthodox Churches

Some of the 15 different national churches in Orthodoxy have a foothold in the United States through their immigrant groups. The Church of Romania, for example, oversees the Romanian Orthodox Archdiocese in North America, just as the Church of Serbia oversees the Serbian Orthodox Church in North America. In these cases the differences are mostly in ethnicity and language, not theology, doctrine, or worship style.

There's also a set of denominations that practice the rites of Orthodoxy, but are affiliated with the Roman Catholic Church. These are called Eastern Rite Catholic Churches, or Uniate Churches. The name "uniate" comes from the agreement of Christians in the Ukraine in the late sixteenth century to recognize the authority of the Roman Catholic Church. Uniates number about half a million in the United States; they retain their Orthodox rites and even manage their own affairs under a patriarch, in exchange for acknowledging Rome's supreme authority and the work of the later church councils. The largest of the Uniate churches in the United States is the Ukrainian Catholic Church, but you should also include in this group any church with Maronite, Malankarese, or Malabarese in the title.

> **Lo and Behold**
>
> Because Orthodoxy spread east from Asia Minor into the Persian Gulf region and India, it is often mistakenly assumed that Orthodoxy contains elements of Eastern religions, like reincarnation and even polytheism. Nothing could be further from the truth.

Orthodox Churches can also be autogenic, or self-starting. These churches are not considered by the ecumenical patriarch or the other patriarchs and metropolitan as part of the international Orthodox communion. The African Orthodox Church in the United States is an example. George Alexander McGuire, a black Episcopalian priest, started this church in 1921 when he decided that the Episcopal Church wasn't up to the challenge of confronting racism. It has only about 5,000 members in the United States, but made great strides in South Africa following its transplantation there.

Overall, U.S. Orthodox churches are healthy by virtue of Greek, Slavic, and Middle Eastern immigration in the early part of the twentieth century, and plenty of natural increase in the years since. More recently, thousands of religious seekers from the outside have discovered Orthodoxy, attracted by its traditions and its rich worship environment. Each year new converts add to the total 5 million U.S. Orthodox Christians. And that's a measure of how far Orthodoxy, like other Old World Christianities, has come in adapting to American's free marketplace for religion.

The Least You Need to Know

◆ Orthodoxy can claim to have the oldest traditions in Christianity, but it is newer to the United States than either Protestantism or Roman Catholicism.

◆ Orthodox Christians value each part of the trinity equally, and do not agree with those who think the Holy Spirit came from both God the Father and God the Son.

◆ Icons or religious images are important in Orthodoxy because they are thought to reveal the presence of God to the believer.

◆ The Orthodox Church in America is historically Slavic, and especially Russian, while the Greek Orthodox Archdiocese of America is, well, Greek.

◆ Orthodox Christians differ from Roman Catholics in mode of baptism, bread used in communion, marital status of clergy, idea of papal superiority, and so on, but they have more similarities than you might realize.

Part  3

Liturgical Protestantism

Protestants believe that the Roman Catholic and Orthodox churches are too caught up in material objects and religious symbols, and give too much authority to their officials. They have other complaints, too, but some Protestants aren't ready to throw out all of the formalities that give stability and order to Catholicism and Orthodoxy. These are the liturgical Protestant denominations.

In the chapters making up Part 3, you'll learn that the liturgical Protestants didn't throw out the sacraments when they went to reform Catholicism. They also use manuals to guide their rather formal worship services, and written documents called confessions to express their beliefs. And their churches are pretty ornate as well. It's in the liturgical Protestant denominations that you're likely to find the biggest pipe organs and the largest stained-glass windows.

Chapter 9

The Protestant Mainline

In This Chapter

- ◆ Take account of Protestant efforts to build communities of belief through written confessions of faith

- ◆ Understand the importance of formality in worship to certain Protestant denominations

- ◆ Learn the different ways that mainline Protestants try to influence society and culture

- ◆ Find out more about the Congregational Church, one of the oldest U.S. denominations

It's become fashionable in recent years to lump the older Protestant denominations together and call the mixture "mainline Protestantism." This term is as confusing as any applied to Christian groups in the United States. Sometimes it's used to identify churches that are socially liberal, like the ones that advocate for gay rights or oppose capital punishment. In other cases it refers to a certain style in worship: very traditional and reserved. But it can also refer to the kinds of people who actually worship in these churches, specifically well-heeled churchgoers from the upper classes. Maybe it's time to retire the term.

But there are some important connections to be made among the older Protestant denominations, even if we have to use the label "mainline Protestant." Protestant churches like the United Church of Christ, the Protestant Episcopal Church, the Evangelical Lutheran Church in America, the Presbyterian Church (U.S.A.), and the United Methodist Church, among others, have long histories here that reach back into the colonial period. Many of them use confessions, or lists of doctrines, as foundations of their faith. They typically have very organized worship services that don't change very much from generation to generation. And they care very much about social service, particularly to their local communities.

Steeple Talk

Confessions are written statements of faith authored by groups of Christians who share certain beliefs in common. They usually cover a wide range of topics, including salvation, the church, the Bible, the nature of God, the use of sacraments, and much, much more. As important as they are, they do not supercede the Bible in authority by those who use them. They are not to be confused with the Roman Catholic practice of confession of sins to a priest.

Edifications

Writers of confessions were almost always theologians or professors at European universities who wrote extensively on theological topics. Philip Melanchthon wrote the Augsburg Confession, which helped to give shape to Lutheranism, while serving as professor of Greek at Wittenberg University.

Creeds and Confessions

Some Protestant denominations use creeds and *confessions*, while others reject them out of hand. Why? What makes one Protestant denomination more inclined to embrace a confession than another? Much of it has to do with timing. Protestant denominations that have a direct line back to the sixteenth century—the start of the Protestant Reformation—are more likely to draw theological inspiration from a written confession of faith.

So what are confessions? These are lengthy documents produced by early Protestant reformers. Philip Melanchthon, one of Luther's theologian friends, wrote the Augsburg Confession in 1530 in order to show Holy Roman Emperor Charles that Lutheranism wasn't so far from Catholicism. The confession highlighted points of agreement, but then it also stressed the doctrine of salvation by grace through faith and the importance of the Bible. It ended by rejecting priestly celibacy, compulsory confession, withholding the cup from the laity in the Eucharist, and other Roman Catholic practices.

Other confessions followed. The Swiss reformers associated with Ulrich Zwingli and John Calvin wrote the Helvetic Confession (1536) to try to bridge the differences between Luther and Zwingli on the sacraments. Calvin wrote a confession for French Protestants, the Gallic Confession (1559), which itself inspired the famous Belgic Confession (1561). Later, the widely used Second Helvetic Confession (1566) grounded Calvin's ideas in the texts of the early church councils, the writings of the earliest Christian bishops, and of course the Bible.

Maybe the intent of the Helvetic, Belgic, and Second Helvetic Confessions was to show how Protestants and Catholics were really cut from the same Scriptural and creedal mold. But in practice the confessions turned out to have political value. They gave an increasingly Protestant Netherlands a rallying point in its drive for political independence from Catholic Spain. Same with German Protestant princes under the Catholic Holy Roman Emperor. Add Scottish efforts to withstand an English takeover in the sixteenth century. Confessions stoked the fires of national feeling when nations were just starting to form.

Edifications

Protestant denominations usually don't require their members to adhere to a written confession of faith. In one rare instance, Scottish Presbyterians in Pennsylvania in the 1720s required clergy candidates to subscribe to the Westminster Confession of Faith in order to be ordained. This is the origin of the subscription movement, advanced by conservative Christians in the Protestant mainline as a way to prevent further theological innovation.

So confessions served both theological and political purposes. They offered concise summaries of the basic positions held by the emerging Protestant churches, and gave religious expression to the aspirations of emerging national groups. They were, and are, important, but keep in mind that confessional Protestants don't equate them with Scripture. They still hold to the idea that the Bible is the sole authority on matters of faith. Confessions merely offer abbreviated versions of the theological positions that brought particular Protestant churches (Lutheran, Dutch Reformed, Swiss Reformed, Presbyterian, and so on) into being in the first place.

Episcopalians are included in the Protestant mainline. They have a direct connection to the earliest days of the Protestant Reformation, value traditional forms of worship, and make use of written articles of faith.

The Formal Style in Worship

Critics sometimes refer to mainline Protestants as God's "frozen" people. Unfair, some reply. And yet mainliners are serious about keeping their denominational heritage alive. Not that they don't accept change. Traditions are living expressions of a reverence for the past, and therefore do develop and evolve. As they confront change, though, mainliners use confessions, historic theological writings, and the Bible as touchstones for thinking through possible responses.

That joke about God's "frozen" people doesn't just relate to mainline Protestants' views about doctrine and theology. In fact, it may have more to do with how they go about worshipping God. Mainline Protestants have an instinctual dislike for spectacles of religious enthusiasm. No quaking, shaking, jumping, dancing, shouting, laughing, fainting, or any other outburst of emotion is allowed on the church floor. Save it for the barbecue afterward. Or never. So what is worship like in the mainline? Glad you asked.

> **CAUTION**
>
> **Lo and Behold**
>
> Because mainline Protestants value tradition, that doesn't mean they can't adapt to changing circumstances. Some mainline Protestant groups have even experimented with two services on Sunday, one traditional and one contemporary. The traditional service holds to the historic liturgy of the denomination, the other uses pop music, spontaneous sessions of praise and individual testimony, and high technology.

Sacraments

Protestants in the mainline started out by taking Catholic practices and subtracting the ones that didn't pass muster with the Bible. After he thought about the sacraments for a while, Luther concluded that only two have a strong biblical warrant: baptism and communion.

> **Everybody Said Amen**
>
> Mainline Protestants differ from other Protestant groups in their method of baptism. Generally, they tend to sprinkle water on the head, rather than fully immerse the body in a tank of water.

In general, Protestants believe that these two sacraments enable the believer to encounter God. Be careful here: Protestants—mainline or otherwise—don't think that the Eucharistic elements actually transform into the body and blood of Christ. Lutherans think they encounter the presence of Jesus, but the material object doesn't itself transform into the body of Christ. The other five sacraments don't possess any special power in bringing the believer into God's presence. Protestants still ordain, marry, anoint with oil, confess sins, and confirm new members. Along the way, though, they caution that these are conventions of the church and of the people of God, not vessels of divine grace or mandates from heaven.

Liturgy

Expect to find a very traditional kind of worship service when you go into a mainline Protestant church. Older Protestant denominations retained many of the elements of worship that Christians practiced for centuries. After all, Jesus used a traditional celebration—the Jewish Passover meal—to teach his disciples about the meaning of his impending death.

Everybody Said Amen

Protestants sometimes use the adjectives "high" and "low" to describe the worship style in their churches. These terms came into use in the seventeenth and eighteenth centuries when certain English bishops and ministers tried to reintroduce Catholic formalities into the Church of England. They were called the High Church Party. So high church means formal and pseudo-Catholic, low church means informal and primitive (by the way, "primitive" is how religion scholars describe churches that are close in form to the church of the early Christians).

Worship in the major Lutheran denominations provides an illustration. Confession and forgiveness opens the service, followed by a hymn, greeting, and the Kyrie (an appeal to the Lord for mercy, borrowed from Catholic rites). The service then moves to prayers of the day, Scripture reading, sermon, another hymn, recitation of the creed, more prayers, presentation of gifts and tithes, the Lord's Prayer, communion, more prayers, and then a benediction. There are local and seasonal variations, but the format is pretty consistent from place to place, and hasn't really changed much over the centuries.

The Word

Luther never said he was going to reinvent Christianity. Rather, he was a devout Catholic (to be precise, a monk under strict Augustinian vows) who wished to revise Catholic practices in light of Scripture. So the Word takes center stage in Lutheranism, and most of the older Protestant denominations.

Edifications

Catholic priests get assistance in the mass from deacons, while Protestant ministers have liturgists at hand to help them in worship. Deacons go through training and ordination in order to handle the sacramental elements with appropriate reverence and care. Liturgists, on the other hand, typically read the Bible aloud and assist with responsive readings and prayers in unison.

The different parts of traditional Protestant liturgy are bathed in scriptural language. In fact, during the first part of the service the believer *prepares* to hear the Word. Once prepared, the believer actually *hears* the Word. Then the minister *proclaims* the Word in the sermon. Finally, the believer *responds* to the Word through acclamation, prayer, and giving gifts.

The elements of the liturgy all point the believer toward the Word. Mainline Protestant groups use a pretty formal set of rituals to get this job done. Protestant denominations that aren't part of the mainline still stress the Word, but do so in a way that doesn't smack of Catholic liturgy. We'll get to those groups in Part 2 when we discuss the Pietist denominations.

A Social Vision

Mainliners inherited a tradition from the first Protestant churches of the Reformation that makes them pretty unique among Protestant groups. Each of these denominations originally aspired to unite with the state and completely regenerate the social and political order. In fact, at one time or another nearly all of the so-called mainline Protestant denominations were actually the official state-sponsored church in a particular nation, state, or colony.

Old habits die hard. Lutherans, Swiss and Dutch Reformed, Presbyterians, and Congregationalists had a vision for making society more and more righteous. In certain cases, that meant taking over the instruments of civil authority and bending government in the direction of God's covenants with Abraham and Moses. In other cases, it meant using the church to promote justice in social and economic relations. Today their heirs have a pretty high level of comfort in dealing with politics and with the world outside the church walls.

Edifications

John Calvin tried to turn Geneva, Switzerland, into a Christian commonwealth in the 1530s, having gotten an ordinance passed that required citizens to "live according to the gospel and the Word of God." His highly regimented system required excommunication of unrepentant sinners, and moral policing by civil authorities.

You may be surprised to learn that mainline Protestants believe the kingdom of God that Jesus talked about in the Gospels is actually present among us.

They believe that they have a responsibility to promote the kingdom by helping the hungry, the poor, the sick, and the oppressed. They also tend to think that church and government are partners in this effort.

These tendencies distinguished mainline Protestants from other Protestant denominations in the early years. This later group, starting with Mennonites and later including Baptists, Quakers, Pentecostals, and dozens of other denominations, started off with a more spiritualized idea of the kingdom of God and with a greater suspicion of government. They were initially reluctant to build relationships with secular institutions out of fear that doing so would corrupt the church.

Sure, these misgivings eventually waned in some of the nonmainline Protestant fellowships. Quakers of the eighteenth and nineteenth centuries began to work in earnest for social reform (most notably the abolition of slavery) and Baptists today are very active in politics. Still, community involvement and social activism are central to the self-identity of the mainline Protestant denominations.

Ecumenism

The mainline Protestant denominations promote a spirit of Christian cooperation and unity through ecumenical organizations and movements.

They forge partnerships in missions and outreach, they pool resources to feed the hungry, and they issue calls for world peace. Ecumenical organizations have increasingly been active in politics, especially in favor of liberal political causes like environmental protection, civil rights advocacy, and economic support for the poor. The largest U.S. ecumenical organization, the National Council of Churches, took out 30-second spots on national television to ask the U.S. government to give the United Nations weapons inspections more time to work before going to war in Iraq in 2003.

Protestant groups disagree on whether unity and close cooperation is really desirable. This issue splits some denominational families: the Presbyterian Church (U.S.A.) belongs to the National Council of Churches, while the Presbyterian Church in America does not. The Evangelical Lutheran Church in America belongs, but not the Lutheran Church—Missouri Synod (a separate Lutheran denomination).

Becoming Mainline

What does mainline actually mean, you ask? The word "mainline" came into use in the 1970s to describe the older Protestant churches located off the Pennsylvania

Railroad's main line, which served the established, well-to-do communities to the west of Philadelphia. The key word here is older. Among the oldest denominations in the United States is the Congregational Church, which today forms part of the denomination known as the United Church of Christ.

The Congregational Church

A little history will help here. Calvinism came to England in the 1550s, but not everyone in England was ready for it. English Calvinists—also called Puritans—were sometimes harassed for their efforts to purify the Church of England of its "Catholic" elements. Some left for the continent of Europe. Others went to the British colonies in North America. The Puritans who came to Massachusetts Bay Colony in the 1630s tried to create a model for the perfect Christian community on earth.

Steeple Talk

Congregationalism is a system of church government in which local churches pick their own ministers and handle their own affairs. The churches are held together in a larger denomination through associations of the ministers who work together to maintain doctrinal unity.

Eventually they created a system, called *Congregationalism*, which established policies for church membership and the management of church business. Each local church had a great deal of authority in the selection of ministers, and laypersons were empowered to decide important matters before the congregation. Local churches were linked together by a ministers' association, which policed the local churches for violations of the Westminster Confession of Faith. Of course, this looked very different from the system of bishops that governed the Church of England.

Congregationalism received the support of the colony's civil government, and thus became an established church. It produced some of the great theologians of U.S. history, such as Cotton Mather (1663–1728) and Jonathan Edwards (1703–1758), and it produced Harvard College as well. In the eighteenth century, its dominance over New England society was challenged by the revivalist preachers of the Great Awakening and by the liberal tendencies of Enlightenment thinkers. Eventually, the state of Massachusetts disestablished Congregationalism, and the church was cast onto the marketplace for religion with the rest of the U.S. Christian denominations.

The United Church of Christ

The UCC, with its roots in Congregationalism, started out as a very Calvinist organization, which means deep theological reflection is valued in the denomination.

Besides Jonathan Edwards, Congregationalism also produced theological minds like Charles Chauncey (1705–1787), among the earliest to promote the idea of universal salvation, and Horace Bushnell (1802–1876), who birthed many of the core ideas of modern theological liberalism. These ideas include the notion that language can never completely express truth, which of course led many to interpret the creeds and even the Bible differently than your garden-variety Calvinist.

> **Everybody Said Amen**
>
> Think of Congregationalist and United Church of Christ leaders as the New York Yankees of U.S. theology. Among the many important figures in this tradition is Washington Gladden (1836–1919), who is mostly responsible for the Social Gospel movement of applied Christian ethics. This is a forerunner to the theological preoccupation with social justice in liberal circles today.

This theological innovation continued into the twentieth century, though it must be said that not all Congregationalists were happy to be associated with theological liberalism. Bushnell was even tried on charges of heresy in 1850 before the General Association of Congregational Ministers. Today, the Congregationalist tradition of theological speculation continues within the UCC amid dissention by conservative groups like the UCC People for Biblical Witness.

The UCC as we know it today is a product of mergers between the Congregational Church and much smaller Calvinist and Reformed denominations like the Congregational Methodist Church (1897) and the Evangelical Protestant Church of North America (1925), and the Evangelical and Reformed Church (1957). The denomination serves 1.4 million Christians in 6,100 churches across the United States. It is predominantly liberal in outlook, characterized by political action against war, poverty, and racial discrimination, and ecumenical cooperation with other Christian groups and religions. Perhaps its most telling feature is congregational independence, as seen in its policy of letting local churches decide for themselves whether to ordain gays, lesbians, or bisexuals to the ministry.

Unitarianism

Like the UCC, Universalism grew out of the Congregational Church. Technically, the Unitarians are now known as the Unitarian Universalist Association. They got their start back in the eighteenth century at the hands of several Congregationalist ministers (eventually to become Unitarian) who began to question the Calvinist doctrine of original sin. This doctrine taught that all people are born with a sinful nature and need to be reconciled to God through Jesus' death, burial, and resurrection. Debates over this doctrine opened the larger question of whether Jesus was really God in human form.

Edifications

Thomas Jefferson was deeply influenced by Joseph Priestly and other philosophers who questioned the supernatural aspects of religion. He produced a version of the New Testament that eliminated references to things that couldn't be proven through reason, like Jesus' virgin birth and the resurrection.

Unitarianism became a movement in Boston in the early nineteenth century when Harvard appointed a Unitarian theologian to a professorship in Divinity, a man named Henry Ware. Ware, like other Unitarians of the time, denied the doctrine of the Trinity and believed in the oneness of God. The ensuing public debate over the Trinity merged with older debates over the doctrine of original sin and by 1825, enough Congregationalists in the Boston area were persuaded by the Unitarian position to form the American Unitarian Association, with its 88 founding churches.

Current Unitarians hold that God is not one in three persons but rather a single entity. They also believe God is good and human beings are good, too. This makes Jesus not an incarnate God sent to redeem a sin-ridden humankind, but a great moral teacher filled with God who did great things as an example for us all. Unitarians also believe in Universalism (hence the longer name), or the notion that God is a loving God who will save everyone in the hereafter. They don't think the Christian Bible is an exclusive source of spiritual guidance and truth, and in fact draw from lots of religious traditions and even science, nature, and human intuition to promote spiritual growth. Unitarian Universalist churches hold two key principles in common: congregational independence and toleration for all forms of religious belief and practice.

The Least You Need to Know

- Mainline Protestants got their name from the Pennsylvania Railroad's main line near Philadelphia, which was lined with churches from the older, established denominations.

- Traditional Protestants typically use historical confessions of faith to express their core beliefs.

- Denominations in the mainline like the Evangelical Lutheran Church in America, the United Church of Christ, and the Presbyterian Church in the U.S.A. have formal services for worship that change very little with the times.

- The Congregational Church, with its origins in colonial Boston and Harvard, is one of the oldest Protestant denominations in the United States, and gave rise to the United Church of Christ and the Unitarian Universalist Association.

Chapter 10

Episcopalians

In This Chapter

 ◆ Find out how the Episcopalian Church grew out of the Church of England

 ◆ Consider the ways that episcopal organization makes the Episcopalian Church different from other Protestant churches

 ◆ Learn about the Book of Common Prayer, a guide to Episcopalian faith and practice

 ◆ Understand the connection between the Episcopalian Church in the United States and other Anglican churches worldwide

Ever see a church with a red door? More than likely, it's your local Episcopalian church. They say that church doors were painted red in the medieval period to signal that they were, in fact, churches, and that anyone fleeing danger could find sanctuary within. The story goes that soldiers in battle could escape their enemies by seeking out the red door, since no soldier would be allowed to pursue his enemy inside a church. In time, red came to symbolize Christ's blood shed for sinners and the spiritual sanctuary that religious seekers could find behind the church doors.

It's also tempting to suggest that Episcopalian red doors are red because of the denomination's connection to the Church of England. England's national color is red. The English national soccer team and the Buckingham Palace guards wear red. England's national flag celebrates the patron saint of England, Saint George, and it is a red cross on a white field. Of course, all Americans remember the redcoats of the Revolutionary War. Next time you walk or drive by a red door on an Episcopalian church, think about the church's long association with Christianity in England. It will help focus your attention on certain aspects of the church's history, organization, and doctrine.

The Church of England

Let's be clear: You can't understand Episcopalianism apart from its mother church. Episcopalians are part of a global fellowship of Christians called the Anglican Communion, a family of nation-based denominations spawned by the Church of England in places once controlled by the British Empire. When the Empire and the Church of England departed, they left behind Anglican churches, and in the United States, the *Anglican* Church is officially known as the Protestant Episcopal Church in the U.S.A. (or Episcopal Church, U.S.A. for short).

Steeple Talk

Episcopalians are also called **Anglicans**. The word "Anglican" derives from the Latin word for English, and since the Episcopal Church came out of the Church of England, the label Anglican works just as well.

Technically, the Church of England separated from the Roman Catholic Church in the 1530s, about the time the Reformation reached its fever pitch in Europe. From that point on, English monarchs from King Henry VIII to Queen Elizabeth II (today's queen) headed the Church of England, not the pope. That fact invited reformers to lobby the kings and queens, along with their ministers, to get rid of the Catholic elements of the church.

They had some spectacular successes. Henry VIII got rid of monasteries and put the English translation of the Bible into the churches. His son Edward VI let priests marry and installed the Book of Common Prayer as the standard liturgy, which completely altered the Latin mass that the English church had used on Sunday mornings for centuries. Then Edward sent Catholicism packing with his famous Forty-Two Articles, a fairly faithful rendition of Protestant doctrine. But then Elizabeth I (Henry's daughter by Anne Boleyn) took over in 1558 and put a stop to the Protestant makeover. She preserved the bishops, the saints, many church ceremonies, and, of course, the headship of the monarch over the church.

Edifications _____

The Episcopal Church has one of the most colorful starting points of any of the Christian denominations. Henry VIII separated the Church of England from the Roman Catholic Church because the pope wouldn't annul his marriage to Catherine of Aragon. Parliament and the Archbishop of Canterbury performed the dual service of making the annulment legal and putting Henry VIII at the head of the church. Eventually, Henry VIII would marry five other women, two of whom he had executed by having their heads severed with an axe.

Those who wished to continue the makeover (like, say, getting rid of images and ceremonies, bishops, and the very formal Book of Common Prayer) grew more and more frustrated. Some went to Plymouth and Massachusetts Bay Colonies to show England how to do the Reformation right, but those who stayed behind finally got the ear of Parliament in the 1630s and 1640s. In a showdown the likes of which the world has never seen, Parliament went to war against the king and his supporters; Parliament won, sealing its victory by chopping off the head of King Charles I in 1649. Chaos ensued, with several powerful factions struggling to redefine the Church of England.

By 1660, English Christians had grown sick of all the religious controversy and political violence. They put the king's heir back on the throne and reinstalled the bishops with their Book of Common Prayer. The Church of England as we know it today, with its unusual combination of Protestant and Catholic elements, had come into being.

Divided Loyalties

The Church of England went everywhere English settlers went during the seventeenth and eighteenth centuries. Puritans in several of the New England colonies still considered themselves part of the Church of England, though less so by the middle of the seventeenth century. Church of England attendance was high among the professional class in colonial seaports like Newport, Philadelphia, and Charleston. But it was especially strong among the tobacco planters of the southern colonies. Anyone living in Virginia, for example, was considered a member unless he or she formally dissented. Settlers were required to attend at least once a month, on penalty of five shillings or 50 pounds of tobacco.

On the national level, seven signers of the Declaration of Independence are buried in the churchyard of Christ Church in Philadelphia, which is an Episcopal church. Some 28 of the 55 men who attended the Constitution Convention in Philadelphia maintained affiliation, though we should acknowledge that it's hard to know what that

Steeple Talk

Vestries are local boards in the Episcopal Church composed of influential members of the congregation. Typically, they are elected to three-year terms and meet once a month. Their duties range from building maintenance to administration of church programs to securing funds to pay the minister.

means. Benjamin Franklin and George Washington are on that list and both were notoriously skeptical of many Church of England doctrines. Washington, the story goes, always left church in the middle of services so he wouldn't have to take communion.

In fact, the Church of England faced a major crisis in the 1770s. Lay Anglicans split down the middle for and against independence and often used meetings of the local boards (called *vestries*) to vent their political disagreements. Anglican ministers vowed to support the king as part of their original appointments, so they were branded Tories when they wouldn't renounce their oaths. Many clergymen fled to British-occupied zones or Canada. It's a miracle the church survived the war at all.

Protestant Episcopal Church in the U.S.A.

With independence, the Church of England didn't officially exist in the United States. Now, Anglican ministers had no bishop to look to for leadership, no financial support from England's Society for the Propagation of the Gospel, and no sympathy from a population deeply suspicious of their loyalties. But the majority of Anglicans who supported independence still valued the traditions, doctrines, and worship of the church.

So the Church of England transformed itself into the Protestant Episcopal Church in the U.S.A., an independent denomination. And what about the differences between the English and American versions? Episcopalians adopted the articles of the Church of England with a few slight modifications. They also accepted the basic format of the Book of Common Prayer, but translated its prayers, ceremonies, and rites into American lingo. Remember, it's been said once or twice that England and America are two countries separated by a common language. And for the record, a "lorry" is a truck, "potato chips" are french fries, and "loo" is a toilet. The Book of Common Prayer and the constitution of the church also purged references to the king, quite naturally.

Lo and Behold

One of the major differences between the original English and the first American prayer book in 1789 is that the Americans dropped the Athanasian Creed. This creed is a long explanation of the trinity and the dual nature of Jesus as both God and man. It also warns that if you don't believe in this creed, you won't be saved.

Once the new American Episcopalians had their prayer book, a constitution, and a set of bishops in place, they were ready for the nineteenth century. They built colleges and seminaries, mission organizations and social service clubs, and of course pitched in with other Protestant groups in shaping American politics. More U.S. presidents have identified themselves as Episcopalian than any other denomination (11 total), including Franklin D. Roosevelt and George H. W. Bush. The National Cathedral in Washington, D.C., the sixth largest cathedral in the world, is Episcopalian. Even though he was a Presbyterian, Woodrow Wilson's buried there.

Everybody Said Amen

The Protestant Episcopal Church isn't the only Anglican denomination in the United States. There are several others, including the Anglican Catholic Church, the Reformed Episcopal Church, and the National Organization of the New Apostolic Church of North America. Their membership is small, and they aren't recognized by the Anglican Communion, the international body of Anglican churches. For the most part, their disagreements with the main body of Anglicans lie in the areas of the Eucharist and church authority.

Today, more than 2.3 million people maintain membership in about 7,400 Protestant Episcopal Churches in the United States. And as many as 3.4 million identify themselves as Episcopalian or Anglican in surveys. They are united by a reverence for tradition and the ceremonies of the church. But feelings aren't the only thing keeping them together. Two props hold the denomination's structure firmly in place: the bishops and the Book of Common Prayer.

Can Protestants Really Have Bishops?

Episcopalians worship in churches that are organized very much like other Anglican churches worldwide. Each local church has a presiding minister, who is called either a rector, vicar, or priest. The rector answers to a local vestry. Put a dozen or more churches together and you have a diocese, administered by a bishop. There are no archbishops in the U.S. Protestant Episcopal Church.

Instead, the denomination is steered by a triennial General Convention that is uniquely American. The body meets in two separate chambers, sort of like the U.S. Senate and House of Representatives. In the House of Bishops, only bishops can participate. The House of Deputies has four priests and four laypersons from each diocese in attendance. If you want to change some policy of the church, you have to get agreement from both chambers.

This turned Episcopalianism in the direction of American-style democracy. Bishops are considered spiritual leaders and have official duties at the regional, national, and international levels. But in the United States, laypersons play a very large role in administering church affairs through their local vestries, diocesan councils, and the General Convention. Such a tradition goes all the way back to the colonial period, when ordinary Anglicans in places like Virginia had to make lots of decisions about the church in the absence of permanent ministers or local bishops.

Edifications

The Episcopal Church celebrates diversity in its ranks. You can be a member of an Episcopal Church and still call yourself an evangelical, a Catholic, or a theological liberal. You can even find a growing number of charismatic Episcopalians, with their stress on the gifts of the Holy Spirit like faith healing, speaking in tongues, and enthusiastic worship.

Administration aside, lay Episcopalians express their spirituality in ways other than the script written into the Book of Common Prayer and directed by bishops. Some Episcopalians call themselves evangelicals and stress the personal experience of conversion and moral regeneration over the formalities of the church. Some rectors and bishops not only participate but are counted among the leaders. Evangelicals argue with traditional Episcopalians who stress the denomination's liturgy, sacraments, and articles of faith. These positions trace their start back to the early nineteenth century, when evangelicals like Bishop William Meade debated those who followed England's Oxford Movement, which made positive comparisons between Anglicanism and Roman Catholicism.

Lo and Behold

The Oxford Movement of the Church of England began in the 1830s. It is also called Tractarianism because of the tracts written by a number of theologians, including Edward Pusey, a professor of Hebrew at Oxford University. They thought evangelical-leaning Anglicans were misguided in their emphasis on personal conversion and morality. Tractarians proclaimed the historic traditions of the church, the sacraments, the apostolic succession of the bishops, and Anglicanism's other Catholic elements.

Keep in mind that other denominations have bishops, too. These include churches that broke away from the Church of England and the Protestant Episcopal Church in the U.S.A., like the United Methodist Church, the African Methodist Episcopal Church, and the Church of the United Brethren in Christ, among others. But churches outside the Anglican tradition may have bishops as well, like Mennonites and Amish. Many Protestant groups believe that the practice of the early Christians of picking overseers (or *episkopos* in Greek) from among the congregational elders to supervise groups of churches makes it sufficiently apostolic and primitive to be continued in the present age.

This Episcopal Church symbol is used throughout the United States. A big red cross in the center represents the cross of Saint George, symbolizing the Episcopal Church's link to the Church of England. The nine smaller crosses signify the original nine dioceses that formed the Protestant Episcopal Church in the U.S.A. in 1789.

(Reproduced with the permission of the Domestic and Foreign Missionary Society PECUSA)

Book of Common Prayer

The Book of Common Prayer is the other unifying element of the church. Episcopalians inherited this manual of Christian belief and practice from the Church of England, though you should bear in mind that other denominations use worship manuals, too, particularly the Roman Catholic Church and the Lutheran denominations. The Episcopalian prayer book is revised periodically, but the core remains the same.

Creeds and Doctrines

The Book of Common Prayer includes the Apostles' and Nicene Creeds. These are considered to be vitally important elements of Episcopalian belief. They unite Episcopalians with the Christians of the early centuries of the faith, and they unite them with other Christians in the Catholic, Orthodox, and most Protestant communions. The ancient creeds are also used in ecumenical conversations among Episcopalian, Catholic, and Protestant groups as a basis for further dialogue and even cooperation.

Edifications _____

The Episcopal Church is at the head of the line among Christian groups seeking greater unity across denominational boundaries. William Huntington, a rector in Massachusetts and later New York, wrote a book in 1870 that identified four common elements that could provide broad agreement: Scripture as the Word of God, the two sacraments ordered by Jesus, the Apostles' and Nicene Creeds, and the institution of bishops. The last one has been a major sticking point for many Protestant groups.

You can find a lot of other documents in there as well. The Articles of Faith are included, which is a long list of doctrinal positions on the nature of God, the church, sin, the sacraments, the role of the ministers, and so on. So is the Chalcedon Creed, which was written in 451 in order to clarify that Jesus was both fully human and fully divine. There's also a catechism used to train children and new converts.

Instructions for the Eucharist

As one of two sacraments established by Jesus himself, so the Episcopalians argue, the Eucharist holds a special place among Anglican rites. Episcopalians believe that the real presence of Christ is in the communion elements, which falls short of the Catholic doctrine that the bread and wine become the actual body and blood of Jesus, but doesn't go along with some of the other Protestant churches, which deny that anything supernatural is involved.

The Book of Common Prayer explains the Episcopalian understanding of the communion rite, but it also instructs the rector on how to perform it appropriately with relevant prayers and Scripture readings. Episcopalians take communion weekly, and more often during the special seasons of the liturgical calendar.

The Eucharist is delivered in a highly structured and ceremonial way, like any other part of Episcopalian worship. This formality suits a denomination that values formality and insists on refinement throughout the church. Worship takes place in a very elegant space, with rectors, acolytes (candle lighters), choir members, and others dressed in colorful robes. This ceremony sets a tone for the kind of reverence the church expects from those receiving the Eucharist.

Everybody Said Amen

Think of the Eucharist, or communion, as the most tangible thing that separates the Christian denominations. They disagree on what it means, how it is administered, and who is qualified to participate. Episcopalians use words like "real presence" to describe what the Eucharist entails, and they open the communion table to anyone who has been baptized in any Christian church.

Private Devotional Aids

Included in the prayer book you'll find suggestions for performing religious services in the home, as well as individual devotional aids to help Christians along in their faith journeys. Like Catholics and Orthodox Christians, Episcopalians generally emphasize the corporate nature of the church and performing religious observances as a body, but this doesn't mean that home prayer, Bible reading, recitation of the creeds, and other devotions are excluded.

Of course, Episcopalians seeking greater spiritual maturity can turn elsewhere for help. And many do. They use the Bible itself, Bible study helps, psalters, and hymnals. Since the Episcopalian Church embraces a diversity of opinion within its ranks, many seek wisdom from other Christian traditions and even other religions.

The Anglican Communion

Christians follow the Anglican way in places like Brazil and Bangladesh, Melanesia and Myanmar. The Episcopal Church of the Sudan has 24 dioceses with churches in the Sudan, Kenya, and Uganda. Of course, you should add the churches of the Commonwealth, which includes some former colonies like Canada, Australia, Papua New Guinea, and the Bahamas that still consider Queen Elizabeth II to be their head of state. A whopping 83 million Christians across the globe belong to an international organization called the Anglican Communion.

What does this mean in practice? The Anglican Communion is a way for Anglicans outside of England to demonstrate their loyalty to the church's traditions, the historic episcopacy—the bishops—and the Book of Common Prayer. The Anglican-style churches in these different places aren't required to join. And they can leave any time they want. But staying put gives them common fellowship with millions of other Christians. It also allows them to coordinate their missionary and relief work. Finally, they get a ticket to the once-a-decade Lambeth Conference.

CAUTION

Lo and Behold _____

The Archbishop of Canterbury is the head of the Church of England. Why isn't the head of the church located in London, you ask? Good question. Canterbury started off as a Roman town, and was later taken over by the Saxons. In 597, Pope Gregory dispatched a monk to Canterbury to establish Roman Catholicism in Britain, which he did by building a monastery. So Canterbury got its position by being the first town in England with a Christian presence.

The Lambeth Conference

The Lambeth Conference convenes every 10 years in England. Bishops from all the Anglican Communion churches throughout the world propose changes and vote on resolutions. Importantly, these resolutions are not binding on American Episcopalians until the General Convention in the United States agrees to them. Lots of other things happen at these conferences as well. It's kind of like a big Christian festival of prayer, singing, and celebration. Anglican interest groups also use the occasion to meet together to coordinate strategies for bringing about change in the Anglican Communion.

The 1998 Lambeth Conference brought bishops from dozens of countries, and in fact was called the Rainbow Conference by some of its attendees.

(Image credit Andrew Day Design/Rosenthal)

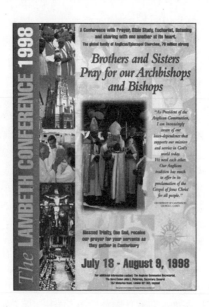

Edifications

Bishop Barbara C. Harris is a trailblazer. In 1988, she became the first women to be consecrated as a bishop not only in the United States, but in the entire worldwide Anglican Communion.

The last three or four Lambeth Conferences have produced quite a stir in Anglican circles worldwide, including the United States. Recent conferences encouraged Anglican Communion churches to permit women's ordination to the offices of deacon and priest. The 1978 conference recommended consecration of women as bishops, which many member churches decided to follow. At the Lambeth Conference 10 years later, 11 women bishops attended.

The Anglican Communion and Human Sexuality

The 1998 Lambeth Conference took up the issue of human sexuality and resolved to uphold "faithfulness in marriage between a man and a woman in lifelong union" and sexual abstinence in singleness. This view has been interpreted as a conservative position on homosexuality, and its approval is thought to have hinged on the votes by a conservative delegation of bishops from Africa, who stand opposed to progressive bishops from industrialized nations. In the United States, some priests bless same-sex unions, while others protest their actions. The pro-gay organization Integrity and the conservative American Anglican Council lobby in support of their divergent views on the role of homosexuals in the church.

In 2003, the General Convention of the Episcopal Church, U.S.A. voted to accept the election of an openly gay minister, Rev. Gene Robinson, as bishop of the Diocese of New Hampshire, which was greeted with a mixed reaction in the worldwide communion. Bishops from Nigeria, Uganda, Egypt, Central Africa, and elsewhere have indicated that this move would put the entire communion in jeopardy.

Perhaps compromise is possible. After all, Episcopalians have a long tradition of compromise, going all the way back to Queen Elizabeth's delicate balance between Catholic and Protestant factions in the sixteenth century. Episcopalians in the United States have their own striking examples of political opposites working together. Two of the original bishops in the United States, Samuel Seabury and William White, were ardent Loyalist and patriot, respectively, and yet without their cooperation it's doubtful the church would have outlasted the colonial period.

The Least You Need to Know

- The Church of England is the mother church to scores of Anglican churches worldwide, including the Episcopal Church in the United States.

- Episcopalianism, also called Anglicanism, blends together Catholic and Protestant elements, so some scholars place it in a separate category of Christianity.

- The Episcopal Church nearly didn't survive the 1770s because it was associated with the English monarchy and most ministers were Loyalists.

- Anglicans have very formal worship services, so they are rightly called "liturgical" in their expression of faith.

- The two things that give Anglicans unity are the bishops of the church and the Book of Common Prayer.

Chapter 11

Lutherans

In This Chapter

- ◆ Consider the importance of the Bible to Lutheran faith and practice
- ◆ Understand the importance of ethnic differences in the shaping of Lutheranism today
- ◆ Find out why Lutheranism evolved into several major denominations in the United States

Lutheranism is the granddaddy of all the Protestant traditions in the United States and elsewhere. What began with one guy and a piece of paper nailed to a church door flowered into a religious movement—Protestantism—that embraces more than 350 million people worldwide today. More than 23 million of these Protestants identify themselves as Lutheran, with about a fourth of those living in the United States. Everybody has heard of Martin Luther, but what is Lutheranism? For that matter, what do Lutherans believe today, and how do they practice the faith differently than other Christians? Read on, and you'll find answers to these and other questions.

Faith Alone, Grace Alone, Word Alone

As an Augustinian monk, Luther was obsessed with one basic question: How can a God who demands perfect justice become reconciled with sinful, wicked people? Or to put it another way, how does God actually *save* sinners? For centuries the church taught that sinners needed to confess to their priests, perform penance, observe the sacraments, and otherwise follow church teachings. Luther did all these things, and yet guilt and uncertainty remained. Luther's obsession with salvation led him to believe that Jesus' death and resurrection are the only things that sinners need, and that the various religious observances that Roman Catholicism required did nothing to affect the condition of a believer's soul. Luther's belief in faith alone (sola fides) and grace alone (sola gratia) produced one of the core principles of Lutheranism: justification by grace through faith. It was a short path to a third sola, Word alone (sola Scriptura), since Luther thought that justification by grace through faith was pretty clearly laid out in the Bible.

> **Lo and Behold**
>
> Luther's Ninety-Five Theses didn't invent Lutheranism. All it did was make a number of points about the use of indulgences in the Roman Catholic Church, and invite other theologians to debate them. His later pamphlets and tracts developed the principles of justification by grace through faith and priesthood of all believers, which became the core principles of Lutheranism.

Luther indicted the Roman Catholic Church practice of indulgences in his celebrated paper, the Ninety-Five Theses (1517). This was essentially an invitation for his fellow theologians at Wittenberg to debate their usefulness in reconciling the sinner with God. In later writings, Luther called into question many aspects of the Roman Catholic mass, the supernatural functions of priests, the five sacraments not established by Jesus, and indeed the entire Catholic system for getting one's sins forgiven. He denied the pope any special role in interpreting the Bible for ordinary Christians, and he criticized the worldly power and wealth of the church. He even said that the pope was the "Antichrist" mentioned in the Bible.

Of course, you don't call the Pope the Antichrist in 1520 and expect to escape without consequences. Luther was excommunicated by the church and tried in absentia by the Holy Roman Emperor. He went into hiding and spent the next 10 years sorting out what faith alone, grace alone, and Word alone really means in practice. Along the way he came up with a new set of instructions for how to conduct religious services, some hymns for congregational singing, and a catechism for instructing youth in his new principles of faith. It's here that Luther laid the foundation for the eventual Lutheran denomination.

Priesthood of All Believers

Luther's famous "solas" naturally led him to the doctrine of the priesthood of all believers. In Roman Catholicism, priests help to bridge the gap between God and humanity by administering the sacraments, which brought grace into the lives of sinners in a very mysterious and supernatural way. By contrast, Luther taught that salvation is an intensely personal matter between the sinner and God. No priest or church official should be thought of as a go-between.

So priests got a makeover in the hands of Luther. They were given no special power to bring grace to believers through the sacraments and no special authority in setting church doctrine. Luther flatly rejected the sacrament of *ordination*, since he thought it falsely elevated certain Christians above others. But Lutherans still have ministers, so the question becomes, what do they do? Since Luther put the Bible in the center of the Christian faith, reading and proclaiming Scripture became the centerpiece of Lutheran worship. At risk of oversimplification, Lutheranism and other Protestant denominations feature the sermon, or proclaiming the Word, in worship, while Catholicism and Orthodoxy feature the Eucharist with priests supervising the miraculous transformation of the elements into the body and blood of Jesus.

The priesthood of all believers is among the most revolutionary concepts in world history. It closed the gap between ordinary Christians and church officials. It brought common people without fancy titles or expensive educations to assert their voice in church affairs. And many could now conceive of a day when women might be permitted to supervise worship or preach a sermon in church.

Steeple Talk

Ordination is a ritual of the church in which priests are consecrated to perform divine service in administering the sacraments. At least that's the Catholic view. Protestants ordain ministers as well, but consider it to be more ceremonial than supernatural.

Edifications

If you want to get it straight from the source, you should read Luther's most influential books. Among these are *Two Kinds of Righteousness* (1518), *Treatise on Good Works* (1520), *Freedom of a Christian* (1520), *Bondage of the Will* (1525), and *Lectures on Galatians* (1535). In fact, the last three are still in print (Fortress Press, 2003, Fleming H. Revell, 1990, and Kregel Publications, 1987, respectively).

Lutheran Worship

Luther wanted all to work out their faith individually with God. And yet Luther still thought the church was terribly important. Lutheran churches have a couple of key unifying elements. The Book of Concord provides doctrinal unity for those of the Lutheran persuasion. It includes the Formula of Concord of 1580, which is a lengthy confession of faith, and the Augsburg Confession of 1530, which is an early statement of Luther's positions on key points of difference between him and his opponents. It also includes the ancient creeds, and Luther's Shorter and Longer Catechisms. But that's where the standardization stops. Unlike Catholicism with its breviary (worship manual) and Episcopalianism with its Book of Common Prayer, Lutheranism allows for a little more diversity in the way that worship is carried out.

Steeple Talk

The Lutheran **Book of Worship** directs ministers and worship leaders as they organize Lutheran religious services. It suggests liturgical activities that are pretty standard across the Lutheran denominations, and that gives Lutheran worship a rather formal appearance. But these are only suggestions; Lutherans aren't required to follow it verbatim.

Edifications

Liturgical Protestant denominations like the Lutherans often use organs to accompany hymns and for musical transitions from one part of the worship service to another. Organs first appeared in churches in the sixteenth century, but really took off when Johann Sebastian Bach (1685–1750) began to compose organ pieces specially designed for Lutheran services.

Lutherans generally follow a plan first set out by Luther himself in books like *Order of Mass and Communion* (1523) and *German Mass and Order of Service* (1526). These texts continue Catholic traditions like collective prayers and chants, observance of special days and seasons of the liturgical calendar, and of course litanies of Scripture to be used for different occasions. Luther supported the practice of congregational singing, so he wrote hymns and suggested others, and encouraged the use of polyphonic choruses in worship. Luther stopped short of a full-blown liturgical revolution, and yet pioneered many of the worship elements that are characteristic of Protestantism today.

Lutherans speak of "patterns" in worship that provide some unity and consistency across the Lutheran landscape. There are three main components:

- ◆ Preparation for the Word
- ◆ Hearing the Word
- ◆ Responding to the Word

Typically, Lutherans enter church with an organ prelude resounding in the sanctuary, then they participate in a collective confession of sins and affirmation of forgiveness. Important note: Lutherans don't confess to priests individually; they do it as a group within the flow of a Sunday worship service. Then they sing a hymn, perform the Kyrie (borrowed from the Catholics), sing another hymn, and offer the prayer of the day.

The interior of this Lutheran Church in Altoona, Pennsylvania, is plainer than the interiors of Catholic and Orthodox churches. It also has the title of Luther's hymn, "A Mighty Fortress Is Our God," painted over the arch in the front of the church.

(Permission for use from the Library of Congress)

All of this is preparation. The hearing of the Word then follows. Someone reads from the Old and New Testaments, the Psalms, and one of the Gospels, interspersed with alleluias to acclaim the Word. Then the minister delivers the sermon, which is thought to be part of the proclamation of the Word. When this is over, Lutherans then respond to the Word by singing hymns, offering prayers and gifts, reciting the creed and Lord's Prayer, remembering Christ through communion, and closing with more prayer.

But Lutherans don't insist on liturgical uniformity. So long as reading and proclaiming the Word remains the centerpiece of the service, the worship is thought to be Lutheran in spirit. Actually, it is thought to be *evangelical* in spirit, which is the word Luther himself used to describe religious practices that conformed to his sense of what the Bible teaches. That explains the evangelical part of the names of several major Lutheran denominations.

CAUTION

Lo and Behold

Lutherans preserved two sacraments in the Reformation: baptism and communion. They don't believe the bread and wine actually become the body and blood of Jesus like Catholics, but the "true body and blood of Christ" are "in, with, and under bread and wine." Most other Protestants deny the presence of Christ and consider the practice to be purely symbolic.

Ethnic Dimensions

It would be a mistake to assume that you have to be German in order to be Lutheran. Lutheranism spread very rapidly to the entire Baltic region and parts of Eastern Europe. These different cultures produced slight variations within Lutheranism, which then became an important factor in how Lutheranism developed in the United States.

German Lutheranism

Nevertheless, Lutheranism began in Germany. Luther won favor with a number of German princes, including his own, Frederick the Wise. In these states, Luther organized churches using the German mass, the German-language Bible, and the Augsburg Confession. All people living in these territories were considered part of the church, and their children were baptized as members. They were also subject to compulsory education using Luther's catechisms. The secular princes appointed superintendents to ensure that religion was observed in their territories, and had the power to fire ministers who weren't performing their duties. These attitudes followed German migrants to the New World, becoming part of Lutheranism's denominational tradition in the United States.

> **CAUTION**
>
> **Lo and Behold**
>
> The German princes worked with the Lutheran ministers to create what they called *landeskirchen,* or territorial churches that included everyone living under a prince's jurisdiction. Anabaptists, like Mennonites, preferred *gathered churches,* which included only those who professed faith in Christ.

Scandinavian Lutheranism

The kingdoms on the Baltic Sea were ready for Lutheranism. Danish, Norwegian, Swedish, and Finnish people resented Rome and all produced early instances of reform activity. When German Lutherans openly challenged the pope and the Holy Roman Empire, the Scandinavian conversion to Lutheranism followed soon after. Denmark's Christian III (1503–1559) arranged to have the Bible and many of Luther's works translated into Danish. He organized the church into districts with superintendents, later administered by bishops, and made himself the supreme head of the church.

The Danish conversion to Lutheranism signaled similar changes in the north. Christian III also inherited the kingdom of Norway and forced it to convert to

Lutheranism. Soon, Sweden's king, Gustavus Vasa (1496–1560), took notice of events and led Swedish Christians out of the Roman Catholic Church. They quickly got a Swedish-language Bible, Swedish hymns, and a Swedish mass, all inspired by Luther. Yet, Swedish Lutheranism retained a few more Catholic elements than its German counterpart, particularly the idea of the apostolic succession of bishops. And this version of Lutheranism found its way to Finland when Gustavus Vasa imposed it on the country during his reign.

Edifications

Luther believed that people have little control over whether they will be saved or not. This led him to disagree with Erasmus, a famous critic of the Catholic Church, who believed that people have freedom to choose their own destiny. The free-will-versus-predestination debate would rage on for centuries afterward.

Evangelical Lutheran Church in America

The largest denomination of Lutherans in the United States, the Evangelical Lutheran Church in America, bears the marks of this ethnic diversity. It is the by-product of a series of mergers between different U.S. Lutheran denominations, each with its own distinct ethnic and national traditions.

The story of how the ELCA came into being is remarkable. German Lutherans who migrated to the United States faced one major question: Do they stick with their native languages and the historic Lutheran confessions, or assimilate to the Anglo-Protestant culture? Some felt strongly about staying German and Lutheran, others wanted to downplay their linguistic and doctrinal differences with other Christians. Rival organizations formed around these positions, with the first group centered in Pennsylvania, and the second ranged across New York, Ohio, and Indiana. Scandinavian immigrants further complicated this picture, and at one time there were as many as 150 distinct Lutheran organizations operating in the United States.

In the last 20 years, the different strands of Lutheranism finally began to come together, resulting in the ELCA (founded in 1988). This denomination of Lutherans is the largest in the United States, with more than 5 million members in 10,000 churches. It is only one of several, but you should keep something in mind

Everybody Said Amen

You can understand quite a bit about Lutheranism in the United States if you know about the debate between two Lutheran theologians in the nineteenth century, Samuel Schmucker and Charles Krauth. Schmucker thought Lutheranism needed to adapt to the American setting, while Krauth insisted on strict adherence to Luther's principles.

about this denomination: As the product of numerous mergers, it is different from the other Lutheran denominations in its willingness to downplay ethnic differences, particular Lutheran traditions, and strict confessionalism in the interests of greater unity.

The ELCA still uses the Book of Concord and generally follows historic Lutheran teachings on the Bible and the two sacraments. ELCA Lutherans consider the Bible to be the inspired Word of God, to be used as the rule for faith and practice. They baptize at infancy to begin the work of grace in the child's life and believe that the real presence of Christ is in the bread and wine of communion. They also use a conventional format for organizing their services, though many congregations are experimenting with newer worship styles that include contemporary music and multimedia technology.

Steeple Talk

Full communion describes the formal relationship among several mainline Protestant denominations, including the ELCA and the Presbyterian Church (U.S.A.), the Episcopal Church, and the United Church of Christ. They recognize one another's confessions, ministerial ordination, and membership standards, so that people can move freely across denominational boundaries.

The ELCA is divided into 65 districts, or synods, that send about a thousand clerical and lay representatives to a biennial Churchwide Assembly. It elects a presiding bishop to a four-year term, and a church council that administers the day-to-day affairs of the denomination. The ELCA is very open to working with other Christian organizations. It is part of the National Council of Churches and has voted to maintain *full communion* with other mainline Protestant denominations like the Presbyterian Church (U.S.A.), the Episcopal Church, U.S.A., and the United Church of Christ. This means that the denominations can exchange ministers and members with little or no trouble.

Lutheran Church–Missouri Synod

Where the ELCA is flexible, accommodating, and ecumenical, the Lutheran Church—Missouri Synod remains committed to the historic Lutheran confessions and the doctrine of Biblical inerrancy. These two issues are not the entire story. The LCMS is very active in education, missions, and publishing. And it operates a system of elementary and high schools that is the second largest in the United States, behind the Roman Catholic parochial school system.

But to understand how the LCMS differs from other Protestant denominations and from the ELCA, you have to go back to the two big issues that maintain the division.

The Missouri Synod started like many other Lutheran organizations, with German immigrants leapfrogging the Atlantic coast and settling in the Midwest. These immigrants originally left Germany partly because of the growing liberalism in German Lutheranism and the growing cooperation between Lutheran and Reformed churches in the old country. These settlers—mostly in Ohio, Michigan, Indiana, and points west—wished to preserve their heritage. They thought the Lutheran confessions were faithful to Scripture, and ecumenical relationships among the denominations invited too many tradeoffs and compromises.

Edifications

Many of the LCMS institutions are named Concordia, which reflects the denomination's respect for the Formula of Concord and its chief legacy, the Book of Concord. This remains the authoritative expression of Lutheran doctrine.

The shaded region in the map indicates the extent of counties in the United States where Lutherans compose more than 25 percent of all individuals who adhere to a religious organization.

(Source: D.B. Barrett, World Christian Encyclopedia [Oxford: Oxford University Press, 1982])

The LCMS adheres closely to the Book of Concord, which includes the Augsburg Confession, the ancient creeds, and Luther's catechisms. They also understand the Bible to be *inerrant*, or without error, which makes them a little different from Lutherans in the ELCA, who believe the Bible is inspired by the Holy Spirit, but not without error. This difference of opinion about the Bible separates Christians in other Protestant denominations as well.

This view gives the 2.6 million–member LCMS a more "conservative" feel than the ELCA. The German language was used in worship services until the 1930s. Today, women are not

Steeple Talk

Inerrant is a doctrine popular among Protestant denominations in which the Bible is thought to be without error in the original manuscripts. This view is a refinement of the traditional Christian understanding that the Bible is the inspired Word of God. Those who hold the inerrant view believe the Bible is inspired by God *and* without error in its original form.

permitted to become teaching pastors in the LCMS, whereas they are in the ELCA. Also, the denomination tends to take literally the description of creation in Genesis chapter 1, with its six 24-hour days. You can find other "conservative" positions, but be careful how this word is applied. LCMS is very much in the vanguard in the media and in education, for example, and in 2001 voted overwhelmingly to assist in the resettlement of refugees to the United States and to study ways to make representation in their national convention more equitable.

Another separate Lutheran denomination, the Wisconsin Evangelical Lutheran Synod, lists nearly half a million members and is very close in doctrine and spirit to the LCMS. The WELS and LCMS differ from the ELCA in how they approach society outside the church walls. The WELS and LCMS believe that taking strong moral stands (on divorce, abortion, homosexuality, the content of Hollywood movies) provides a biblical witness to a culture that desperately needs moral clarity. The ELCA believes that working closely with other denominations and welcoming everyone into the church is the best way to minister to a broken and fallen world. So Lutherans can be part of a common tradition, and yet have different points of view about the relationship between Christianity and the larger world.

The Least You Need to Know

- Luther and his followers stressed the importance of God's grace and faith in Christ to salvation, and denied that any human effort could affect the state of one's soul.

- Lutheranism adopted the idea of the priesthood of all believers, which changed the role of the minister in Lutheran churches.

- Nearly all Lutherans consider the Book of Concord to be a faithful expression of Scripture and a useful guide to faith and practice.

- Ethnic and national differences kept Lutheranism from uniting in the United States, since the different immigrant groups had different ideas about how best to organize the church.

Chapter 12

The Reformed Denominations

In This Chapter

- ◆ Learn concepts like total depravity, predestination, and presbyterian
- ◆ Consider the historic ethnic differences between the different Reformed denominations
- ◆ Find out how the evangelical and fundamentalist movements affected the Presbyterian Church in the United States

If Martin Luther is the Reformation's Butch Cassidy, then John Calvin is its Sundance Kid (minus all the shooting). Both worked to rid the church of corruption; Luther's efforts eventually gave rise to Lutheranism while Calvin helped to engineer the Reformed tradition. The Reformed tradition includes part of the United Church of Christ, all the Presbyterian denominations, and any church with "Reformed" in its name. By looking at the legacy of John Calvin and other like-minded people, we'll understand some of the differences between the Reformed/Presbyterian denominations and other Christian churches.

God's Sovereignty

Reformers of the sixteenth century tried to answer one basic question: If Catholic indulgences don't save your soul, what does? Luther answered "justification by grace through faith." Calvin liked this answer, but he went a little further. After he thought a while about God's grace, Calvin was drawn toward the idea of God's sovereignty.

He concluded that God is the supreme ruler of the universe and causes all things to work according to an overriding purpose.

Lo and Behold

Did God cause evil? Denominations in the Reformed tradition believe that God is in complete control over all creation, which opens them to charges that God must then be the author of evil. They reply that sin is a defect of human will, evident in Adam and Eve's inability to obey God's clear instructions.

Human Depravity

Calvin's understanding of God's sovereignty rests on the conviction that all people are inherently sinful. He didn't think of sin as an action that could be erased with some offsetting deed. Instead, he thought of it as a congenital birth defect that everybody inherits just because they are human beings—an awful fact of human existence that no human effort can remedy.

Everybody Said Amen

A handy way to remember the basics of Calvinism is TULIP. The letters in this acronym stand for total depravity, unconditional election, limited atonement, irresistible grace, and perseverance of the saints. This complicated set of doctrines was designed as a replacement for the Roman Catholic understanding of salvation, though it came into being only after Calvin's students began to work through his writings and identify what they believed to be the core principles of his theology.

The source and nature of human sinfulness is widely debated within Christian circles. Some Christians speak of a "sin nature" that can't be escaped, just as one can't change the color of one's skin. Others believe that "sin is in the sinning," which means that people sin when they commit actual misdeeds or fail to do good when presented with an opportunity.

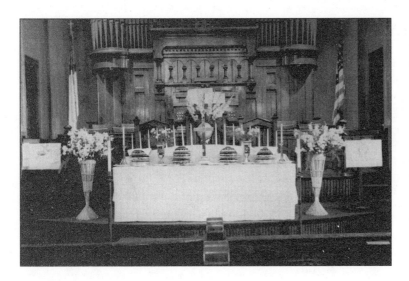

Reformed churches have two stands in front, one for preaching and the other for reading the Word, symbolizing the importance of Scripture (far left and right). And they have communion tables, not altars, since nothing is being sacrificed (center).

(Permission for use from First Presbyterian Church, Huntington, Indiana)

God's Grace

Human beings are deficient, Calvin thought. We are completely powerless to avoid the eternal punishment awaiting our souls in the afterlife. Indulgences, good deeds, the pope, and any other human action amount to nothing. If so, how do people get saved? The answer: God's grace. Despite our failed attempts, God graciously saves some people even though they don't deserve it. In fact, God's grace is so irresistible that those who are saved cannot be otherwise. If this is puzzling, then chalk it up to man's incapacity to know the mind of God.

In Calvin's view, God takes the initiative in bringing grace to those who are saved. But just like his notion of human depravity, this is a point of disagreement among Protestants. Calvinists give God all of the responsibility in saving the lost; others say no, that people have some responsibility to respond correctly to God's divine leadings.

> **Everybody Said Amen**
>
> An example of a Protestant group that disagrees with the Reformed denominations' position on human initiative and responsibility is the Methodists. John Wesley and his followers thought that humans had more responsibility and choice in the matter than John Calvin's Reformed theology would allow.

Divine Providence

Calvin's view of human depravity and God's grace leads naturally to a stress on God's omnipotence and omniscience. These terms mean, respectively, all-powerful and all-knowing. If you take these terms literally, Calvin and Reformed Christians can be understood to believe that all human history is predetermined. People are robots acting out some sort of cosmic script that God wrote before the beginning of time.

Edifications

God's providence means simply that God sustains all of existence through divine power, participates in creation—which includes helping people make decisions—and leads the world toward the final ends that God has designed.

But this is a misrepresentation of the Reformed view. Reformed theologians use the word "providence" to describe how an all-powerful God maintains the universe and participates in its continued operation. They don't think of God as a clockmaker who designs the thing and then lets it run on its own, and they don't think of God as a puppeteer who controls the minute details of everyday life. Instead, they describe a God whose will cooperates with human wills to secure God's ultimate intentions in the world.

Predestination

As you can see, Calvin and other Reformed thinkers dealt with some thorny problems, like fate, destiny, determinism, free will, and so on. And this brings us to the idea most directly associated with Calvin and Calvinism, and that is predestination. Predestination is the idea that God actively wills that certain souls will be saved, leaving others to deal with the consequences of sin on their own.

Lo and Behold

How can infants be damned if they haven't sinned? Many philosophers over the centuries have struggled with this problem. Calvin said they are damned because sin is an inherited nature, not an act, but provided for this by keeping the Catholic rite of infant baptism.

If this sounds unjust, keep in mind that Calvin discussed predestination in connection with a comprehensive theory of God's sovereignty over all creation. This theory holds that God actively governs the universe and steers events in order to obtain God's ultimate purposes. Along the way, God's will is revealed as some choose salvation and others damnation. Most importantly, God's grace becomes known as some escape the punishment that all should suffer as a result of our sinful nature.

The Reformed Tradition

The beginning point of Reformed theology is an appreciation for God's sovereignty. But a tradition is a living thing that grows, adapts, and changes. The Reformed thinkers first broke away from Martin Luther over communion. Luther wished to retain something of the supernatural in the Eucharist, and insisted that the real presence of Christ is in the elements. Ulrich Zwingli, a Swiss reformer, disagreed. He thought that sacraments were ordinances of Christ that enabled believers to demonstrate their faith, instead of being spiritual events in which believers receive the grace of God.

Zwingli and Calvin focused on the importance of the sacraments of communion and baptism in drawing people together in a community of faith. You take communion as a group, and you baptize infants as a sign of their inclusion in the church. Scripture taught Reformed thinkers that Christians, like the Jews before them, are God's elect. Soon, reformers like Theodore Beza of Geneva developed the idea of God's elect into an elaborate system of covenants between God and humanity. Infant baptism and communion were understood as signs of the covenant between God and the chosen people. And so the Reformed tradition went forward with its distinctive *covenant theology*.

Steeple Talk

Covenant theology provides a way for Reformed theologians to describe God's contractual way of doing business. God made covenants with Abraham and Noah, which were replaced by a new covenant for Christians. If we are obedient to the terms of the covenant, spelled out in the Gospels, God will fulfill the promises of salvation and eternal life. Some think covenant theology laid the foundation for many liberal political ideas that culminated in American democracy.

Reformed denominations in the United States find inspiration in the numerous confessions of faith drawn up by Zwingli, Calvin, and other like-minded thinkers. These documents stress the final authority of Scripture, the Reformed understanding of the sacraments, and the manner by which God's grace extends to the elect. The reason there are so many Reformed confessions is because Reformed churches developed along national lines. The Swiss produced the two Helvetic Confessions (1536, 1566), the Dutch produced the Belgic Confession (1561) and the Canons of Dordt (1618). Later, the Scots would produce a Scottish Confession of Faith and help English Calvinists with their Westminster Confession (1643–1648). These became the charters of faith for the established churches in these countries.

Like other Protestants, Reformed Christians use written confessions to organize themselves into communities of faith. These confessions are secondary to Scripture in authority, used when Scripture doesn't speak directly to issues in dispute. Migrants from countries with Reformed churches came to the United States and quickly formed separate denominations. But all who acknowledge their common heritage in the Reformation and the Reformed denominations today consider all the confessions to be part of this heritage.

Church Governance: Presbyterianism

The Reformed churches stress God's sovereignty and describe their relationship with God in terms of covenants, which makes them a little different from other Protestant denominations in the United States. But another difference has to be included in this list: presbyterianism. This is a peculiar way of linking congregations together into a network of churches.

Presbyterianism has to be distinguished from episcopal organization, which is the standard form in the Orthodox, Roman Catholic, and Episcopal churches. Episcopal organization, if you recall, uses bishops consecrated by a chief bishop (like the pope or council of patriarchs) to govern dioceses, or groups of local churches organized into districts. Like episcopal organization, presbyterianism recognizes the importance of knitting churches together into a larger body in order to encourage mutual support and doctrinal consistency.

Steeple Talk

Session, presbytery, and **synod** are the words used by Reformed Christians of Scottish and English heritage to describe levels of local, district, and regional church governance. In the Dutch Reformed tradition, these levels of government are called consistory, classis, and coetus.

That's where the similarities end. Presbyterianism is essentially a minidemocracy. Each church has a *session* composed of elected elders. Church sessions send elected representatives to a district meeting, called a *presbytery*. Presbyteries send representatives to a regional body called a *synod*, which elects representatives to a national meeting. In the Presbyterian Church (U.S.A.), this is called the General Assembly. In the Reformed Church in America, the national body is called the General Synod.

In this arrangement, authority flows upward from local churches to ever-broader levels of government. But local churches confer on these larger bodies the power to ensure that they follow the guidelines of the denomination, as outlined in their constitutions and books of church order. More specifically, the national bodies are responsible for making changes to their general guidelines, and the regional and district bodies are responsible for holding local churches and ministers accountable. For example, Rev. Theodore Parson Clapp was excommunicated in 1832 by a Mississippi presbytery for teaching a doctrine of universal salvation, which of course is very

un-Calvinist. In our own time, the
Presbytery of Cincinnati defrocked a
local minister in 2003 for marrying same-
sex couples in defiance of denominational
policy in the Presbyterian Church
(U.S.A.).

Several denominations that are considered part
of the Reformed tradition, like the United
Church of Christ, are not governed according
to presbyterian principles. They are congrega-
tional in the sense that local churches recognize no binding authority above themselves in the management of their affairs. The UCC is congregational because
English Calvinists argued over church government back in the seventeenth century,
and those who left to come to the American colonies during this dispute happened to
belong to the faction that argued for congregational organization.

> **Edifications**
>
> In Greek, the word for elder is
> *presbyter*, hence the name. The
> word shows up in the letters of
> Paul to the new churches of
> Asia Minor, so many Protestant
> churches use the office of elder
> as the basis of church govern-
> ment.

Reformed Church in America

Just like Lutherans, Reformed Christians came to the United States with ethnic and
national identities in tow. Most of the Reformed Christians from Germany ended up
in the Evangelical and Reformed Church, now part of the UCC, while those from
Scotland tended to enter the Presbyterian Church. As for the Reformed Church in
America, well, think Dutch.

The Dutch brought the Reformed faith to settlements on Manhattan and Long
Islands, the Hudson River Valley, and New Jersey during the earliest years of colo-
nization. Many wished to maintain ties with the
mother church in Amsterdam, but this became
increasingly hard to do, especially when later
generations of colonial-born church members
learned English and adopted English customs.

Although the Dutch Reformed community left
the colonial period ready to compete in the free
marketplace for religion in the infant United
States, it carried forward an old question that
divided Lutherans as well: Should the church
hold fast to the Old World confessions and
church traditions, or should it adapt to new

> **Everybody Said Amen**
>
> The Reformed Church in America
> and the Christian Reformed
> Church value the writings of
> Abraham Kuyper (1837–1920),
> a Dutch minister who eventually
> became the prime minister of the
> Netherlands. He wrote exten-
> sively about God's sovereignty
> and the relationship between
> Christianity and politics.

surroundings? In some ways the fact of migration already answered the question, but divisions nonetheless remained.

The Dutch Reformed Church finally made its peace with America, dropping the Dutch from its name and becoming the Reformed Church in America (RCA) in 1867. But the RCA had to revisit this issue when a huge clump of new Dutch migrants settled in Michigan and Iowa in the 1840s and 1850s. These new Dutch settlers joined the denomination, but didn't appreciate the established Americans' weakened commitment to the Reformed confessions and Dutch Calvinist traditions. So most of them quit the RCA and formed the Christian Reformed Church.

Christian Reformed Church

Both the older RCA and the newer Christian Reformed Church (CRC) are confessional, liturgical, and Reformed in theology. And Dutch, too. But the CRC is more so. The mingling of native-born Americans with recent Dutch immigrants on the eve of the Civil War proved an unhappy marriage, and the recent immigrants left the RCA to form the CRC in 1857. The fledgling denomination grew steadily, and today the denomination numbers 300,000 in about 1,000 churches, mostly in the Midwest.

What's the difference between the RCA and the CRC? The RCA and the CRC disagree on how best to respond to changing times and places. For example, as the women's movement crested in the early 1970s, the RCA ordained its first woman minister (1973). By contrast, the CRC allowed its regional bodies to ordain women only in 1995. Both have women ministers today, and yet the RCA embraced this change much earlier than the CRC. The ways that the RCA and the CRC respond to change seems to parallel the experience of Lutherans in the Evangelical Lutheran Church in America and the Lutheran Church—Missouri Synod. One stresses the importance of ministering effectively in a changing society, while the other stresses the importance of standing firm on long-standing doctrinal and moral principles.

Edifications

When did women become ministers? Here are some key dates:

Quakers: 1660s

Congregationalists (United Church of Christ): 1853

Mennonites: 1911

United Methodists: 1939

Episcopalians: 1976

Presbyterian Church (U.S.A.)

Episcopalianism came here by way of England, Lutheranism by way of Germany and Scandinavia, and the Dutch Reformed Church by way of the Netherlands. The

Presbyterian Church (U.S.A.) first came by way of Scotland and the Scotch-Irish communities in Ireland. All these denominations are now much more diverse, but these European and British beginning points are critical to their denominational self-identities.

The PCUSA is the result of a merger of numerous strands of Presbyterianism, with its main thread having originated in Scotland in the seventeenth century. The Roman Catholic Church in Scotland turned Calvinist during the Reformation, following the lead of reformer John Knox (ca. 1510–1572). English kings in the early seventeenth century tried to force episcopal government and the Church of England's Book of Common Prayer on the Scots, which only increased their devotion to Calvinist presbyterianism. During the Civil War that pitted the king and his supporters against the Scottish army, and then Parliamentary forces, Scottish Presbyterians collaborated with English reformers to write the Westminster Shorter and Longer Catechisms and the Westminster Confession of Faith (1643–1648).

When Scottish Presbyterians began to migrate to an arc of frontier settlements that ranged from Georgia to New York, they brought their commitment to the Westminster Confession along with them. American Presbyterianism broke into factions over *revivalism* in the eighteenth century and over interdenominational cooperation in the early nineteenth century. This latter division roughly corresponded to the sectional division of the northern and southern churches over slavery. Presbyterianism officially divided at the Mason-Dixon Line in 1857, a rift that didn't completely heal until 1983 when northern and southern Presbyterian denominations pulled together to form the current PCUSA.

Lo and Behold

Many of the Scottish Presbyterians who came to the United States didn't come from Scotland, but rather from the Scottish settlements in Northern Ireland (Ulster) established by the English crown. That's why the people of Scottish descent are sometimes called Scotch-Irish.

Steeple Talk

Revivalism is a Protestant practice of convening special meetings to convert new people to Christianity or encourage spiritual renewal among established Christians.

Recent Presbyterian history witnessed both division and reunion. Presbyterians disagreed over certain elements of the Reformed tradition, like predestination and election, total depravity and infant damnation, and the restriction of communion to members of the church. The bottom line in many of these disputes has a familiar ring: How much can the American Presbyterianism stray from the Westminster Confession and still be Presbyterian? The PCUSA today is drawn into factions over confessional standards, with a large-scale Confessing Church movement emerging within the denomination that seeks member congregations willing to ascribe to the historic confessions of the Reformed tradition, rather than make adjustments in light of contemporary social, cultural, and political change. They hope to use their numbers to influence policy decisions in the General Assembly.

Presbyterian Church in America

The largest group of Presbyterians after the PCUSA is the Presbyterian Church in America. The PCA is the product of some of these theological and confessional disputes in the twentieth century. In the 1970s, the PCA joined together Presbyterian denominations that opposed ecumenical efforts that eventually led to the National Council of Churches and the World Council of Churches. These denominations also accepted the emerging inerrancy doctrine devised in the late nineteenth century in opposition to scholars who treated the Bible as just another human-generated document.

> **Everybody Said Amen**
>
> Protestant denominations use their annual national meetings to take positions on a range of social and political questions, such as abortion, euthanasia, capital punishment, war and peace, and welfare policy. The resolutions of these national meetings are a good place to start in trying to figure out the denomination's relative liberalism or conservatism.

The PCA believes that the Bible teaches against ordination of women and that the Bible teaches a restrictive policy on divorce and remarriage. In many ways, the word "conservative" applies to the denomination, as it resists departures from positions that Presbyterians adopted in the sixteenth through early twentieth centuries. This includes all of the principles that comprise the Reformed conception of God's sovereignty, including total human depravity, the concept of predestination, and Christ's limited atonement for the elect.

But the PCA shares things in common with other Presbyterian denominations, such as a commitment to an educated ministry. The credentials that all Presbyterian denominations require for the ministry are among the highest of all Protestant denominations, including a Master's degree in divinity, comprehensive exams in Scripture and theology, and clinical pastoral training. This tradition started with the earliest Reformed theologians, who modeled theological sophistication in their own careers, and stressed the importance of an educated ministry (in light of Reformed emphasis on reading Scripture firsthand and the all-important sermon).

Ordination in Presbyterian denominations is a rigorous process involving advanced training, written exams, and ongoing presbytery-level review.

(Photo by the author)

Other Reformed Denominations

These denominations are by no means the only Reformed denominations in the United States. There are others, but unfortunately there's no way of generalizing about the disagreements they have with their larger denominational siblings. Denominations like the Cumberland Presbyterian Church and the Orthodox Presbyterian Church maintain their independence because they reject predestination (the former) or hold to a different view of the Bible's origins (the latter). In the end, the differences among Reformed denominations may seem razor-thin to outsiders, but the people who make up their membership consider them crucial.

> **Everybody Said Amen**
>
> Reformed ministers on TV include Robert Schuller (RCA) with his *Hour of Power* and D. James Kennedy (PCA) and the *Coral Ridge Hour.*

The Least You Need to Know

♦ The Reformed tradition teaches that the Word is the ultimate authority in human affairs, over the authority of kings, popes, and church policies.

♦ Calvin and other reformers stressed God's sovereignty, which means that only God's grace and faith in Christ can save peoples' souls.

♦ The Reformed tradition left behind half a dozen or so written confessions of faith, which are complicated statements of doctrine considered to be faithful to the Bible.

◆ The Reformed Church in America and the Christian Reformed Church are historically Dutch, while the Presbyterian Church (U.S.A.) and the Presbyterian Church in America are historically British—though all are now much more diverse.

Part 4

The Pietist Churches

After the dust started to settle from the Reformation, a few Protestant leaders started to question the obsession of the early Reformers with theology, doctrine, and scholarship. In Germany, a movement began that downplayed the importance of book learning, intellectual refinement, and theological pedantry. Soon, the movement got a name: Pietism.

In this part, you'll learn that the Pietists didn't care very much about denominational boundaries. To their way of thinking, policing these boundaries brought people to the point of theological and doctrinal hairsplitting. And that took the focus off of Jesus Christ. The Pietist teachers found an audience among the early Anabaptists and Brethren, and dropouts from the Church of England like the Quakers and Methodists. Unlike the Lutherans, Presbyterians, Episcopalians, and Reformed churches, the Pietists seek to escape formalism in worship and association with politics in favor of authentic encounters with the Savior. And it is in the Pietist churches where you'll find large numbers of African American Christians.

Mennonites, Amish, Brethren

In This Chapter

◆ Learn the meaning of the term "Anabaptist"

◆ Consider the ways in which Mennonites, Amish, and Brethren are linked

◆ Discover how the paths of Mennonites and Amish diverged

◆ Find out how and why Amish communities adapt to economic, social, and cultural change

During the last few years, I've made it a habit of attending an annual missions conference in New Wilmington, Pennsylvania. During the trip, I usually go jogging a few times, and my established route takes me on a 3-mile tour through Amish country. I see well-tended fields, horses chewing at a few tufts of grass, a few boys in plain blue clothes finishing chores. Perhaps you have a mental image of Amish life that fits this description. But like anything else, there is more to Amish life than meets the eye. What you'll find if you look more closely is a lifestyle that is infused with faith, carefully pieced together using guidelines drawn from the Bible.

If the Amish read the same Bible, pray to the same God, and honor the same Jesus as other Christians, then why is their lifestyle so different? To answer this question we have to consider the Amish in light of the Anabaptist tradition to which they belong. Anabaptists, which also includes Mennonites and various kinds of Brethren, reject Catholic, Orthodox, Lutheran, and Reformed views about salvation and membership in the church. They separate from the world to provide an example of faithful living and to guard against its corruptions. They want as little to do with government as possible and refuse military service.

But Anabaptist groups differ among themselves, too: Mennonites and Amish disagree on how much separation from the world is desirable, for example. In fact, most Mennonites look like everyone else in outward appearance. Read on, because without a good grasp of the Anabaptist tradition and without a good sense of how Mennonites, Amish, and Brethren differ from one another and from other Christians, you'll leave a gaping hole in your understanding of contemporary Christianity.

The Anabaptist Way

Anabaptists like the Mennonites, Amish, and Brethren share a common set of principles. These were established in the earliest years of the Reformation, and gained further definition as the years wore on. Today, they are still very much at the center of Mennonite, Amish, and Brethren belief, even if the different Anabaptist groups don't always agree on how to put their principles into practice.

The Gathered Church

Those of the Anabaptist persuasion have one basic goal in mind: They want to ensure that everyone in the church actually *belongs* in the church. They don't think church attendance or membership should be compulsory or automatic, but that the church should comprise all those who've actually made a personal commitment to Jesus.

Edifications

The gathered church concept laid the theological foundation for what became known as the "free church" movement. Technically, free churches are those that refuse to recognize the authority of an officially sponsored church hierarchy in nations that actually have an official church. Today, the term "free church" is used to describe nearly any congregation that recognizes no earthly authority beyond itself, religious or secular.

The early Anabaptists disagreed not only with Roman Catholicism, but also Luther and Calvin on this point. In different ways, the early reformers tied church membership to citizenship and residence in a variety of places throughout Germany, Switzerland, the Netherlands, Scandinavia, and Eastern Europe. Anabaptists didn't like this idea. Instead, they formed *gathered churches* of the faithful whose only motive for participation was devotion to Christ.

Infant vs. Adult Baptism

Of course, this basic goal has far-reaching consequences for how Anabaptists practice the Christian faith. They don't believe in infant baptism, for example. Zwingli and Calvin kept infant baptism because they believed it served as a sign of the extension of the church's covenant with Christ to new additions to the church family. Luther kept it because he thought the faith that accompanied the ritual provided the necessary spiritual cleansing, which was provided by those who prayed for the baptized child.

Nonsense, Anabaptists reply. In their view, Scripture teaches that baptism should follow a personal commitment to Christ, or the inner baptism of the Spirit. Through baptism, believers testify to the spiritual cleansing that Jesus performs when he saves their souls. Anabaptists understand the ritual as an outward sign of a believer's spiritual conversion and commitment to live a new life in Christ as part of the gathered church.

> **Steeple Talk**
>
> **Anabaptist** comes from the Greek word that means rebaptize. Early Anabaptists got their name because they insisted on being rebaptized as adults, after having been baptized as infants into the Roman Catholic Church.

Self-Denial

Anabaptists are known for their plainness in dress, speech, mannerism, home decor, and church design and worship. Mennonites, Amish, Brethren, and others believe the root cause of sinfulness is disobedience, of putting one's own interests above God's. So they stress self-denial, and warn their fellow church members of the dangers of pride.

This self-denial must be expressed in the plainness of one's style of life. No conspicuous luxuries are permitted, so forget that widescreen plasma television with satellite linkup and TiVo. Sensuous pleasures lead the mind astray and should be avoided. Originally, Anabaptists disallowed alcohol, gambling, dancing, and other worldly entertainments. Many still do, though Mennonites have been more inclined to direct the Anabaptist notion of self-denial toward Christian service to others, not long lists of prohibited activities.

This building reflects the simplicity of churches in the Anabaptist tradition. Take note of the separate entrances for women and men.

(Permission for use from the United Brethren in Christ Archives)

Anabaptists believe that true religion lies in the heart and in fellowship with other believers, not in rituals or decorations. So they typically worship in churches without lots of ornamentation. Of course, this might also be a legacy of their early years under persecution (by Catholics *and* Protestants), when they had to meet in places like caves and boats at dock for fear of being tortured and killed for their faith. At any rate, external surroundings are a secondary concern. What really matters is one's personal experience with God and participation in heartfelt worship with like-minded souls.

Church and State

Relations between the Anabaptists and the governments of Europe in the sixteenth century were sour. Early Swiss Anabaptists like Conrad Grebel (c. 1498–1526) and Felix Manz (1490–1527) grew impatient with Ulrich Zwingli's plan to cooperate with Zurich's civil authorities in bringing about the reformation of the church. So they gathered together into separated churches, in defiance of the city council's wishes. They also rebaptized the adults, which Zwingli didn't very much like.

Both Grebel and Manz wound up in prison and Manz was later sentenced to death by drowning in the River Limmat. Later Anabaptists thought cooperating with the state was just another way for corruption to enter the church. So the Anabaptists formed gathered churches with no connection to the government. In many ways this foreshadowed the pattern in the United States. But at the time Luther and Calvin thought this practice led to schism, or disunity in the church.

Edifications

Apparently, the first adult to be baptized in the Anabaptist tradition was Georg Blaurock, a Roman Catholic priest in Zurich who agreed with Conrad Grebel's protests against infant baptism. In January 1525, Grebel baptized Blaurock, who then turned around and baptized Grebel.

The Peace Tradition

Christians who follow the Anabaptist way differ from most other Christians in their opposition to war. This position can be traced all the way back to the years when Anabaptists first signaled an intention to limit their cooperation with the state. But the Anabaptists became committed to pacifism after two of the more infamous episodes of the Reformation: the Peasant's War and Münster.

In the Peasant's War of the 1520s, some peasants in Saxony rebelled against their feudal lords for various economic and social oppressions, but they were led by Thomas Münzer, a zealous reformer who rejected infant baptism and the use of icons in the church. Münzer also believed that the Holy Spirit spoke to him, just as it did with the writers of the Bible. Luther branded Münzer a fanatic and advised civil authorities to brutally suppress his movement. Now men who were loosely classed with Anabaptists had taken up the sword and brought Germany to the brink of chaos. A decade later, at Münster (1536), a group of Anabaptists took over the city until a coalition of Lutheran and Catholic princes reclaimed it by force. They accused the ousted Anabaptist leaders of communism, polygamy, and a host of other scandalous practices.

Since the events at Saxony and Münster, Anabapists have preached against the use of violence. They believe that Jesus taught this idea in the Sermon on the Mount when he said, "Blessed are the peacemakers." (Matthew 5:9) They disagree with other Christian groups that hold the *just war* position in which violence is justified by reference to Christian ethics and scripture. Today, Mennonites, Amish, Brethren, and Quakers (a non-Anabaptist denomination) who are asked to serve in the military can request conscientious-objector status, which enables them to serve in noncombatant roles, or to be discharged altogether.

Steeple Talk

Just war refers to a war that some Christians believe is justified, so long as it meets certain criteria. The criteria offered by Roman Catholic theologian Thomas Aquinas has been widely adopted: (1) War must be waged by a state's supreme authority, not a faction or party; (2) War must have a just cause, like avenging a prior wrong; (3) War must have a rightful intention, like advancing a good or avoiding an evil. Pacifists believe war is never justified.

The Mennonites

Among the oldest and largest of the historic European Anabaptist churches is the Mennonites. There are several Mennonite denominations in the United States, and their divisions owe to ethnic traditions and disagreements about adaptation to the U.S. environment. Even so, they are united by a common set of principles left to them by early Anabaptists and by their namesake, Menno Simons.

Lo and Behold

One study found more than 160 Anabaptist martyrs in the Netherlands in the sixteenth century. Michael Sattler's case is typical. Having authored the Schleitheim Confession, Sattler was burned alive in 1527, but not before he had his tongue cut out and large pieces of flesh torn off with hot tongs.

Let's start with Simons. Simons was a Catholic priest in Friesland, in what is now the northern part of the Netherlands. He came to Anabaptism just after the Münster debacle in 1536 and began to organize gathered churches throughout the Netherlands and northern Germany. He taught his followers to demonstrate their new birth in Christ through adult baptism and separation from worldly politics and culture. Simons stressed a literal reading of the Bible, which meant that believers weren't allowed to take oaths and that women should worship in church with their heads covered, among other things.

To be a Mennonite in the early years was to be a martyr or a refugee. Mennonites left Switzerland, Germany, and the Netherlands by the thousands amid persecution. Many Swiss and German Mennonites went to Pennsylvania and organized gathered churches in relative freedom; others migrated to Russian-held lands in the seventeenth and eighteenth centuries, eventually landing in the Midwestern United States and Canada in the nineteenth and twentieth centuries.

Edifications

Mennonites accept the Dortrecht Confession of 1632, which confirmed pacifism as part of their identity. It reads: "We must not inflict pain, harm, or sorrow upon any one, but seek the highest welfare and salvation of all men, and even, if necessity require it, flee for the Lord's sake from one city or country into another, and suffer the spoiling of our goods; that we must not harm any one, and, when we are smitten, rather turn the other cheek also, than take revenge or retaliate."

Menno Simons and the later Mennonite ministers tended to dislike written confessions, preferring instead to consult with the Bible as the rule of faith. But Mennonites draw some inspiration from early Anabaptists who drew up the Schleitheim Confession (1527). In this document, Anabaptists claimed to be "separated from the world in everything" and taught a doctrine of shunning members who fell into worldliness in order to keep the church pure. A hundred years later, Dutch Mennonites wrote the more widely adopted Dortrecht Confession (1632) which identified the problem of universal sin and affirmed the provision of salvation through Christ, the requirement of personal conversion for salvation, the symbolic nature of the sacraments, separation of the church from the state (especially in the form of pacifism).

Everybody Said Amen

John Howard Yoder (1927–1997), a Mennonite theologian who taught at the University of Notre Dame, was known for his book *The Politics of Jesus* (1972). This book rejected the might-makes-right doctrine of secular politics and asked Christians to live by the radical ethics of Jesus as witnessed in the Gospels, especially the part about loving one's enemies.

Currently, Mennonites affirm the confessions produced within their tradition, but they allow for ongoing conversation on theological topics. This aspect is perhaps the result of the influence of Pietism, a religious movement among Protestants in seventeenth- and eighteenth-century Germany that stressed devotion to Christ and union with the divine, even to the point of spiritual ecstasy. In more recent times Mennonite theologians like Harold S. Bender and John Howard Yoder encouraged Mennonites to come out of their shell a little. In response, the Mennonite Church

U.S.A., the major Mennonite denomination (there are more than a dozen others), emphasizes the importance of community, nonviolent civil disobedience, and social service, along with the older convictions about demonstrating one's personal commitment to Jesus in day-to-day living.

Understanding the Amish

The Mennonites and Amish are kindred spirits, but they are not interchangeable. They share a common point of origin in the early Anabaptist movement, and they share a common heritage in the major Anabaptist confessions of faith. Back in the seventeenth century, however, the Amish became a distinct communion within the Anabaptist family.

Lo and Behold

Don't go looking around for the church building when you go to Amish country. Amish meet for worship in the houses of church members, usually on a rotating basis. Women and men sit in separate sections, and girls and boys are separated as well. Preaching tasks rotate, with sermons typically chanted in Pennsylvania German dialect. Scriptures and hymns, though, are in the German language.

The Amish got their name in the 1690s when a Swiss Anabaptist named Jakob Ammann and some like-minded friends began to argue with other Swiss Brethren (who eventually took the name Mennonite) over Pietism. Some critics accused the Pietists of being too emotional and mystical, and Ammann was among their number. So Ammann told them to stick to the Anabaptist confessions of faith and to reject buttons, buckles, ribbons, lace, and other pride-inducing luxuries. Trimmed beards were out of the question, since they smelled of vanity. Most importantly, Ammann felt the need to practice *Meidung*, or shunning. This meant that members of the church who failed to live according to these standards were not only excommunicated from the church, but ostracized from the community as well.

Scores of Mennonite churches in Europe adopted Ammann's positions. These churches eventually sent migrants to America, starting in the 1710s, settling in close proximity to Mennonite communities. In the colonial years these were mostly found in Pennsylvania, owing to its climate of religious toleration and availability of good farmland. Soon, the Amish-Mennonite population came to be known as Pennsylvania Deutsche, simplified today (however misleadingly) as *Pennsylvania Dutch*. But Pennsylvania Dutch culture moved west into Ohio, Indiana, and even farther west into Iowa, Nebraska, and Canada, as Amish patriarchs sought new farmland for their sons and grandsons in the nineteenth and twentieth centuries.

A common misconception about Amish is that they don't change with the times. They do, but they decide as a community how best to go about it. The church bishops and elders (strictly limited to older men) determine whether a proposed change violates the *Ordnung*, German for discipline or order. These rules put into practice Anabaptist virtues like self-denial, humility, togetherness, separation, obedience, and so on. Entertainments or technologies judged to promote individualism and to destroy the rhythms of family life are rejected. If you see an Amish farmer on the telephone, don't consider him a hypocrite, since the Ordnung approach gives rise to an ongoing process of evaluation and decision making.

In fact, Amish communities, embracing about 100,000 people in the United States, do adjust to a changing economic and social environment. Recent studies show that less than half of Amish heads of household make a living through farming. Amish workers earn their keep in a variety of ways, like construction, furniture making, handicrafts, and tourism. You can find lots of Amish workers in industry as well. Be careful about making generalizations. Decisions regarding economic and social life in Amish communities are locally made and locally applied. What goes on in one Amish community may be different than another, and the concept of Ordnung permits this local variation.

> **Everybody Said Amen**
>
> Generally, Amish Christians selectively use technology. Farm machinery is acceptable so long as it can be towed behind a horse. Telephones are, too, but only in phone shanties attached to poles outside the house. Amish aren't permitted to drive cars, but can ride in cars driven by others. And there are no restrictions on modern medical procedures at the local hospital.

The Brethren Churches

At one time, both Mennonites and Amish used Brethren to identify themselves. When you see the word "brethren," think Anabaptist, since it refers to Christians who were influenced by the ideas of early Anabaptist reformers in Switzerland, Germany, and the Netherlands.

Hutterites, for example, share much in common with Mennonites, but also, literally, share things in common. That's right, they practice a kind of communism. The Hutterian Brethren were organized as a movement in sixteenth-century Moravia, now part of the Czech Republic. Persecution soon chased then into Slovakia, Transylvania, and the Ukraine, where their *bruderhofs*, or collective farms, were sometimes courted by monarchs looking to develop unused land. Hutterites fled to the United States and Canada in the 1870s, and again during World War I, as Russia and other European powers demanded their wartime service. Today some 40,000 U.S. and Canadian Hutterites live communally, speaking German and living plainly.

Various other denominations have Brethren in the title, like the Church of the Brethren and the Brethren in Christ Church. The former is perhaps the largest, and is famous for its earlier nickname: Dunkers. Strongly influenced by Pietism, the Church of the Brethren prefers to talk about personal faith in Christ and the nature of spiritual experience, rather than theology or doctrine. They practice adult baptism like other Anabaptists, but dunk three times forward. In addition to the traditional Anabaptist positions of biblical authority, pacifism, and simple living, they anoint the sick with oil and practice humility by washing one another's feet.

Bruderhofs like the Maple Ridge Bruderhof in New York (founded in 1985) generally follow historic Anabaptist principles while featuring communal living.

(Photo courtesy of Maple Ridge Bruderhof)

Brethren denominations, as with other Anabaptist groups, prefer to give their local congregations a great deal of independence. They select their own ministers and give them freedom to preach from the Bible. This sets the Anabaptist churches apart from many of the mainline Protestant denominations that instruct churches to use standardized worship manuals like the Episcopal Church's Book of Common Prayer or the Lutheran Book of Worship. This independence means that local churches, whether Brethren, Mennonite, Amish, or another sect, have wide latitude to follow trends in Christianity, or resist them. As a result, Anabaptist heritage is expressed in highly diverse ways as you go from gathered church to gathered church.

The Least You Need to Know

- Mennonites, Amish, and Brethren churches share a common ancestry, and a common Anabaptist heritage.

- Mennonites desire to live out the Gospel of Jesus Christ, which they understand as living simply, keeping a community-centered ethos, and working for peace and justice.

- Amish communities don't resist all change but instead evaluate the potential impact of new ways of living in light of the Ordnung, or discipline.

- Brethren denominations share an Anabaptist heritage with the Amish, but like the Mennonites, have been more influenced by Pietism.

Chapter 14

Baptists

In This Chapter

♦ Consider the importance of voluntarism to Baptist faith and practice

♦ Find out the meaning of the phrase "born again"

♦ Learn about Primitive, Missionary, Free Will, General, Regular, and Independent Baptists

After Catholics, Baptists register in polls and surveys as the largest group of Christians in the United States. Their fellowship is large, with some 18 percent of the population, or about 34 million people, claiming membership in one sort of Baptist denomination or another. One of the many Baptist denominations, the Southern Baptist Convention, is the largest religious denomination in 39 percent of U.S. counties. That's second only to Roman Catholicism's 40 percent. In 15 of 50 U.S. states, the SBC has more than 1,000 churches. Again, that's just one of the Baptist denominations. You can find First Baptist Churches from Bar Harbor, Maine, to Berkeley, California. Baptists come in all shapes and sizes: black and white, conservative and liberal, town and country—you name it.

You may well ask, if Baptists are so diverse, how can anyone make generalizations about them? Good question. But don't start pulling your hair out just yet. A closer look reveals not only a few motifs common among the Baptist denominations, but also a few major fault lines that run through the Baptist community. Stick with it and you'll gain an understanding of the most significant vein of Protestant Christianity in a country where the majority identifies itself as Protestant.

Calvinist Beginnings

To understand Baptists in the United States is to understand the path of a Christian fellowship that starts with John Bunyan (who wrote *Pilgrim's Progress*) and Roger Williams, and continues through the lives of Martin Luther King Jr. and Billy Graham. But the starting point lies in an exile church composed of radical English Calvinists in Amsterdam. During the English Reformation, a few congregations formed separated churches without bishops, icons, altars, and other Roman Catholic forms. The authorities executed a couple of London ministers in 1593, and the rest found refuge across the English Channel in Amsterdam.

CAUTION

Lo and Behold

The similarity in names and doctrines between European Anabaptists and English Baptists may lead you to believe that the former created the latter. Not so. English Baptists owe a lot more to English Puritanism's obsession with creating the purest possible church on earth, and with various Calvinist ideas that the Puritans popularized in the sixteenth and seventeenth centuries.

One of these exile churches, under John Smyth, became the seed of the Baptist fellowship that would flower in the United States. Smyth carried English Calvinism to its logical conclusion: To really make God happy, you need to exclude anyone who isn't a Christian from the church, and you need to keep the church uncontaminated by any association with worldly power. In Amsterdam, Smyth came across Dutch Mennonites who agreed with these two points. But how do you figure out who's a Christian? The Mennonites had a solution: Ask people to make a public profession of faith in Jesus Christ, and seal their commitment with baptism. Smyth liked this solution, and adopted believer's baptism.

Baptists formed on American soil under the same sort of circumstances. English Calvinists formed a colony at Massachusetts Bay and developed policies about church membership and church-state relations that a few, like Roger Williams, didn't like. Williams, minister at Salem, believed these policies led to impurity in the church and was banished for openly criticizing them. Williams eventually formed what became the first Baptist church in America in Providence, Rhode Island. You'll see that this insistence on purity and separatism is a running theme in Baptist history.

The Voluntary Principle

Williams hit on something that Baptists would later cherish as a cardinal rule of faith: the idea that churches ought to be composed of those people who've made a conscious choice to be included. Membership is voluntary, not compulsory. Baptists are considered Christians by their own *free will*.

Steeple Talk

Free Will Baptists don't accept the view that certain people are chosen by God to be saved, and have no power to control their ultimate destiny. They prefer to think that Jesus Christ makes salvation available to everyone, and that human beings are involved in making the decision to convert. Three or four smaller Baptist associations refer to themselves as Free Will Baptists in order to proclaim their doctrinal position.

But that raised an important issue for Baptists. The problem is this: If Baptists began as Calvinists, and Calvinists believe that all souls are predestined for either salvation or damnation, then how can they also believe in free will and choice? This question broke Baptists up into two camps, one called Particular Baptists and one called General Baptists. General Baptists decided that Christ died for all people and thus anyone could be saved. Particular Baptists responded that God could save only particular people: the "elect" for whom Christ died.

Yet colonial Baptists worked around their internal disagreements about predestination and free will and grew their numbers. They benefited from inspired ministers like Shubal Stearns (1706–1771) and Daniel Marshall (1706–1784), who had visions for spreading the great revival of the 1740s and 1750s to the religion-free zone along the southern frontier. They organized frontier congregations in Virginia, the Carolinas, and Georgia; so many churches started so quickly that the center of gravity for colonial Baptists began to move from Rhode Island toward the south.

Everybody Said Amen

Are all of the world's religions as aggressive as Christianity in seeking out new converts? Islam offers a parallel. Muslims proselytize widely; one of their missionary groups, the Tablighi Jamaat, got into the news in 2002 when reporters discovered that they helped to convert John Walker Lindh, the so-called American Taliban, to Islam. Tablighi Jamaat typically work part-time, and teach near mosques and on college campuses in the United States and elsewhere.

Thousands became members following highly emotional conversion experiences, often during soul-winning campaigns led by enthusiastic frontier preachers. So Baptists came to a distinct understanding of the church. In their view, the church includes all those who have experienced conversion and baptism. This is important to remember: The act of baptism is not thought of as a means by which the sinner is saved, but instead is considered an indication of the believer's desire to be included among others who have also made a public commitment to Christ.

Twice-Born Christians

In the United States, Baptists were more prepared than other Christian denominations to compete on the open market. They preferred sudden, authentic conversions to lengthy catechisms as a means of bringing people into the church. They allowed unrefined preachers to fill their pulpits rather than wait around for seminary-trained professionals to finally arrive. And they wanted their sermons delivered straight from the Bible. Most important, they permitted local congregations to operate pretty much independently of a higher body. Franchising the Baptist brand didn't require a great deal of overhead.

But Baptists expected, and still expect, new converts to live as twice-born people. What does it mean to be twice-born anyway? When Jesus told a Jewish priest named Nicodemus that in order to see the kingdom of God he must be born again, the guy asked, half in jest, if Jesus meant that we needed to crawl back into our mother's womb a second time.

Steeple Talk

Born again refers to an intense spiritual experience in which a person comes to terms with sin and asks for forgiveness. Many born-agains remember it as a moment of deep spiritual vision and even ecstasy. Pat Robertson, television host and founder of the Christian Coalition, uses words like "suddenly" and "at this moment" to describe the changes he felt inside during his born-again experience.

We should probably address this directly, since 39 percent of Americans claim to be *born again*, and among Protestants that number is 53 percent. Among Baptists, its 69 percent. When Christians speak of being born again, they speak of an intensely personal experience of spiritual regeneration. Twice-born Christians are immediately transformed both within and without, or as the articles of faith of a national Baptist association puts it, the new birth "is instantaneous and not a process." Before, they may have wanted to satisfy all their lusty urges. Afterward, they want to please God and demonstrate the fruits of the Spirit, like love, joy, peace, patience, and all the other fruits listed in Galatians 5:22–23. Bible ever in hand, they point to 2 Corinthians 5:17, which says "Therefore, if anyone is in Christ, he is a new creation; the old has gone, the new has come."

This photograph from 1940 shows a congregation assembled for full-immersion-style water baptism.

(Permission for use from the Library of Congress)

This motif tells us that Baptists have a very spiritualized understanding of the faith. They don't have a heavy investment in material objects, images, ceremonies, rituals, and other things common among Catholics, Orthodox, and even liturgical Protestants. Generally, Baptist services place the sermon at the center, with unscripted prayers, hymns, special music, and Scripture reading before, and offerings, hymns, and more prayers after. If anyone's going to get baptized, it's usually done toward the end of the Sunday service in a large tank toward the front of the church. Rural churches often break away to baptize in a local stream.

> **Everybody Said Amen**
>
> Since the sermon is such a vital part of Baptist worship, ministers carefully prepare them, and often leave them for posterity. Sermons of one of the more famous Baptist ministers, Charles Spurgeon (1834–1892) of London, have become a publishing phenomenon. You can find them in scores of editions, and they are used as textbooks in some Baptist seminaries.

Some Fault Lines

A recent CNN story quoted a Baptist minister as saying, "In Baptist tradition, the local congregation is where it all happens." That about says it all. Baptists are governed locally, which means they don't have a strong national or international structure that can be broken up over some theological, doctrinal, or ethical issue. There have been, however, a few fault lines on the Baptist landscape that inevitably divided Baptists into loose categories, and served as the basis for national *associations* of local churches, which is what the Baptists call denominations.

Regular and General Baptists

Regular Baptists believe in something close to predestination: that God predestined some for salvation and others for damnation. In earlier times they were more inclined to worship in a reserved manner and value the original Baptist charters like the Philadelphia Confession and the New Hampshire Confession (1833). Today, Regular Baptists consider themselves fundamental, meaning they've identified a few key principles of faith and have taken a firm stand in support of them (like the authority of the Bible, deity of Jesus, necessity of Jesus' death for salvation, and so on).

General Baptists hold the view that Jesus Christ died not for a select group of people, but for everyone. Few Baptists today describe themselves strictly as General Baptists (about 75,000 belong to an association called General Association of General Baptist Churches, for example), although millions of Baptists in other associations hold a similar view.

Everybody Said Amen

You might be able to remember the Primitive and Missionary Baptists better by their nicknames. The former are called Hard-Shell Baptists because of their strict application of predestination, while the latter are called Soft-Shell because of their flexibility about doctrinal matters in the interests of evangelism and conversion.

Missionary and Primitive Baptists

In 1814, Baptists created the General Missionary Convention, which mounted a fund-raising campaign for foreign and domestic mission work. The intent was to promote collaboration among local churches and coordinate efforts in the area of evangelism. But other Baptists considered missionary societies to be unbiblical and believed they limited the independence of the local church. Most important, they thought God would somehow get the elect into the church without human effort. Soon, Baptist churches began to align themselves with the

Primitive Baptist position, characterized by jealous defense of local church autonomy, literal interpretation of the Bible, and staunch commitment to predestination. Missionary Baptists, on the other hand, are those who believe that some coordination beyond the level of the local church is desirable.

Major Baptist Denominations

The Regular, General, Missionary, and Primitive categories are not Baptist denominations, but gravitational fields that pull Baptists into regional and national associations. In fact, Baptists say they don't have denominations in the strict sense of the word, since they don't recognize the authority of regional or national governing bodies over the local church. Still, it makes sense to learn a little more about some of the associations because they give local Baptist churches that affiliate a measure of identity in a country where national denominations are important ways of organizing the Christian faith. And it makes it easier for people in my line of work to count and map them.

National Baptist Convention

Baptists in the National Baptist Convention are overwhelmingly African American, and they trace their roots back to the slave and free black communities of the Old South. Today, Christianity is stronger in the African American community than in the white population: 55 percent of African Americans attend church, as compared to 39 percent of whites. And most African American Christians, more than 90 percent, belong to one of three major families of Protestants—Baptists, Methodists, and Pentecostals.

Get ready for a curveball. Actually, four *different* African American Baptist associations use the name National Baptist Convention: the National Baptist Convention U.S.A., the National Baptist Convention of America, the Progressive National Baptist Convention, Inc., and the National Primitive Baptist Convention. When put together, a total of about 12.3 million Christians are affiliated with these organizations.

The differences among these associations are more apparent than real. Associations formed in the nineteenth and twentieth century to promote missions, education, and publishing eventually divided over the handling of funds or election of officers. To give but one example, the National Baptist Convention U.S.A. divided in 1960 over whether to allow Dr. J. H. Jackson to serve a second four-year term as president, which would have violated convention policy. Those who believed he shouldn't be allowed left the association to form the Progressive National Baptist Convention, Inc.

Core Baptist principles transcend the divisions: Biblical authority, congregational independence, restriction of membership to the saved and baptized, and separation of church and state.

American Baptist Churches in the U.S.A.

Some local Baptist churches are more open to collaborative work with other congregations than others. Those that formed the American Baptist Churches in the U.S.A. offer an illustration. This association of 5,800 churches and about 1.6 million members pulled together earlier associations that formed in the nineteenth and twentieth centuries. Which means that the ABC-USA leans more toward the Missionary Baptist outlook of earlier times, which supported coordination among the local Baptist churches in the North. In many ways, the ABC-USA looks a lot like other denominations in the Protestant mainline. It offers local churches a common lectionary, participates in ecumenical organizations like the National Council of Churches, and runs a more centralized operation (they actually have a full-time general secretary with a professional staff of directors).

Lo and Behold

The American Baptist Churches are commonly thought of as the northern Baptist denomination, but that isn't quite right. Part of the problem in defining the church lies in the fact that it's a fusion denomination, and one part of it used to be called the Northern Baptist Convention. Today, ABC-USA churches are concentrated in northern states, but also have strong contingents in places like California, Florida, and Washington, D.C.

ABC-USA might then be thought of as a liberal Baptist counterpart to the more conservative associations like the Southern Baptist Convention and the General Association of Regular Baptist Churches. Be careful here. Their ecumenical spirit, celebrations of diversity, support for women's ordination in the ministry, and commitment to economic and racial justice give this impression, but the ABC-USA still values local congregational independence. Positions taken by the General Board, liberal or otherwise, are not binding on local churches, and congregations are not marched out of the association for what they teach from their pulpits.

General Association of Regular Baptist Churches

An array of Baptist churches formed the General Association of Regular Baptist Churches in 1932 because they thought other Baptist associations had become too modern in their outlook. This separation occurred during the height of the fundamentalist-modernist controversy, in which Protestant theologians and church leaders battled over how to approach the Bible. GARBC churches came down on the side of the fundamentalists, and today hold the view that the Bible is infallible and inerrant in all matters of which it speaks. They think it's not enough to say, as the ABC-USA says, that the Bible is divinely inspired and provides the most authoritative guide to knowing and serving God.

The 90,000 members of the association (about 1,400 churches), centered in the South, Midwest, and mountain states, are culturally conservative as well, claiming the need to separate themselves from theological liberalism and compromising accommodation to a changing world. Generally, GARBC churches teach their high schoolers to stay away from rock music and movie theaters, and preach against homosexuality, abortion, and feminism. Some GARBC Baptists even distance themselves from conservative evangelical Christians like James Dobson, Charles Colson, and Billy Graham, who they believe are too willing to borrow language and concepts from non-Christians and to fraternize with Catholics and liberal Protestants.

Southern Baptist Convention

The granddaddy of all Baptist associations is the Southern Baptist Convention, at least in terms of size. With 42,000 congregations, it swamps all other Protestant denominations. The SBC has its roots in the pre-Civil War South, having organized itself in 1845 when the main Baptist association at the time refused to allow slaveholders to become missionaries. Pro-slavery gave the SBC an initial rallying point, but almost destroyed it during the Civil War. African Americans left the church to form their own associations. Thousands more left, mostly whites, to join the Primitive Baptists in their opposition to coordinated and centralized mission work.

Baptists are all over the map, but the shaded areas mark counties where Baptists make up over half of all professing Christians.

(Source: D.B. Barrett, World Christian Encyclopedia *[Oxford: Oxford University Press, 1982])*

But the SBC weathered these storms and surfaced in recent years as the flagship Baptist association in the United States. Congregations join together in local associations and state-level conventions in order to support colleges, universities, seminaries, nursing homes, hospitals, Christian camps and retreat centers, and missions, to name

Edifications

The Southern Baptist Convention is a big association with some Texas-sized churches, including Jerry Falwell's Thomas Road Baptist Church in Virginia, with its 22,000 members, and First Baptist Church in Dallas, with 28,000 members.

a few things. An annual convention meets to stake out positions on a range of contemporary religious, social, and political issues. Importantly, a church can be a Southern Baptist Convention church and not participate in any of these broader associations. That's a measure of the local independence that SBC churches value.

The major preoccupation of SBC churches is bringing people who are not saved into a personal relationship with Jesus Christ so that they, too, can be born again. To accomplish this task, the SBC believes that separatism of the sort practiced by GARBC churches is too extreme. In fact, they say that churches must strike a balance between accepting everything outside the church walls and fussing over each and every shortcoming in the world. The SBC believes that if you don't affiliate with other churches because they are impure, then you may end up like Roger Williams, America's über-Baptist. He is said to have arrived at the conclusion that nobody belonged in the church except himself and his wife. And he wasn't too sure about her, either.

Rather than strict separatism, SBC churches have in fact joined in the political fray over the last generation. Experts give SBC churches lots of credit for the election of Republican Party candidates in the 1980s and 1990s, especially through grassroots organizations like Rev. Jerry Falwell's Moral Majority and Pat Robertson's Christian Coalition (Falwell is an SBC minister, Robertson isn't). But political engagement has

Lo and Behold

Baptists claim that the Bible is the sole authority in matters of faith, yet they go ahead and write out lists of doctrines like Philadelphia Confession, the New Hampshire Confession, and the more recent Baptist Faith and Message. Is this a contradiction? Well, Baptists say no. They consider the doctrines to be an explanation of Baptists' beliefs to non-Baptists, not a binding charter to which each and every congregation must subscribe.

its costs. In the wake of the September 11, 2001, terrorist attacks and the war in Afghanistan, the SBC became the focus of controversy when former SBC President Jerry Vines declared in a widely quoted sermon that the prophet Mohammad was a demon-possessed pedophile. Battle lines were drawn as Tom Brokaw accused Vines of preaching hate, while prominent SBC ministers accused the media of anti-Christian bias.

Add to this the usual internal squabbles that all U.S. denominations experience. SBC churches are still dealing with the fallout from the pronouncement of the Baptist Faith and Message (2000), which took conservative positions on several key issues regarding the inspiration of the Bible, the nature of salvation, and women's roles in family and society. Though out of context, one part of it reads, "A wife is to submit herself graciously to the servant leadership of her husband." This prompted former president Jimmy Carter to renounce his association with the SBC. If the SBC splits—sheer speculation here—it would only be the latest instance in a long history of denominational shifts, splits, morphs, and fusions within the Baptist family, within Protestantism, and within Christianity itself.

The Least You Need to Know

- Baptists and Anabaptists are different: Baptists were more influenced by English Calvinism than by developments in Switzerland, Germany, and the Netherlands, as were the Anabaptists.

- Baptists believe that only those who have made a personal commitment to Jesus and have been baptized should belong to the church.

- The word "association," rather than "denomination," best describes Baptist organizations, since they jealously guard the independence of the local church.

- The largest Protestant denomination in the United States is the Southern Baptist Convention, which doesn't actually think of itself as a denomination in the traditional sense.

Chapter 15

Methodists

In This Chapter

- ◆ Learn why Methodists got their name back in the eighteenth century

- ◆ Consider the importance of the German Pietist movement to the founder of Methodism, Englishman John Wesley

- ◆ Understand the aspects of Methodism that distinguish Methodists from most other Protestant denominations

- ◆ Find out how Methodists define Christian perfection, one of their unique doctrines

A church marquee caught my eye recently; it read, "Happy 300th Birthday John Wesley." That got me thinking. Wesley's birth is a lot closer in time to Columbus's voyage to the New World than to our own age. Yet Wesley's movement, called Methodism, seems as modern and contemporary as the United States itself, mostly because it was so well fitted to succeed in America. One observer even called Methodism "the most American of Churches." How's that so? Methodism spun off a number of other important American denominations, like the African Methodist Episcopal Church and the Wesleyan Church. Also, many of the telling aspects of American Protestantism are most clearly identified with Methodism, like revivalism, freedom of choice, and personal morality. Their importance within American religion requires everyone to understand a little better the movement that John Wesley started what seems like only yesterday.

Points of Departure

Methodism started with John and Charles Wesley in the 1730s. These two brothers were educated to the ministry at Oxford University, where they participated in a club for reading Scripture, conducting devotions, and observing communion. During a trip to colonial Georgia, John came under the influence of Moravian Pietist Christians. He attended a Church of England service upon his return to London in 1738 and felt his heart "strangely warmed" during a reading of Martin Luther's *Commentary on Romans*.

This experience led to a pilgrimage to Germany to meet Count Zinzendorf, the famous Pietist thinker. John came back to England ready to apply a lot of what he learned. He preached the Pietist doctrine that Christians mustn't just say they're Christians and go to church, but must also live as if the grace of God was at work in their souls. He urged them to greater practical devotion to God and to greater holiness in lifestyle. Wesley's brother Charles joined these rallies, writing and translating hymns that eventually formed the core of most Protestant hymnals in the United States.

> ### Everybody Said Amen
>
> John and Charles Wesley started the Methodist movement, John through his sermons and organizing, Charles through his music. Some hymns by Charles Wesley include Protestant warhorses like "O for a Thousand Tongues to Sing," "And Can It Be That I Should Gain," and "Christ the Lord Is Risen Today." You've probably heard of another Charles Wesley favorite, "Hark! the Herald Angels Sing."

Wesley's outdoor rallies eventually found their way to the United States, as in the case of this Methodist camp meeting at Sing Sing, New York (1868).

(Permission for use from the Methodist Archives and History Center of the United Methodist Church)

Wesley's evangelical zeal and his willingness to adopt unconventional methods lent to his rallies an air of spectacle. Nothing like it had ever been seen in England. John Wesley pushed this even further by organizing his converts into classes to continue the process of spiritual development following his departure, and he appointed people to lead and direct these groups in his absence. The outlines of a denominational order had begun to form, even though John Wesley's break from the Church of England wasn't complete until 1784.

Methodists took their name from the jesting John endured in the Holy Club at Oxford in the 1720s and 1730s. John's rigorous spiritual discipline became legendary and his mates chided him by calling him a *methodist*, which eventually stuck. Methodism came to the American colonies with ordinary farmers and artisans in the 1760s, but soon missionaries like Joseph Pilmoor and Richard Boardman, and later Francis Asbury and Richard Wright were sent along to organize the congregations into a national body. Francis Asbury would eventually become known as the father of American Methodism.

> **Steeple Talk** _____
>
> **Methodist** came to describe a group of Christians who followed John Wesley in his observance of special devotions within the Church of England. The name was first given in jest, but it stuck anyway.

The Manner of Methodism

The basic thing you need to know about Methodists is that they offered a very different perspective on the process of salvation than that held by other Protestants. Methodists didn't think that certain people were predestined for salvation, and therefore they didn't agree with Calvinists that salvation is limited to the chosen few.

Methodists believe that God knew which people would choose salvation when presented with the choice. This is not to say that God does the choosing. Human beings are able to know about God, and are ultimately responsible for choosing to follow God sometime during the course of their lifetimes. Methodists believe that when people freely choose to accept the truths of God, they permit the work of grace to eliminate their sins and transform their souls.

> **Lo and Behold** _____
>
> It comes down to choice. Methodists believe that salvation is open to all, and that people have the capacity to choose either for or against God. They picked this idea up from their founder John Wesley, who picked it up from Jacob Arminius, a Dutch critic of Calvinism in the late 1600s.

According to the Methodists, God's grace saves people in three ways:

1. Prevenient grace

2. Justification

3. Sanctification

God gives us prevenient grace early on in the process of salvation, which is described as a gentle nudge, a feeling that something isn't quite right and an urge to think about ultimate things. In doing so, we discover our sinfulness and the eternal penalties of sin and acquire an inward desire to seek God's forgiveness.

Edifications

John Wesley could pinpoint the precise moment on May 24, 1738, when his heart was strangely warmed and he became convinced of his need for faith in order to be saved. He told and retold this story on his various travels, which cemented the importance of the sudden conversion experience within Methodism and within the broader evangelical Protestant community.

This experience leads to repentance, and the next way in which God's grace saves people. Methodists believe that God reaches out to those who repent with love and forgiveness, counting Jesus' death as a sufficient compensation for their sins. Technically, this is called justification: forgiveness of past sins.

The final step is sanctification, which is the signature feature of Methodism. After the believers' sins are forgiven, or justified by Christ's work on the cross, their hearts are transformed by the Holy Spirit. Now they desire to do good, to live holy lives, to strive for righteousness. Grace is at work within their hearts to enable them to live according to God's will and to resist sinning in the present.

Faith That Works

Methodists expect the work of grace in the lives of believers to produce results. The usual works will do; start with the fruits of the spirit like love, joy, peace, patience, kindness, and other virtues listed in Galatians 5:22–23. If you don't evidence these virtues, maybe the conversion you claim to have made never happened in the first place.

To Methodists good deeds don't actually save you from damnation. Grace does. Good deeds are actually the end result of saving grace and a regenerated soul. Methodists say that the Holy Spirit *imparts righteousness* during the process of sanctification. Believers who receive the second work of grace receive the desire and the power to practice the Christian virtues.

Steeple Talk

Imparted righteousness means that the righteousness one requires in order to be reconciled with God is actually imparted. The righteousness becomes real, actual, and evident in the life of the believer. Other Protestants believe that righteousness is imputed, whereby God ascribes to the sinner the righteousness necessary for reconciliation. In this case, righteousness doesn't materialize in the actual daily life of the believer.

These points may seem trivial, but they influence how Methodists practice the faith. Now Methodists have a way of holding people to a higher standard of personal morality. This is something *all* the early reformers wanted during the Protestant Reformation. This higher standard was expected from those who joined the Mennonite and Amish churches in Europe and the United States, and it was the driving force behind the Pietist movement that shaped Protestant evangelicalism in the centuries to follow.

Christian Perfection

Wesley had given Christians a blueprint for how to follow Jesus' instruction in Matthew 5:48: "Be perfect, therefore, as your heavenly father is perfect." Leaders of Methodism developed a few tools to help push new converts in this direction. The class system made its way to Methodist congregations throughout the British Empire. Each class had its own leader who was responsible for ensuring that believers made progress toward sinless perfection. Organizers also put together books and magazines to aid them in their study of the Scriptures.

These tools are intended to lead the believer into *Christian perfection*, as distinguished from absolute perfection. In the case of Christian perfection, the believer achieves freedom from sin, defined as a voluntary transgression of a known law. This allows for unintentional sins and character defects. Methodists deny that they teach the possibility of absolute perfection, of which only Jesus Christ was capable of achieving. They also deny that Christian perfection is the result of human effort alone.

Steeple Talk

Christian perfection refers to the attainment of a state of righteousness, which is understood as freedom from sins committed through conscious choice. Methodists believe that this limited kind of perfection is not solely the result of human effort, but also of human collaboration with the Holy Spirit.

Revivalism

Let's put it all together. According to the Methodists, nobody is considered to be a lost cause since nobody is preselected for damnation. If so, then everyone's soul is up for grabs. Yet, God prompts, leads, and eventually transforms once the spiritual pilgrim makes a conscious choice to listen, follow, and eventually commit. And new Christians can expect grace to assist in their progress toward Christlike holiness.

Methodism offered preachers a practical theology that inspired them to actively seek conversions. The Wesleys demonstrated this aspect at various outdoor meetings throughout England. In the United States, Methodists identified certain locations along the frontier as preaching stations, and assigned traveling ministers to visit a set of them arranged in a circuit that could be completed in about two or three months. Circuit-riders like Lorenzo Dow and Peter Cartwright soon became icons of American Christianity. These practices matured into a key Methodist tradition, the camp meeting. At these meetings, ministers preached the revival message, seeking conversions and exhorting the faithful to higher levels of morality.

Edifications

Lorenzo Dow (1777–1834) is one of the most colorful figures in American religious history. Methodists waffled on whether to license him because of his eccentricities, but he traveled the Methodist circuits anyway. He claimed to have met the prophet Nathan and to have been taken to heaven in a whirlwind, where he met God, Jesus, and Gabriel. He drew a large following among the camp-meeting crowd launching into hysterical fits of enthusiasm and sarcastic tirades against other Protestant ministers.

This short book from the 1960s indicates the strength of the revivalist tradition among American Methodists, Baptists, and Pentecostals in more recent generations.

(Image credit: Revell)

STEPHEN F. OLFORD

HEART-CRY FOR REVIVAL

Introduction by ALAN REDPATH

United Methodist Church

The United Methodist Church, the major U.S. Methodist denomination, draws together many different strands of Methodism that developed over the entire sweep of U.S. history. These strands all trace their beginning point to Francis Asbury, perhaps the most important missionary dispatched to the American colonies by John Wesley himself. Asbury took advantage of Methodism's unusual blend of centralized administration and revivalistic, popular religious expression to make it the largest U.S. denomination before the Civil War.

Asbury was a shrewd organizer. He laid the entire country out on a grid, plotting circuits and organizing them into districts and conferences. He was careful to provide a structure for the church, and yet permitted flexibility. He followed Wesley, who was famous for wanting to include everyone: "Dost thou love and fear God? It is enough! I give thee the right hand of fellowship."

> **CAUTION**
>
> **Lo and Behold**
>
> Unlike Baptists, Methodists never experienced a desire for separated, independent churches of believers set apart from the rest of society. The UMC describes itself as "connectional" (local congregations are linked together) and values what a denominational system can provide to individual churches: mutual responsiveness and accountability.

In the nineteenth century, the Methodist Church survived major schisms over slavery and perceived worldliness. The latter schisms resulted in the so-called Holiness denominations like the Free Methodist Church, the Pilgrim Holiness Church, the Church of the Nazarene, and the Church of God (Anderson, Indiana). The main body of the Methodist Church tried to unite with its historically black Methodist counterparts at the end of the nineteenth century, but to no avail. In 1939, the northern and southern branches of Methodism that separated over slavery reunited, and then fused with the Evangelical United Brethren in 1968 to make up the current United Methodist Church.

> **Everybody Said Amen**
>
> Methodists don't have martyrs like the Mennonites and Quakers, but they do celebrate people like John Wesley, Francis Asbury, and Richard Allen as heroes of the faith. Christians today argue about what constitutes martyrdom. If missionaries are killed in automobile accidents while on the mission field, are they martyrs? Some say yes, others say no. Roman Catholicism avoids these debates because it has a centralized, bureaucratic process for evaluating claims of sainthood.

In the UMC, clergy from local districts elect bishops to govern regional conferences, who in turn appoint new clergy to fill empty pulpits within their jurisdictions. Each conference meets annually, with both clergy and laypersons representing the districts. The annual regional conferences send clergy and lay delegates to a General Conference every four years to discuss important policy issues facing the church. Churches are expected to implement the policy decisions taken by the General Conference. UMC churches align themselves with a very fat Book of Discipline, and use some of the formalities in worship associated with the Church of England, with (of course) a heavy dose of Charles Wesley's hymns.

It's fair to say that liberal and evangelical trends in Christianity affected UMC's member congregations in the same way as other major Protestant denominations, and similar internal divisions are evident. Conservative groups like the Confessing Movement and supporters of *Good News Magazine* complain about the denomination's tolerance of radical bishops and weak stand on the issue of Biblical authority. But liberal groups like Affirmation and In All Things Charity complain that the denomination isn't moving fast enough to incorporate gays, lesbians, and transgendered persons into the life of the church. All groups claim to be grounded in Methodist principles, since the Wesleys supported the authority of the Bible, but also welcomed everyone committed to Jesus Christ into the church.

African Methodist Episcopal Church

Methodists moved into the nineteenth century with separate organizations for whites and for African Americans, much like their fellow Pietists, the Baptists. The African Methodist Episcopal Church found its Francis Asbury in the person of Richard Allen.

Edifications

United Methodists have become known for their diversity of opinion on social and political questions like abortion, gay rights, capital punishment, and U.S. foreign policy. Want some evidence? Look no further than two prominent Americans who belong to the United Methodist Church: Sen. Hillary Rodham Clinton and President George W. Bush.

In one of the more famous episodes in U.S. Christianity, Allen and a group of free blacks were refused equal treatment in seating and administration of the sacraments at Saint George Methodist Church in Philadelphia in 1787. In protest against racial injustice and apartheid, Allen organized a separate church in a blacksmith shop, and later joined forces with other black Methodist churches that began in similar circumstances in Philadelphia and Baltimore.

Allen's AMEC was interchangeable with the white Methodists in doctrine and church government. It accepted American Methodism's general rules of church order and its system of districts and conferences with bishops at the top. There were a few differences, though. At the start, he limited membership in his church to descendents of the African race and ensured that the local congregation would select its own minister. This demonstration of African American leadership and self-determination inspired thousands to join and the AMEC took off.

The AMEC taught the importance of personal piety and moral perfection, clearly part of the Methodist tradition. But Wesley's commitment to some of the formalities of the Church of England didn't resonate. Worship focused on spiritual regeneration and expressiveness. As the white Methodist Church became less revivalist and more middle-class in the nineteenth century, the AMEC continued to attract African American factory workers and sharecroppers. Racial and class divisions kept the white Methodist Church and the AMEC from uniting in the 1880s and 1890s, despite a sustained series of conferences aimed at racial reconciliation and reunion.

Several African American Methodist denominations cropped up to rival the original AMEC. The African Methodist Episcopal Zion Church is an example. It began when African Americans left the white Methodist Episcopal Zion Church in New York City in 1796 to form a separate congregation, having experienced the same kind of discrimination that Richard Allen experienced 10 years earlier among white Methodists in Philadelphia. A denomination formed itself in 1821 from African American Methodist congregations in the surrounding area. The AMEC with its 2.2 million members and the AMEZ with its 1.2 million are like-minded in organization and doctrine.

Church of the United Brethren in Christ

Methodists like Francis Asbury and Richard Allen were movement builders. The environment of the early United States both encouraged and demanded it. Another example of movement building in the early years of U.S. history is today's Church of the United Brethren in Christ, the product of a merger instigated by a Mennonite bishop and a German Reformed minister in 1800. At its founding, the CUBC shared Wesley's sentiments that fellowship in Christ knows no denominational boundaries, so long as it contains true Christian piety.

In fact, the founders drew inspiration from German Pietism and the beginnings of the Methodist Church. The Mennonite bishop, Martin Boehm, eventually took membership in the Methodist Church, and the German Reformed minister, William Otterbein, became good friends with Francis Asbury. Otterbein assisted with Asbury's consecration, and Asbury gave the eulogy at Boehm's funeral. Boehm and Otterbein preached the importance of personal conversion and holy living among the German settlers of Pennsylvania. Their paths crossed in 1767 at a revival meeting of German

Protestants in York, Pennsylvania, which were not unlike Methodist camp meetings. Otterbein, upon hearing Boehm preach, exclaimed, *"Wir sind Brüder!"* (We are Brethren!) Apparently, you can still visit the barn where Otterbein gave the eventual denomination its name.

> **Everybody Said Amen**
>
> One of the most influential bishops in the history of the Church of the United Brethren in Christ is Milton Wright (1889–1929), who provided leadership to the denomination from his home in Dayton, Ohio, while his sons Orville and Wilbur Wright meddled around with flying rubberband machines and added custom features to bicycles. Later they would revolutionize aviation at Kitty Hawk, North Carolina.

The CUBC adopted episcopal governance like the Methodists and filled pulpits with deeply spiritual, if untrained, laypersons. It even used the Methodist circuit-riding system to meet the needs of leaderless churches. To the CUBC, depth of spiritual commitment rated more highly than theological sophistication or formal credentials. Today, the CUBC reflects this evangelical and Pietist heritage. It stresses the importance of the conversion experience and ongoing devotion to Christ. A large group within the CUBC left the denomination over procedural matters in the 1880s and eventually joined with the United Methodist Church, leaving the remnant to move in step with the broader evangelical movement over the last several generations.

The Least You Need to Know

- Methodists emerged from the Church of England in the 1780s, and became an independent American denomination under the leadership of Francis Asbury.

- Methodists share Pietist sentiments with Mennonites and Baptists, like resistance to stale intellectualism and desire for intense spiritual experience with Christ.

- To Methodists, everybody is a candidate for salvation, which makes them work hard to present the Gospel to people who haven't heard about Jesus.

- Like other major Protestant denominations, the United Methodist Church is a fusion denomination that embraces a wide diversity of opinions and backgrounds.

Chapter 16

Quakers

In This Chapter

- Learn how the Society of Friends earned the nickname "Quaker"
- Find out how the idea of an Inner Light shapes Quaker views about the Spirit, Jesus, salvation, the Bible, and other aspects of the Christian faith
- Consider the importance of silence and sincerity in Quaker meetings
- Understand the Quaker social conscience, which works to promote peace, equality, and justice in the world

There isn't a Christian group in the United States with a more misleading name than the Quakers. If that was all you had to go on, you'd assume they're holy rollers, tumbling, jerking, and twitching their way through Sunday services. Nothing could be further from the truth. In fact, some Quakers meet as a group and wait in silence for the Spirit to move someone to speak. Others use paid ministers to lead services that don't seem all that different from liturgical Protestant churches. So let's clear the air right away: Quaker is a nickname for the group, and their actual name is the Religious Society of Friends. You'll soon find out how they got both names.

The importance of the Friends churches to Christianity in the United States far outweighs their numbers. There are a little more than 100,000 Quakers in the United States, a fraction of the number of Catholics, Baptists, or Methodists. Yet, the impact of their work in the areas of social reform, social service, and education is hard to overlook. Then, too, Friends pioneered a very unusual blend of ideas and practices that some other Christian groups eventually adopted with success. They don't have creeds and they don't observe sacraments or rituals. Their meetinghouses have no altars, stained glass, elaborate organs, or special seating for church officials. Friends teach about equality, togetherness, and peace, and place at the center of their faith the idea of a believer's direct and intimate experience with God. In the end, it's hard to find a group that tries harder to recreate the spirit of Christianity as it was practiced during the first century after Christ.

The Inner Light

The notion of an Inner Light makes Quakers unique among U.S. Christians. They believe that within every human soul you can find a certain element of God's spirit. It is thought to help each person not only to understand the difference between good and evil, but to understand his or her connection to everyone else in the world.

> **CAUTION**
> **Lo and Behold**
>
> Many Friends don't have the same views about the Bible as Protestants. They think Protestants are too fixated on the Bible as the ultimate rule of faith and practice. Instead, they teach that the inspiration of the Holy Spirit extends to both the writers of the Bible and to those who follow the Inner Light. The Holy Spirit is the ultimate authority, not written words.

The idea of an Inner Light puts Friends at odds with a great number of other Christians on the issue of sin. They don't believe that human beings are inherently sinful and condemned to eternal punishment. Instead, they teach that a person must nurture and care for the seed of God within, to make it grow before the seed of evil develops and takes over. Think of it as tending a garden. If you water and fertilize and weed your garden, the right kind of plants will grow. If you don't, you'll be eating chickweed come harvest.

Who Is Jesus?

Some of the questions raised about Friends by other Christians involve their understanding of Jesus Christ. Most Catholics and Protestants believe that people are inherently sinful and await punishment in the hereafter, and Jesus died as a sacrifice for their sins so they can reach heaven through faith in him. If Friends don't believe that human beings are inherently sinful, does that mean they don't believe Jesus to be a savior who died for people's sins?

Friends are famously skittish about creeds and theological formulas, so it's hard to pin down an explicit statement about what Jesus Christ does to save people. An early writer with some standing among Friends, Robert Barclay, affirmed that Jesus' birth and death was necessary as a sacrifice for sins and that his sufferings purchased the grace that people need in order to be reconciled to God. Barclay taught that people should look to the light within, since they will find Christ there and see him crucified for their sins. If they repent and become saved, they will spiritually experience his resurrection and permit His dominion over their hearts. To become saved is to experience God directly, firsthand, by virtue of the Spirit who dwells within one's soul.

Being Convinced

And yet Friends don't really talk about coming to the faith in quite the same way as other Christians. If you want to become a Catholic, you have to go through confirmation. If you want to be included in most of the Protestant churches, you have to experience conversion. Friends don't use words like confirmed or converted, but instead speak of becoming *convinced*.

This argument isn't over just semantics. Friends describe coming to the faith as a process, not a once-for-all event. To be convinced is to accept the idea of an inward light, and to begin following the will of God as the light so leads. Over time, those who consistently follow the Inner Light will achieve victory over sin, having learned to become completely obedient to the will of God. So convincement is just the first step in a gradual process of perfecting one's obedience to Inner Light's leadings.

> **Steeple Talk**
>
> **Convincement** is the way that Friends describe a believer's conscious decision to listen to the Inner Light and follow its leadings. It grows out of the Quaker departure from Catholicism and Protestantism on the issue of how God relates to humankind and how believers achieve union with Christ.

As the seed of God within grows, it is expected that the believer will live in Christlike fashion. This means living simply, speaking truthfully, and serving others. The idea of the Inner Light doesn't mean that Friends are withdrawn and introspective, or that they think of religion in purely spiritual terms. They think of the inward and the outward as opposite sides of a coin, fused together in a seamless whole. Convincement on the inside corresponds with virtuous living and with acts of love and mercy on the outside.

A Society of Friends

Someone had to invent the notion of an Inner Light, which brings us to George Fox (1624–1691). Many Christian denominations are intimately associated with their founders such as John Wesley and the Methodists or Joseph Smith Jr. and the Mormons, and this includes the Friends. Fox left behind lots of writings and a very interesting *Journal*, so Friends can consult with the originator of the concept of the Inner Light and understand better how one particular person lived according to its leadings.

The Meeting System

George Fox lived in heady times. The English Civil War of the 1640s stirred up all sorts of new religious groups, like the Seekers, Ranters, Fifth Monarchy Men, and so on. Fox circulated widely throughout England, once he arrived at his conception of the Inner Light, preaching to these fringe groups a simple message: You don't need theology, doctrine, or elaborate rituals and churches in order to experience God or to live in obedience to Christ.

From Fox's *Journal* comes this basic idea, still taught by Friends: "The Lord showed me clearly that He did not dwell in these temples which men had commanded and set up, but in people's hearts." Christians who used altars, sacraments, symbols, icons, prayer books, hymns, and other forms had placed a bunch of things made by human hands between themselves and God. Fox put this idea into practice by entering Anglican and separatist Puritan churches and calling the ministers hirelings who worked solely for the money.

Everybody Said Amen

Think of Quakerism as the end result of the Reformation's effort to get rid of all the things that human beings added to the Christian faith since the time of Christ. Luther and Calvin got this process started, but Anabaptists didn't think they went far enough. However, Quakers think that the Anabaptists didn't go far enough either, since they kept baptism, communion, ordination of ministers, and other practices that kept people from having a direct experience with God.

For all his efforts, Fox earned some time in jail, along with a lot of other Quaker ministers. I like to tell my students the story of James Nayler, who allowed his followers in Bristol to recreate Jesus' triumphal entry into Jerusalem with Nayler playing the role of Christ. The point was to call the church to a primitive kind of

Christianity. Nayler was charged with blasphemy and had his tongue bored through with a hot poker. The persecutions of Fox, Nayler, and hundreds of other early Quakers were commemorated in a book by Joseph Besse called *Sufferings of the People Called Quakers* (1753), which gave the movement some martyrs to inspire them to greater devotion.

But early Quaker complaints about hireling clergy, spiritually dead steeple houses, and empty rituals left them with the obvious problem: How would they express their faith in the absence of these forms? Fox responded by developing a unique system of meetings. He organized weekly meetings for worship on First Days (he stopped calling the days of the week by their pagan Roman names), with monthly meetings for business that joined together several weekly meetings. Quarterly meetings dealt with disciplinary issues in subordinate monthly meetings, and yearly meetings developed policy for different regions of the Atlantic world. The meeting system is still in use today, characterized by its highly egalitarian and democratic format.

> **Edifications**
>
> Believe it or not, Friends pioneered streaking and mooning. Early Quakers protested empty religious rituals by going *naked* as a sign in public places. Apparently William Simpson of Lancaster was accomplished in this area, stringing together a series of naked appearances at churches and marketplaces over a three-year period in the 1650s. Later Friends abandoned the practice.

A New Voice: Women Ministers

The meeting system arrived in the colonies years before the Society of Friends' most well-known Quaker, William Penn, did. Friends started West New Jersey in 1676, attracting thousands of their persecuted co-religionists in the years to follow. Soon enough, Pennsylvania was chartered as a refuge for religious dissenters in Britain and Europe. And surprisingly, the meetings adopted a practice that was quite radical for its time: the encouragement of women in the ministry.

First of all, what does it mean to minister as a Friend? Fox followed the example of Jesus, who didn't use schools of theology, complicated ordination procedures, or special sacramental rites to set the disciples off from the rest of his followers. They were fishermen, tax collectors, and common folk whom Jesus blessed with spiritual power. Fox believed that anyone who

> **Everybody Said Amen**
>
> An indication of the prominence of women in early Quakerism is the printed petition sent by 7,000 women in 1659, which demanded freedom from paying the tithe to support Church of England clergy. It's hard to find another Christian fellowship that encouraged the spiritual and social voice of women as early as the Society of Friends.

received an "opening from the Lord"—a deep spiritual truth revealed by the Inner Light—should share it with others. Seekers could mull it over and if it proved to be sound, add it to their own fund of knowledge and wisdom. Friends considered the inner teacher to be gender-blind when it comes to dispensing revelations.

The first woman memorialized on a circulating coin by the U.S. Mint happens to be a member of the Society of Friends. Susan B. Anthony was active in both the abolitionist and women's rights movements of the pre-Civil War years.

(Photo by the author)

A Plain Style

Besides equality, Friends strive to act upon another principle as well: sincerity. Indeed, Friends protest all forms of insincerity, both inside and outside the meetinghouse. Inside, some Friends reject all written prayers, hymns, and sermons as insincere, because they reflect the thoughts and feelings of a writer in the past, not the thoughts and feelings of the worshippers in the present. Other Friends allow sermons from paid clergy, but still emphasize absolute honesty and integrity.

Early Friends taught plainness in speech, gesture, and dress. If you truly follow the Inner Light and seek Gospel purity, then it will affect the way you furnish your house and fill your wardrobe. Friends got rid of buckles, lace, ribbons, and other fancy appointments, and refused to stage lavish parties and entertainments. By the 1670s, Friends actually became conspicuous themselves, due to their plain gray clothes, broad-brimmed hats, and odd manner of addressing others. Today's Friends aren't so conspicuous, but they still strive for simplicity in their consumer choices. And they still want sincerity to guide all their social relationships.

Lo and Behold _____

Early Friends used the pronouns "thee" and "thou" when addressing an individual. This form was taught as a way to achieve sincerity in speech. "You" refers to a group, and "thou" to a single person in early English usage, and so Quakers thought it was insincere to use "you" in addressing an individual. In passing someone on the street, hearing him or her say "thee" or "thou" was a sure sign that he or she had joined the Society.

The Quaker Social Ethic

Friends developed a social conscience that dovetailed with that of the Anabaptists in Europe. Like the Mennonites, they had a pretty bad experience with the legal system and acquired an instinct for protesting injustice. Friends received confirmation from the Inner Light since Jesus addressed injustice himself during his earthly ministry. Besides withholding oaths, they refused military service and closed their purses to church tithes and taxes. But they didn't withdraw. Instead, they taught that politics must be made Godly by voting, organizing, and serving according to the dictates of conscience.

They demonstrated this conscience in Pennsylvania. William Penn, as much of a founder of Quakerism as Fox himself, developed Pennsylvania's political institutions. Friends quickly dominated the council and provincial assembly, though issues that pricked their conscience soon surfaced. Periodic requests from England to provide colonial support for wars against France violated their pacifist principles. Friends resigned in droves during the French and Indian War in the 1750s and during the American Revolution.

But they still found ways of influencing the direction of society and politics. Friends meetings began to issue injunctions against slaveholding in the early eighteenth century, and prominent Quakers like John Woolman and Anthony Benezet led the transatlantic movement to eliminate slavery from its outset. The nineteenth-century American Anti-Slavery Society, which kept slavery on the national political agenda, had more than its share of Friends. Other issues benefited from Quaker

Edifications _____

The register of famous Quaker American reformers is long. Start with Woolman and Benezet, then add the abolitionist poet John Greenleaf Whittier and the Grimké sisters, Angelina and Sarah. Include women's rights advocates Lucretia Mott and Susan B. Anthony as well.

energies, too, such as prison reform, women's rights, and education. Today, Friends work for racial reconciliation, third-world economic development, and world peace.

Pacifism united Friends with several other so-called Peace Churches, the Mennonites and Brethren. Friends say this: "There is that of God in everyone." Doing violence against another person is to do violence against that of God, both in the giver and receiver. In the Peace Churches, war represents a failure to address root causes of conflict, like injustice and poverty, and a failure to seek alternatives to violence and armed aggression. Friends were vocal critics of the war with Iraq in 2003, just like every other war that governments waged in the last 300 years. Friends believe that true Christianity lies in standing up for one's principles outside the Quaker community even as the majority moves in the opposite direction.

Speaking of majorities and dissenters, Friends have a very unusual way of reaching decisions on various social, political, and religious questions. They don't vote, which would divide the community into visible majority and minority factions, but instead decide questions by a "sense of the meeting." Friends describe this approach not as complete consensus, but unity of principle and sentiment. They try to avoid showdowns at business meetings and instead, proceed delicately until majority opinions emerge and minority objections are withdrawn.

Friends and Enemies

Despite their desire for unity, larger divisions within Quakerism occurred in the early nineteenth century, usually identified as the Hicksite, Gurneyite, and Wilburite schisms (named for the leaders of the different factions). Hicksites made a connection between the Inner Light and the enlightenment's idea of a light of reason, eventually declaring irrational the idea that God used Jesus as a substitute for humankind in atoning for sins. Gurneyites made a connection with the frontier Methodists and Baptists, eventually leaving the other Friends in order to stage revivals, learn more from the Bible, and conduct worship with pastoral leaders. Finally, the Wilburites liked neither the Hicksites' understanding of Jesus, nor the Gurneyites' stress on the Bible and revivalism. Instead, they were committed to the Quakerism they received from their forebears.

Many Quakerisms

The Hicksite, Gurneyite, and Wilburite streams are important to know about if you want to understand the way Friends are organized today. The major groups—called the Friends United Meeting, the Friends General Conference, and the Evangelical Friends International—are composed of meetings that formerly leaned in one of the three directions.

The Friends United Meeting (FUM) brings together about 380 weekly meetings totaling 45,000 Friends in the United States and Canada, with a number of others located in meetings overseas. Many of the meetings that once hewed toward Gurneyite Quakerism in the nineteenth century eventually pulled together to form this larger fellowship in 1902. In the FUM, each First Day Meeting is its own monthly meeting for business as well, so they just call each congregation a Monthly Meeting. Their worship services can be either planned or unplanned, but silence is still an important component of both styles. FUM continues most of the traditions of early Quakerism, but uses full-time ministers. As the FUM explains, its chief purpose is to prepare others for ministry, rather than control the life of the meeting.

> **Edifications**
>
> The boundaries between major Friends denominations are the end product of an internal controversy over how much Friends ought to adapt to an increasingly Protestant and evangelical culture in the early nineteenth century. They testify to the gravitational pull of the Baptists and Methodists who dominated the American religious scene in the 1800–1850 period.

Another organization that bears the Gurneyite imprint is the Evangelical Friends International (EFI), where you can find 41,000 U.S. and Canadian Friends in a little under 300 meetings. Many more EFI Quakers live overseas than in the United States, with a roughly equal number in Africa, Latin America, and North America. The EFI reflects the nineteenth-century Gurneyite association with other Protestant churches, and in fact refers to its local meetings as churches. They have ministers and advertise a confessionlike document called Affirmation of Faith. The points raised in this document resonate with positions taken by evangelical Baptists and Methodists on the nature of sin, salvation, the Bible, and the voluntary church. But they echo classic Quakerism when they speak of a direct, inward experience of Christ and work in concert with other Friends groups to promote peace.

Friends of the Hicksite variety formed the Friends General Conference (FGC) in 1900, which is not so much a tight-knit organization as a friendly alliance of yearly meetings totaling about 32,000 located in the United States. About a third belong to one yearly meeting alone, the Philadelphia Yearly Meeting. The FGC still calls its local congregations "meetings," and they don't have pastors to lead worship. First Day meetings are held in silence, with audible testimonies from some of the worshippers occasionally breaking the reverie. Those who attend sit in a circle so that no individual person is positioned at the head of the group. Generally speaking, the FGC is the more socially and politically progressive of the three major Friends organizations.

The American Friends Service Committee keeps the pacifist flame burning among Friends by distributing literature and coordinating peace and social justice initiatives among all Friends' denominations.

(Permission for use from the American Friends Service Committee)

You can trace Wilburite tendencies to modern-day meetings as well, mainly under the umbrella of the Religious Society of Friends (Conservative). These meetings, mostly in Iowa, North Carolina, and Ohio, try to keep alive as much of the original expression of Quakerism as possible. All the groups strive to work together on projects of common interest. This includes excellent Friends colleges like Swarthmore, Haverford, Bryn Mawr, and George Fox University, and private high schools like Sidwell Friends in Washington, D.C. And they support the American Friends Service Committee, which, among other peace-oriented projects, offers conscientious objectors with a way to serve during wartime without fighting in combat. Friends received an affirmation of their important role in promoting nonviolence when the American Friends Service Committee was selected, along with a similar Friends group in England, as co-winner of the 1947 Nobel Peace Prize.

The Least You Need to Know

◆ Quakers are distinct for their belief in the Inner Light, which they describe as an element of the divine within that allows the believer to discern and follow God's will.

◆ Without the Friends, it might have taken the United States a lot longer to get African Americans out of slavery, and American women into the voting booth.

◆ All Friends incorporate silence into their meetings, whether they are led by full-time ministers or not.

◆ All Friends, regardless of denominational affiliation, consider peace and non-violence to be a cardinal rule of faith and practice.

Part 5

Homegrown Denominations

Many denominations in the United States are transplants. And yet there's a large population of American Christians who don't look to the Old World for leadership or spiritual inspiration.

Along with their non-European origins, homegrown denominations have another thing in common: Their faith hinges on visitations from God. Here you'll find out more about the Pentecostals, Adventists, Jehovah's Witnesses, and Mormons—especially how personal visitations from God gave their movements a start and in many cases continue to energize their movements today.

Chapter 17

Holiness and Pentecostal Churches

In This Chapter

- Find out about the Wesleyan idea of entire sanctification
- Consider the origins and practice of gifts of the Holy Spirit, like speaking in tongues and faith healing
- Understand what Pentecostals mean when they talk about baptism of the Holy Spirit and fire

The three fastest-growing denominations in the United States during the last 10 years are the Church of Jesus Christ of Latter-Day Saints (Mormons), the Christian Churches, and the Assemblies of God. Their growth rate is separated by less than half a percentage point: 19.3, 18.8, and 18.5 percent respectively. The Assemblies of God, a Pentecostal denomination, are spiritual kin to the Society of Friends (Quakers), but only in the sense that they both talk a lot about the indwelling spirit of God. In fact, that might be where the similarities end. Knowing the differences among the Holiness and Pentecostal denominations will help you navigate some tricky terrain in today's Christianity.

Baptism of the Holy Spirit

The Holiness denominations like the Wesleyan Church, the Free Methodist Church, and the Church of the Nazarene got their start in the nineteenth century when some Methodists altered John Wesley's idea of Christian perfection. John Wesley had taught that the process of salvation entailed a second work of grace, or sanctification. This gave believers power to resist temptation so they could reach a state where they never consciously sinned. Holiness churches reworked this idea, claiming that the first and second works of grace are separated in time, and the second work they called the Baptism of the Holy Spirit.

Steeple Talk

Entire sanctification is a doctrine held by Holiness advocates in the Methodist tradition like the Wesleyan Church, which teaches that all believers receive a work of God's grace in their souls after conversion to eradicate sin and to empower them to live without sinning in the future.

Eventually, the major Holiness denomination, the Wesleyan Church, came to see salvation and perfection as a process involving three stages. First, the Spirit provides initial sanctification, where past sins are forgiven. Second, it provides progressive sanctification, which enables the believer to grow in obedience to the Lord. So far, so good. Then comes the all-important third stage: *entire sanctification*. In this stage, the believer receives complete perfection and freedom from sin through Spirit baptism. This happens at the precise moment when he or she willingly offers himself or herself as a living sacrifice to God. The believer experiences a new desire for holy living along with the power to sustain a high level of personal morality.

It goes without saying that the Holiness and Pentecostal churches limit their membership to those who have made a commitment of faith to follow Jesus. In fact, as part of their effort to encourage believers to experience the fullness of Christ, they insist that members refrain from smoking, drinking alcohol, gambling, attending movie theaters, social dancing, and membership in secret societies, along with all the other vices that most other Christians consider sinful. In the past, Holiness churches had a longer list of prohibitions, including Coca-Cola, lipstick, and attending ball games.

The Wesleyan Church

The Wesleyan Church started at the height of the Second Great Awakening, a national revival fueled by Methodist camp meetings and interdenominational revivals. With practically the whole nation talking about greater righteousness and godliness, some disgruntled Methodists came to believe their denomination was compromising with evil because it allowed slaveholders to be members. In 1843, they formed the abolitionist Wesleyan Methodist Church (which shortened its name to the Wesleyan Church some time later).

Lo and Behold

Don't assume that early Holiness churches, with their conservative message of right living and prohibited behaviors, were also conservative in their views toward women. One of the acknowledged leaders of the Holiness movement was Phoebe Palmer (1807–1874), a New York City Methodist who experienced entire sanctification around 1836 and directed a group called Tuesday Meetings for the Promotion of Holiness. Methodists from all over the country came to hear her speak and to experience the Baptism of the Holy Spirit for themselves, putting her at the epicenter of Holiness spirituality.

Wesleyan Methodists established a chilling precedent for the denomination: If you don't like the direction the denomination is heading, leave. This strategy was known as come-outism. But most rejected come-outism in favor of fixing the denomination's problems from within. And Methodism's internal critics were busy pointing out these problems. They disliked newer, more progressive ministers with seminary degrees, recently installed organs, choirs that began to dress in lavish robes, and new policies that allowed wealthy donors to rent prominent pews. These critics thought only a sustained campaign to promote sanctification could restore John Wesley's vision of biblical Christianity.

This view required a return to Methodism's earlier roots. Methodist ministers seeking renewal organized the National Camp Meeting Association for the Promotion of Christian Holiness, which staged a series of national revivalist conventions starting in 1867 as a way to spread Spirit baptism and greater purity in lifestyle. Soon, this gave way to the National Holiness Association, designed to distribute books and magazines with Holiness ideas. The NHA was pan-denominational: Presbyterians, Baptists, Congregationalists, and others also got involved.

The Holiness preachers—then and now—stood watch for evidence of creeping worldliness in the church. In the late 1880s and 1890s, they complained about progressive Protestant ministers in many denominations. From the Holiness point of view, the progressives had surrendered to Darwinism and evolutionary theory. Also, they wrongly applied secular methods of critical analysis to the Bible. And the progressives misunderstood sin, having blamed urban problems on capitalism, poverty, and poor sanitation, rather than individual moral failure.

Everybody Said Amen

Most of the Pentecostal denominations in the United States trace their roots back to a Methodist come-outer named Charles Parham. Like the Holiness ministers, he didn't think the Christian faith and the Bible should be studied like any other academic subject. So he started a Bible institute in Kansas in 1900 and taught its handful of students that the only way you can tell if a person has received the Baptism of the Holy Spirit is if they speak in unknown tongues. His institute didn't last, but one of its students, William Seymour, went on to lead the Azusa Street Revival in Los Angeles, and Pentecostalism as a movement was born.

A huge block of Methodists followed the early lead of the Wesleyan Methodists and became come-outers. According to one scholar, Vinson Synan, 23 new Holiness denominations sprung up in the seven years between 1893 and 1900. A few of the Holiness denominations predate this rash of new start-ups, like the Church of God (Anderson, Indiana) and the Christian and Missionary Alliance (founded in 1881 and 1887, respectively). You should keep in mind there's no binding union holding Holiness denominations together. They are joined instead by periodicals, speakers, and conferences, and coupled together by a common desire to gain victory over sin, both within the heart and in the world beyond.

The Azusa Street Revival

The Holiness and Pentecostal movements are associated but nevertheless distinct. Holiness came first, then Pentecostalism, which got the idea of Spirit baptism from the Holiness preachers, magazines, and conventions. Some ministers in the National Holiness Association thought that the second work of grace and the Spirit baptism were different events. Now, some began to look for an experience of spiritual ecstasy after the second work of grace had sanctified and empowered them for perfection.

Lo and Behold

Critics of the Fire-Baptized Holiness Church branded its members "Holy Rollers," with its unfortunate negative connotations. Unlike Quakers and Methodists, Pentecostals refused to accept the nickname and it fell out of use. Be warned, Pentecostals will take offense if you refer to them by this name.

These ministers called themselves Pentecostals, in reference to the appearance of the Holy Spirit on the Day of Pentecost in the Book of Acts chapter two. They prayed for a third experience of the Holy Spirit after conversion and sanctification. They called this experience a baptism of fire. The new emphasis on baptism of fire among Pentecostal preachers came to a head at the famous Azusa Street Revival in 1906. The revival, led by an African American Holiness minister named

William Seymour, brought believers from every race and nationality in Los Angeles to an abandoned African Methodist Episcopal Church on Azusa Street. For the next three years, thousands manifested the baptism of fire not only by spasms of jerking and shouting, but also speaking in tongues and healing the sick. Some clergy who arrived to witness the work of the Holy Spirit came as Holiness preachers and left as Pentecostals, spreading the baptism of fire to the North, the East Coast, and even to Europe and South America.

Gifts of the Spirit

Pentecostalism emerged from Azusa Street as a movement when hundreds of Holiness congregations converted to Pentecostalism and formed new denominations like the Pentecostal Assemblies of the World (1907), the Assemblies of God (1917), and several organizations with Church of God in the title. Since they mostly came out of the Holiness movement, which mostly came out of Methodism, which came out of the Church of England, they maintained classic Methodist-Protestant views. Today, the vast majority believe in the Trinity, the fall of humankind into sin, the need for salvation by faith through Jesus Christ, the idea of a gathered church of converted believers, the authority of the Bible, and high moral living. But they are distinct by their practice of the so-called "Gifts of the Spirit."

Speaking in Tongues

You can be a Pentecostal if you believe that faith in Jesus Christ leads to the Baptism of the Holy Ghost and fire, which produces the outward effect of spontaneous speech in unknown languages, or speaking in tongues. The first Christians experienced this blessing from God, as recorded in the Book of Acts. Jesus promised a Baptism of the Holy Spirit, which occurred in chapter 2 when they "saw what seemed to be tongues of fire that separated and came to rest on each of them. All of them were filled with the Holy Spirit and began to speak in other tongues as the Spirit enabled them." (Acts 2:3–4)

Pentecostal teachers say that the gift of tongues, or *glossolalia*, doesn't come to those with unclean hearts, since the Holy Spirit can't

Steeple Talk

Glossolalia refers to the phenomenon of speaking in an unknown language by means of divine power or inspiration. Scholars note that speaking in tongues has been practiced by such disparate groups as French Catholics in the twelfth century, U.S. Mormons in the nineteenth century, and Christians in Wales in 1904. Some say news of Welsh glossolalia hastened the onset of the Pentecostal movement in the United States.

take up residence in a corrupt vessel. This is where the Pentecostals reveal their roots in the Holiness tradition. In preparation for receiving this spontaneous gift, believers must maintain separation from substances and activities that induce sin, since only those with pure hearts can expect continued visitations of the Spirit. These include narcotics, alcohol, pornography, and premarital sex. Going a little further, the United Pentecostal Church International instructs its 600,000 adherents not to have televisions in their homes.

Critics of Pentecostalism have tried to paint speaking in tongues as unbiblical, disorderly, outdated, and even demonic. Pentecostals respond by pointing out its biblical origins and its practical value in building a worshipping community.

(Image credit: Dimension Books)

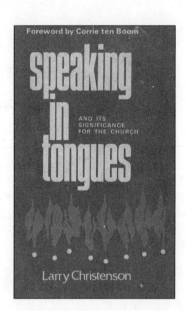

Healing

Numerous Pentecostals believe faith in Christ brings physical healing of the body as well as spiritual healing. They point to passages in the New Testament in which Jesus and the disciples healed the sick and the disabled, and to passages such as James 5:14–15 where anointing with oil, prayers, and laying on of hands are said to restore health. Most Christians believe that prayer can result in miraculous healing, so the Pentecostals don't differ that much from other denominations in this respect. But some Pentecostal ministers go beyond this limited acceptance of faith healing in their claims that fire baptism enables them to channel the healing power of the Spirit into the sick and the lame.

Miraculous healing has a long and storied history in the Christian church, with heavyweights like Tertullian, Cyprian, Saint Francis of Assisi, and Martin Luther providing support. In fact, the most visited shrine in all of Christianity is the Basilica at

Lourdes, France, where it is said that Bernadette Soubirous received a visitation from Mary in 1858 and discovered a spring of healing waters. In this way, Pentecostal teachings fit into a larger Christian tradition beyond Holiness and Methodism.

> **Lo and Behold** _____
>
> It's hard to ignore the distinct social and economic background of Holiness-Pentecostals in the earliest years of the movement. Most came from the poorer classes, and lacked the formal education and cultural refinement that seemed to be growing in mainline Protestant churches. Farmers and mill workers put in a full day's work and then led Holiness and Pentecostal revival meetings deep into the evenings and on Sundays. With few material barriers to entry, the movement appealed to the poorer sort who sought, and received, authentic spiritual experiences.

Prophecy

Speaking in tongues and healing are part of Pentecostal faith and practice. So is prophesying. Typically, believers issue such prophetic utterances (essentially previously hidden truths) during services as the Spirit has given to them to reveal. Non-believers might identify prophecy as something akin to clairvoyance or soothsaying. Pentecostals deny any connection to pagan practices of mind reading or fortune telling, citing biblical precedents and instructions for prophetic belief.

> **Edifications** _____
>
> From tiny seeds came mighty oaks .... The earliest Pentecostal churches were tiny gatherings crowded against the stream banks and horse paths of the southern Appalachian range. But you can't find larger churches today than the Pentecostals. In Seoul, South Korea, the Yoido Full Gospel Church boasts 700,000 members, while the Jotebeche Methodist Pentecostal Church in Santiago, Chile, lists 350,000. In the United States today, some 10 to 12 million adherents are identified as Pentecostal.

You might be able to demonstrate the presence of the Spirit in other ways, too. A small portion of the Pentecostal family teaches that Spirit-filled believers can handle poisonous snakes and drink arsenic without harm, following Jesus' teaching in Mark 16:15–18. Snake-handling churches hit the headlines from time to time when the demonstrations go awry, as when Rev. John Wayne "Punkin" Brown Jr. died at the Rock House Holiness Church in Alabama in 1999 from a bite given by a 4-foot timber rattlesnake. Apparently, Brown had been bitten 22 times before without serious harm, though his wife, Melinda, had died from a snakebite three years earlier at the Full Gospel Tabernacle in Jesus' Name Church in Middlesboro, Kentucky.

Churches of God

There's no centralized organization for Pentecostals, and in fact the whole movement began with the idea of eliminating denominational boundaries. Today, about as many local churches are completely free and independent as are part of larger associations. The Church of God family shows why denominational unity has been difficult to achieve.

There's a denomination called Church of God in Christ, founded in Mississippi in the 1880s and today comprising 5.5 million African American Pentecostals. There's also a Church of God (Cleveland, Tennessee) and a Church of God of Prophesy—which broke away from the Church of God (Cleveland, Tennessee). And there's a Pentecostal Church of God, centered in the Chicago area for urban Pentecostals. Location, race, and alternate visions induced by Spirit baptism help to maintain the boundaries among Church of God denominations in the Pentecostal family.

Everybody Said Amen

The Pentecostal movement began as an interracial fellowship. Revivals at Azusa Street in 1906 reportedly drew Los Angeles's Mexican, Chinese, African American, and white populations together in the belief that Christ's blood had washed away the color line. Denominations soon formed roughly along racial lines, but the spirit of interracial fellowship resurfaced. Many Pentecostals remember the Memphis Miracle of 1994, when hundreds of white and African American ministers gathered to discuss racial reconciliation, and spontaneously washed each other's feet in a gesture of humility and repentance.

Edifications

The Assemblies of God got quite a bit of unwanted publicity in the 1980s when its televangelists, Jimmy Swaggart and Jim Bakker, fell from grace amid sexual scandals. But the denomination earned the admiration of the Christian world by disciplining Swaggart and Bakker, and ultimately revoking their ministerial licenses.

Assemblies of God

Pentecostals didn't think organizing denominations was a good thing to do in the early years of the movement. But the shrieking, tumbling, jerking, and wild prophesying began to discredit the whole idea of Spirit baptism. So influential ministers of mostly white, unaligned Pentecostal churches in the South gathered in 1914 to plan a new denomination that would limit the excesses of Spirit-led Christianity, while also presenting a united front to Pentecostalism's critics.

The Assemblies of God pulled together a number of Pentecostals who began to question the movement's strict separation between sanctification and the Baptism of the Holy Spirit. They collapsed sanctification into conversion, thus nullifying all the careful distinctions that John Wesley's heirs had crafted over the years. Now believers were thought to receive the power of the Spirit at conversion and would grow in grace without having to experience a second spiritual crisis and a corresponding second work of grace. The Assemblies of God still maintain Pentecostal views about speaking and tongues and healing, but have left behind the Wesleyan and Holiness beliefs in sinlessness and perfection. That's where the Assemblies of God and the Church of God denominations differ.

Pentecostals tend to see the Spirit as a flame, while other Protestants think of the dove; both symbols are found in Scripture (Matthew 3:16, Acts 2:3), and together they represent the power and the peace of God. Detail from the logo of the Wesleyan Church's General Conference, 2004

(Permission for use from the Wesleyan Church)

Early in its history, some Assemblies of God members rejected the doctrine of the Trinity. Denominational leaders, fearful of such departures from Christian orthodoxy, produced a Statement of Fundamental Truths (1916), a written constitution of church government (1927), and new planks for the Fundamental Truths in the 1960s to square the denomination with evangelical Protestantism. This put checks in place to limit the range of possibilities for individual revelations from God. Currently, believers in the Assemblies of God consider themselves part of the evangelical mainstream. As a legacy of their Holiness-Pentecostal past, they teach separatism; they don't belong to the National Council of Churches and they prohibit members from participating in a list of worldly activities.

Other Pentecostal Denominations

The Pentecostal movement doesn't have an administrative center like the Roman Catholic Church. Instead, it's a great fellowship of believers who seek an intense encounter with the Holy Spirit, accompanied by extraordinary physical demonstrations. Most of the traditional Pentecostals seek separation from the world and try to practice a primitive, if enthusiastic, kind of faith, without the symbols, sacraments, and programmed worship of the Catholic, Orthodox, or liturgical Protestant churches. This results in lots of independent churches, and smaller denominations that typically formed around charismatic founders like Aimee Semple McPherson and her International Church of the Foursquare Gospel (founded in 1927, with a current membership of 230,000), and Gordon Lindsay's Full Gospel Fellowship of Churches and Ministers, International (founded in 1962, with a membership of 275,000).

Steeple Talk

Full Gospel is a phrase used by some Pentecostals to distinguish themselves from Lutherans, Episcopalians, Mennonites, and even Methodists. They accept classic Protestant teachings on the authority of Scripture, justification by grace through faith, and the priesthood of all believers, but then add things found in the Bible that they believe the other Protestants leave out, like Spirit baptism with signs of speaking in tongues and faith healing, and belief in Christ's imminent return.

Some experts think that the future of Christianity in the United States and the world belongs to the Pentecostals and their spiritual cousins, the Charismatics. The most reliable source for tracking Christians worldwide, David Barrett's *World Christian Encyclopedia*, estimates that about one fifth of the entire world's population of Christians are Pentecostal/Charismatic. That's second only to Roman Catholics. Perhaps that should come as no surprise. The Pentecostals practice a living faith that promises an immediate experience with the divine, which requires no heavy investment in equipment, and knows no racial or ethnic boundaries. When the 20th Pentecostal and Charismatic World Conference convenes in South Africa in September 2004, those in attendance may represent as many as half a billion Christians across the globe.

The Least You Need to Know

- The Holiness denominations like the Wesleyan Church and the Church of the Nazarene began amid calls in the Methodist Church for greater morality.

- Wesleyan Methodists, the first large Holiness denomination, taught a doctrine of entire sanctification, which raised the possibility of living without sin.

- Pentecostal churches believe that following conversion, believers can experience the Baptism of the Holy Spirit, which produces signs like speaking in tongues.

- Pentecostals and Charismatics make up a large and growing fellowship of Spirit-led Christians that is second only to Roman Catholicism worldwide.

Chapter 18

Mormons

In This Chapter

- ◆ Learn about the sacred texts of Mormonism, which include the Bible, the *Book of Mormon*, and the *Doctrine and Covenants*

- ◆ Consider the importance of Joseph Smith Jr.'s revelations to current Mormon faith and practice

- ◆ Understand the importance of the Mormon concept of eternal progression

- ◆ Find out about unique Mormon observances like sealing in marriage and baptism of the dead

Want to learn more about the fastest-growing denomination in the United States today? If so, you came to the right place. Sure, you're probably familiar with a few Mormon-related things, like Brigham Young University and the Mormon Tabernacle Choir. But a lot more education is needed. Despite the visibility of BYU and the Mormon Tabernacle Choir, Mormon beliefs and practices are not as well known. What do Mormons believe about God and Jesus? What do they think happens when they die? What do they do in church on Sunday mornings and special occasions? These are the right kind of questions to ask, and this chapter attempts to answer them.

A Little Background

Mormonism is made in the U.S.A. None of its early leaders claimed to be carrying on an Old World tradition or preserving the ideas of a European thinker. In fact, it's hard to find a denomination in the United States that more clearly bears the imprint of its founder than the Church of Jesus Christ of Latter-Day Saints. Know the founder, and you've gone a long way toward knowing about the denomination.

Joseph Smith Jr.

Joseph Smith Jr. (1805–1844) was a farm boy in Palmyra, New York, with a keen interest in the Bible, even if he didn't formally belong to a church. As a 14-year-old, he received a vision of God and Jesus Christ in human form, directing him to restore the true church on Earth. He also learned that none of the other churches were adequate, and their creeds were an abomination to God. This revelation put him in good company, since rejecting creeds and churches was a common refrain in the early nineteenth century.

> **Edifications**
>
> Like several other founders of denominations in the 1830s, Joseph Smith Jr. did not receive formal theological training, and was not a professional clergyman. Today, the LDS staffs a Church Educational System that in turn administers a network of religious institutes, typically located near college and university campuses. At these institutes, you can take classes like *Preparing for Eternal Marriage*, which "considers the doctrine of celestial marriage and the dating and courtship practices leading to such a marriage."

Smith got a second vision at the age of 17. This time, he spoke with an angel, Moroni, who directed him to a book written on gold plates and buried in a nearby hill. This book, the angel revealed, was left in the earth by an ancient race of people who lived in North America thousands of years ago. Smith found the plates along with two transparent seer stones, named Urim and Thummim, which would help make the unknown characters etched on the plates readable. After a bit of time passed, Moroni gave Smith permission to translate them into English. Plates in hand, he traveled to his father-in-law's farm in Harmony, Pennsylvania, to begin the work. Thus began an odyssey that would change the face of religion in America.

The translation wasn't easy. Smith had to decipher the language, which he called reformed Egyptian, by means of the seer stones. In order to work their magic he had to recite passages to transcribers from behind a screen. The transcribers, Martin and

Emma Harris, never actually saw the plates during the translation, and the angel Moroni eventually took the plates away along with Urim and Thummim. But Smith kept hold of the *Book of Mormon* as translated into English and in 1830, had the manuscript published back in Palmyra.

The Book of Mormon

So what's in the *Book of Mormon?* The *Book of Mormon* contains a number of cross-references to the Christian Bible, like quotes from Malachi and Isaiah, and a condensed version of Jesus' teachings in the Gospel of Matthew. The Lord's Prayer is there, along with a command to practice the Eucharist. But the key feature is the saga of the Nephites, an ancient race of North American inhabitants who left Israel and came to the Western Hemisphere around 600 B.C.E. In North America, they broke into two tribes (Nephites and Lamanites), one faithful to God and the other unfaithful. They battled for centuries, but then Jesus Christ appeared to them, shortly after his ascension as recorded in the Bible's Book of Acts. Jesus brought unity, along with instructions for planting his true church on American soil. A few centuries of peace ensued, but eventually a climactic battle destroyed Nephite civilization. The last survivor, Moroni, son of the Nephite general Mormon, preserved his father's record of that civilization by burying the golden tablets in a hill in western New York. And that's where Joseph Smith Jr. found them.

Everybody Said Amen

Things Jesus told the ancient North Americans, recorded in the *Book of Mormon:*

- "Thrust your hands into my side, and also that ye may feel the prints of the nails in my hands and in my feet"
- "I am in the Father, and the Father in me, and the Father and I are one"
- "Whoso believeth in me, and is baptized, the same shall be saved"
- "Blessed are ye if ye shall give heed unto the words of these twelve whom I have chosen"
- "Blessed are the poor in spirit who come unto me, for theirs is the kingdom of heaven"
- "This is the land of your inheritance; and the Father hath given it unto you"

3 Nephi, chapters 11–26

Heading West

Elements of ancient Judaism and Christianity come together in the Mormon story, which has an exodus, a promised land, tribal warfare, and a visitation from the resurrected Christ. The Mormon *hegira*, or exodus, from Palmyra to Utah territory, with stops at Kirtland, Ohio; Independence, Missouri; and Nauvoo, Illinois, is nothing short of remarkable. It began after Smith and an early convert baptized and ordained one another as high priests and organized a church. Smith adopted the official title of "Seer, a Translator, a Prophet, an Apostle of Jesus Christ, and Elder of the Church through the will of God the Father, and the grace of your Lord Jesus Christ." He received new revelations from God, two of which profoundly shaped the Mormon faith:

1. The Latter-Day Saints would discover the New Jerusalem *on the borders by the Lamanites*

2. Any new revelations from God would be given to Joseph Smith alone.

So Mormons fell under the complete control of Smith and headed west. The congregation left New York in 1831 to join a few Mormons who had started an early mission among Indians in Ohio. More revelations followed in the years to come, including the idea that God and Jesus have fleshly bodies, that Jesus and the Holy Spirit are the offspring of God and a heavenly wife, that there exists a plurality of gods, and that human beings can progress to become gods themselves. Smith's later revelations in the 1830s and 1840s, which became the core of the *Doctrine and Covenants*, are considered by some experts to represent Mormonism's greatest departures from Orthodox, Catholic, and Protestant teachings.

Lo and Behold

Polygamy, or plural marriage, has never been officially sanctioned by the Church of Jesus Christ of Latter-Day Saints. Critics say that Smith practiced it in secret and his converts merely followed suit. This population includes Brigham Young, a notorious polygamist who was sealed to 56 different women, and had 57 children by 16 of his wives. Apparently, 10 divorced him as well. The LDS president advised against the practice in 1890, but the church continues to deal with popular associations between LDS and Mormon extremists. In 2002, Mormons winced when Tom Green made national news for his conviction on charges of bigamy and child rape; Green lived openly with five wives and 29 children in a compound near Nephi, Utah.

Smith allegedly began practicing polygamy as well, marrying some 49 different women according to some sources. His revelations and unconventional lifestyle angered local residents, putting Mormons on the move once again. While visiting Mormon missionaries in Missouri, Smith revealed that Jackson County was the promised land. Mormons built a temple and planted farms, but local hostility forced a repeat of earlier exits from Palmyra and Kirtland. Even though the area near their Missouri settlement was thought to be the site of the original Garden of Eden, Smith assured his followers that Nauvoo, Illinois, was the future home of the Kingdom of God. Built from scratch by Mormons, Nauvoo was governed like a theocracy, and Smith was declared King of the Kingdom of God with command of a paramilitary forced called the Nauvoo Legion. Smith even campaigned for president of the United States in 1844.

When Smith ordered the destruction of an opposition newspaper, non-Mormon neighbors reached their boiling point. Smith was jailed and later lynched by an angry mob. At this point his initial plans to build an empire out west went into high gear under the visionary leadership of Brigham Young. Young organized a pioneer band in 1847 and headed west on an eventful, 100-day odyssey into the very heart of Lamanite country to claim a new promised land. So if Joseph Smith Jr. is Mormonism's Abraham, then Brigham Young is its Moses. Young selected the Salt Lake basin as the site of the New Jerusalem, secured territorial status from the U.S. government, and declared a new state of Deseret. By the eve of the Civil War, Mormons had planted more than 90 settlements throughout the Rocky Mountain region and California, though other Mormons could be found in Ohio, Missouri, and Illinois as a result of disagreements about Joseph Smith's later revelations.

> **Everybody Said Amen**
>
> Mormon vegetarians? The Word of Wisdom, a revelation from Joseph Smith Jr. in 1833, outlined a dietary code for LDS members. It encouraged the consumption of vegetables, breads, and fruits, and forbade alcohol, tobacco, coffee, and tea. According to some Mormon interpretations of the Word of Wisdom and other *Doctrine and Covenants* provisions, eating meat is also discouraged.

Church of Jesus Christ of Latter-Day Saints

Smith, Young, and every Mormon ever since had one goal in mind: re-creating the true church that Jesus originally planted in North America in the time of the Nephites. Those saints were the first saints and Mormons today are the latter-day saints, which puts them in good company—dozens of other denominations at one time believed they were restoring Christianity to its primitive state before history corrupted it with symbols, rituals, and false doctrines.

How does the LDS church work? There are two orders of priests, Melchizedek and Aaronic; the latter manages the day-to-day affairs of the local churches, while the former provides spiritual direction for the entire denomination. Those ordained in the Melchizedek priesthood fill the highest denominational offices, including the First Presidency, the Council of the Twelve Apostles, the group of Seventy, and the High Priests. These are very powerful positions within the Mormon organization. For example, the president is thought to have inherited Smith's prophetic powers, which is a later LDS development. His revelations are entered into the *Doctrine and Covenants* alongside Smith's.

Below the First Presidency, the Council of Twelve acts as a kind of board of directors. They supervise the work of the Seventy, which in turn direct the work of various high priests, bishops, elders, and patriarchs. The Mormon world is subdivided into regions (like archdioceses) and *stakes* (yes, dioceses). And a stake is made up of a bunch of wards. A *ward* is essentially a congregation in which local Mormons observe the different aspects of LDS faith. In a loose sense, a ward is like a parish.

> **Edifications**
>
> The *Book of Mormon* has been a publishing dynamo. Since 1830, 116 million copies have been printed in 102 different languages. For comparative purposes, J. K. Rowling's Harry Potter books number about 90 million in print as of the fall of 2003.

> **Steeple Talk**
>
> **Wards** are individual congregations, each led by a bishop, and **stakes** are districts composed of a number of wards, administered by a stake president.

Eternal Progression

The LDS organization exists to support Mormons in their eternal progression, which is the heart of LDS belief. All of the official doctrines, religious practices, Sunday school lessons, Bible-study workbooks, and so on have this general concept in mind. It explains the nature of God, the relationship between God and humankind, the purpose of existence, the linkage between sin and redemption, the idea behind the church, and what happens at the end of time.

Here's how it all fits together: God is not a changeless, infinite, spiritual being. Instead, God started off ages ago in a condition just like a normal person. Over time, God gradually grew in power and eventually became an exalted man. In a sense, God

> **Lo and Behold**
>
> Does the Mormon belief in eventual godhood for human beings mean that they are polytheists? The LDS says that the Bible teaches in I Corinthians 8:5-6 that there are many gods, but only one God to whom all reverence and worship must be directed.

became God over time. But God retained human form, so that if you could see him, you'd see arms, legs, a head, and so on. There's a shorthand way of describing the nature of God among Mormons: "As man is, God once was."

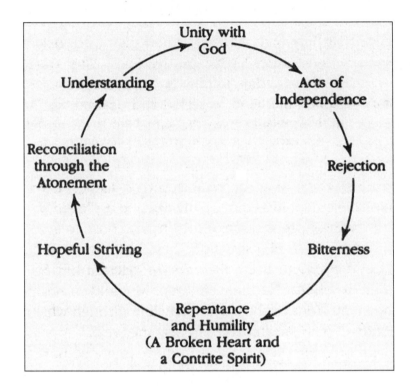

Unity with God

Acts of Independence

Understanding

Rejection

Reconciliation through the Atonement

Hopeful Striving

Bitterness

Repentance and Humility (A Broken Heart and a Contrite Spirit)

This demonstrates the Mormon concept of spiritual progress and development within the life cycle, which is but one phase of an eternal progression that extends from prebirth to the afterlife.

(Reprinted by permission from Bruce C. Hafen, The Broken Heart *[Salt Lake City: Deseret Book Company, 1989])*

That's only half the equation. The above saying continues: "As God is, man may become." The LDS doctrines teach that each and every person was once a spirit that entered a human body at conception. As human beings, they move through the stages of life with the possibility of becoming more and more godlike. If they make the right choices, they actually become gods in the hereafter. This concept leads Mormons to believe in a multiplicity of gods, an idea at odds with the traditional Christian understanding of monotheism and the trinity. Instead of one God in three persons, Mormons believe that Father, Son, and Holy Spirit are three separate gods, with the Father at the top. And all people who progress to the point of godhood eventually join them in exaltation.

And it leads to a different view as to how Jesus Christ helps people to reach the exalted state. Mormons believe that Jesus is like an elder brother, having been born in spirit and flesh along with the rest of humankind by common celestial parents. He suffered and died to provide salvation for all human beings, not just a select few.

He helps people achieve a higher state of exaltation in the hereafter by providing an example of a person who overcame wickedness and lived a perfect, holy life. Believers receive grace through Jesus Christ's suffering and death to aid them in making the correct choices during the earthly phase of their eternal progression.

The final goal of eternal progression is *exaltation*. Believers who have faith in Christ, repent of their sins, and follow the laws and ordinances of the church will reach the highest state. There are two lesser states in the hereafter for those who fail to demonstrate the highest levels of faith and obedience. But you're not stuck at the bottom forever; you can continue your progression in heaven up to the second level. Only those who reach the fullness of celestial exaltation during their lives can live in the highest level, called the celestial kingdom. Hell, on the other hand, is reserved for only a small number of truly despicable people.

Steeple Talk

Mormons use the word **exaltation** to identify the highest level of attainment of an individual in the future celestial realm. It represents the progression of a person to the status of godhood.

Religious Practices

To get saved you have to be obedient to the laws and ordinances of the church—what Mormons call "enduring to the end." The religious practices of Mormonism have a familiar feel to them. You'll find communion, baptism, and special rites for membership and marriage. But these rites are connected to the principle of eternal progression, so they take a different form and meaning within the Mormon community.

Since we're dealing with eternal progression, let's start at childhood. If you are born to Mormon parents, you'll attend services on Sunday and other special occasions, receive a special blessing from your parents through laying on of hands, take religious education classes every morning throughout high school, and observe the various laws and ordinances of the church. These include dietary restrictions like avoidance of tobacco and alcohol, but also caffeinated beverages like tea, coffee, and Coca-Cola. At some point during this process you'll be baptized in the local ward through full immersion, and, if you're male, ordained to one of the priesthoods.

Baptism readies you for the next few steps, which are necessary for full celestial exaltation. Once you've selected a spouse, you'll proceed to a sealing ceremony, which is a bit like marriage but the religious components are different. Mormons believe that you continue with your family after death. What they call *sealing* takes place in a temple with the participants robed in white. Part of your white garments—the undergarments—will stay with you through the rest of your life. Mormons wear them every day under their regular clothing and take them off only for athletic activities, swimming, and other necessaries. They are meant to remind the wearer of the covenants made in the sealing ceremony. Sealing ceremonies in the temple also seal children that may eventually be born to the couple.

Edifications

Generally, crosses and crucifixes are rare among practicing Mormons, either as church decorations or jewelry. Mormons believe that the cross represents the death of Jesus, and they seek to worship a living, risen, and exalted Christ. Early teachings also held that the cross was a pagan symbol associated with the Roman state. Temples and ward buildings have spires, but they aren't topped with crosses. The main spire on the Salt Lake Temple is topped with a statue of the angel Moroni.

Full celestial exaltation is possible only if you proceed through endowment, another ritual that takes place in a temple, not the local ward. Candidates for endowment must pass an interview with a temple bishop and receive the status of recommend. You'll pass if you've done all the things the church requires for salvation up to this point. Endowment ceremonies, like sealings, are closed. All the temple ordinances are thought to be a way for God to give special knowledge and power to the spiritual pilgrim who is seeking progression.

Everybody Said Amen

Some may wonder, why do Mormons have such large families? Mormons tend to have large families at a time when average family size is shrinking in the United States. Many factors account for this, including religious belief. The LDS teaches that families can be together forever through a sealing ordinance performed in the temple, which gives earthly families a cosmic significance, and the LDS promotes a literal interpretation of God's command to Adam, "Be fruitful and multiply." (Genesis 1:28)

If you don't make it through blessings, baptism, and endowment and sealing during this life, don't worry, you still have a chance. Mormons practice something called vicarious baptism. They believe they can baptize others in absentia, thereby giving the deceased the opportunity to follow the correct path in the spiritual realm. If you find the name of a deceased person, you can bring it before the temple authorities, identify a proxy willing to be baptized on their behalf, and proceed to the baptizing ceremony. Because of this practice, Mormons are avid genealogists, and each stake has a microfilm room where church members can scan old census, baptism, death, and burial records for long-lost relatives who might have died without knowledge of God and Jesus Christ.

The Kirtland Temple illustrates a few distinctive features of Mormonism. The gallery is for all specially ordained laypersons, since Mormons don't have a professional clergy. There are no crosses, either, since Mormons believe the cross represents Jesus' death and they prefer to dwell on his resurrection and exaltation.

(Permission for use from the Library of Congress)

These temple rituals are special rites of passage. Sunday services in the local ward, on the other hand, are similar in form to those of many nonliturgical Protestant churches. Hymns, Bible readings, communion, and testimonies are typical. To the Mormons, communion has no supernatural dimensions, as is the case with Roman Catholic practices. Since the rite is merely commemorative, Mormons use water instead of wine to symbolize the blood of Jesus Christ. Also, Mormons don't use professional clergymen, so they fill the balance of their services with personal testimonies from members of the congregation as to the work of God in their lives.

Two other unique practices bear mentioning. Mormons are taught to stockpile a year's worth of food and other supplies in case of emergencies. Church leaders offer advice on what sort of items Mormon families ought to keep in stock. Also, Mormons stress the importance of tithing and giving to the church, which is illustrated by the expectation of two years of full-time missionary work for young people. Some 60,000 Mormon missionaries are at work at any given time, most of them young men and women on break from college. Experts believe that the considerable moral commitment required of Mormons, coupled with their network of missionaries, explains their high rate of growth in recent years.

The Other Mormons

The Church of Jesus Christ of Latter-Day Saints, based in Salt Lake City, Utah, is the largest of the Mormon denominations with 5 million members in the United States, but by no means is it the only denomination. Experts count scores of splinter groups that left the LDS at different times and for different reasons.

One of these, the Community of Christ (which used to be called the Reorganized Church of Jesus Christ of Latter-Day Saints), operates out of its headquarters in Independence, Missouri. The Community of Christ initially formed over questions of succession following Joseph Smith Jr.'s death. In fact, other Mormon denominations like the Bickertonites and Strangites, also formed out of the confusion as to who would succeed Smith as the prophet, seer, and revelator for the Latter-Day Saints.

The Community of Christ has moved closer to conventional Protestant ideas about the nature of God and the path to salvation. It has also permitted the ordination of women and persons of color for more than a hundred years. The larger Utah-based LDS allowed the ordination of persons of color only in 1978. And then there's Mormon fundamentalism, with its insistence on purity of the faith as revealed and practiced by Joseph Smith Jr. This acts as a kind of counterweight to the supposed liberalization of the Community of Christ and other progressive Mormon denominations.

> **Lo and Behold**
>
> Observers estimate that anywhere from 30 to 60 Mormon denominations exist in the United States, though some are as small as a single congregation. Make no mistake: The vast majority (about 97.3 percent) belongs to the Utah-based Church of Jesus Christ of Latter-Day Saints.

The Least You Need to Know

- Mormonism bears the imprint of the revelations and organizational talents of Joseph Smith Jr.

- Central to the Mormon experience is the exodus from New York to Ohio to Missouri and Illinois, and finally to Utah.

- Mormonism is the fastest-growing denomination, with more than 11 million followers worldwide and more than 5 million in the United States.

- To achieve the highest state of exaltation in the hereafter, a Mormon believer must have faith in Jesus, get baptized, and observe certain ordinances like sealing and endowment.

- The major divisions within Mormonism are a result of disagreements about Joseph Smith Jr.'s later revelations in the 1830s and 1840s.

19

Millenarian Churches

In This Chapter

- ◆ Discover the importance of an obscure field of theology—eschatology—to the practice of Christianity in the United States

- ◆ Learn the difference between rival interpretations of the end times, like premillennialism and postmillennialism

- ◆ Consider the importance of premillennial eschatology to contemporary American politics

While paying for a meal at a restaurant a short time ago, I glanced to the side and discovered a pile of glossy brochures. They advertised an eight-day seminar at the local AmeriHost Inn entitled *On the Doorstep of Armageddon*. Speakers promised to inform the audience on topics like "Armageddon: Cosmic Battle of the Ages," "Signs You Can't Ignore," and "Why So Much Suffering." Those in attendance were assured they would leave knowing where we are in prophetic time and what would happen next. And as an obvious reference to the nervy post-9/11 climate in the United States, the brochures declared that "confidence and security can be yours" and that you "would find peace and confidence that lasts."

Looking back, what strikes me as noteworthy is my lack of a strong reaction to the brochures. Maybe that's because our media and popular culture are awash in nightmarish apocalyptic scenarios, from *Mad Max: The Road*

Warrior to *The Terminator* to *Independence Day* to, well, *Armageddon*, perhaps so much that the deluge of final showdowns and days of reckoning dull the senses. The apocalypse even hit the cover of *Time* magazine in July 2002. In the United States, a number of denominations formed over questions regarding Jesus' anticipated return and the doctrines associated with eschatology—the study of end things like heaven, hell, and the final judgment. Read on, and you'll soon find out how thinking about the future affects the way Christianity is practiced across the denominational landscape.

The End Is Near: Christian Apocalypticism

Prophetic belief is a vital component of the Christian faith. To Christians, Jesus Christ's appearance was the fulfillment of Old Testament prophecies in Psalms, Isaiah, Micah, and elsewhere. Jesus himself prophesied that he'd return someday and establish the Kingdom of God on Earth. Jesus made such a claim after the disciples once asked him a fateful question, a question that has fueled speculation among Christians for centuries: "What will be the sign of your coming and the close of the age?" (Matthew 24:3) Jesus launched into a long discussion of things that would happen as the time of his Second Coming approached, like wars and rumors of wars, famines, earthquakes, persecution of Christians, and a general "desolating sacrilege" promised by the prophet Daniel.

CAUTION

Lo and Behold

Be warned that picking the Day of the Lord is a dicey enterprise. In the late 1980s, Edgar C. Whisenant published a book called *Eighty-Eight Reasons Why Jesus Will Come in 1988*, which seems not to have turned out to be as insightful as the author hoped. He followed this up with *Final Shout Rapture Report* in 1989, then annual editions for the next five or six years.

But then Jesus also warned that nobody would know the exact date, time, and location of his return: "But of that day and hour no one knows, not even the angels of heaven, nor the Son, but the Father only." (Matthew 24:36–37) He said he would come as a thief in the night; where two men are walking in a field, one will be taken and one left behind.

Jesus' promised return is Christianity's great hope. Naturally, Christians have busied themselves interpreting current events in light of biblical prophecies. Right away, Jesus' disciples looked for signs of his imminent return, and epistles of the New Testament—letters to the earliest churches scattered throughout the Mediterranean Sea—provided instructions on how to prepare for the end of time.

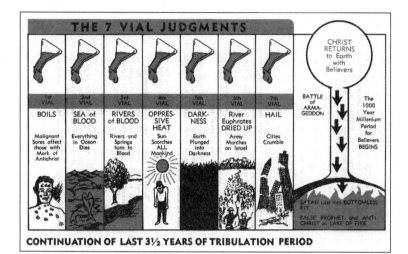

THE 7 VIAL JUDGMENTS

CONTINUATION OF LAST 3½ YEARS OF TRIBULATION PERIOD

Christians believe that Jesus will return one day to bring a final victory of good over evil; this figure, from a mid-twentieth-century book on eschatology, depicts some of the suffering that non-Christians can expect once Christians are taken away to heaven.

(Image credit Salem Kirban)

Prophetic belief continues among Christians today because Jesus promised to return and because his return is needed to initiate the sequence of events that leads to the final judgment and eternity in heaven. Prophecy bridges the gaps between doubt and certainty, fear and comfort, and despair and hope. Maybe the greatest human fear is that we might not matter, that our existence is meaningless. Prophetic belief tells us otherwise. It tells us that our age may have cosmic significance, that we might be living at the end of time, and that Jesus may choose to favor us over other past peoples with the blessing of his return. That's why *eschatology* matters so much to those who practice the Christian faith.

Steeple Talk

Eschatology is the branch of Christian theology that addresses the nature of heaven and hell, the resurrection of the dead, the Second Coming of Christ, the final judgment between good and evil, and eternity. Major Christian theologians like Saint Augustine, Thomas Aquinas, and John Calvin addressed these subjects extensively in their writings.

Everybody Said Amen

The image of a small group of enthusiasts who gather on a mountaintop or a roof to wait for Jesus to come has been the subject of a lot of ridicule and satire. But this has some basis in Scripture. Jesus said, "When you see the desolating sacrilege spoken of by the prophet Daniel, standing in the holy place … then let those who are in Judea flee to the mountains; let him who is on the housetop not go down to take what is in his house." (Matthew 24:15–17)

Apocalyptic Scenarios

Eschatology's importance to Christianity has stimulated lots of discussion about how all of Christ's promises will be fulfilled. Sermons, television programs, books, and magazine articles encourage Christians to think about their hope of resurrection and to take comfort in knowing their eventual destination in heaven. But many Christians don't stop there. They desire to master biblical prophecies about the end times, which has produced various readings of Hebrew apocalyptic literature like Daniel and Ezekiel, and, of course, the Christian apocalypse, Revelation.

Postmillennial

Some U.S. Christians hold to what experts call the postmillennial view about the end times. This view is a particular ordering of events prophesied in Scripture, in which the Second Coming of Jesus and the apocalypse takes place *after* the millennial period of peace and prosperity mentioned in Revelation chapter 20. Once the millennial period expires, Jesus will return, followed by the resurrection of the dead and the final judgment of humanity. Those deemed worthy will enter into heaven, and those deemed unworthy will spend eternity in hell.

The postmillennial view gained its clearest expression in the writing of Anglican clergyman Daniel Whitby (1638–1726), who persuaded many that Christ would return only after humanity took measures to build the millennial kingdom in the present age. Whitby's ideas gave people a vision for defeating ignorance, brutality, disease, and poverty in their midst, since they accepted the idea that they were actually helping to bring the Kingdom of God into being. To make that happen, people were inspired to create inventions, achieve medical breakthroughs, and convert others to the Christian faith. Postmillennialists could point to the progress of humanity in the eighteenth and early nineteenth centuries as evidence of an expanding Kingdom of God. It's safe to say that the majority of Americans were at one time postmillennialists, and many are today.

Premillennial

But the late nineteenth and early twentieth centuries left the postmillennial position in tatters. War, imperialism, disease, and exploitation gave the lie to prognostications that the Kingdom of God is expanding, and that events pointed in the direction of Jesus' eventual return. Some theologians and clergymen in the nineteenth century began to revisit assumptions about the end times, and committed themselves to a position that experts call the premillennial view.

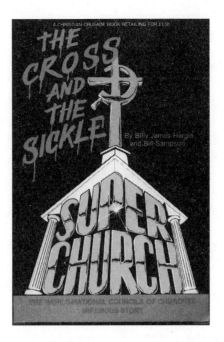

A major sign of Jesus' imminent coming for premillennialists is that apostate churches will unite behind a charismatic religious leader, who will in turn back a political figure known as the Antichrist. To radicals in the Reformation, the pope was this religious leader, and more recently, premillennialists identified the World Council of Churches as the likely culprit for having a too-soft attitude toward "godless," "atheistic" communism.

(Image credit Christian Crusade Books)

So what's premillennialism? Basically, premillennialists place the apocalypse and Second Coming of Jesus *before* the millennial period of peace and prosperity mentioned in Revelation chapter 20. In doing so, premillennialists weave an awful tale of woe for nonbelievers. They say a false prophet, or Antichrist, will appear someday without fanfare and without prior warning to seduce people into thinking he's got all the answers to the world's problems.

Then, the Antichrist will give way to a strong political leader—called "the Beast" in Revelation—who will preside over a one-world government during a horrible seven-year stretch called the tribulation. During the tribulation, a third of the earth will burn, pestilence will bring mass starvation and death, an army of 200 million will kill half of humanity, and the seas will turn to blood.

At the end of this period, Christ will return and defeat the Beast along with the Antichrist and all the armies of the united nations. This so-called Battle of Armageddon will be staged somewhere in the Middle East and then Christ's victory will usher in the millennium described in Revelation chapter 20. It pays to be a Christian prior to the tribulation, by the way, since premillennialists say that Jesus will return secretly in the air to remove them from the earth before it begins. They call this the rapture.

It's hard to overstate the significance of premillennialism in today's Christianity. Premillennialists seek to get their loved ones converted to the Christian faith prior to the rapture, which can come at any time. They also look for signs that the Antichrist and the Beast may be among us. Premillennialists have given eschatological value to various developments in modern history: the formation of the state of Israel, the rise of Hitler, the Holocaust, the creation of the United Nations and the World Council of Churches, the spread of communism, and even the use of new technologies to track consumer purchases or consolidate forms of identification. Some observers say that support for the state of Israel among conservative and evangelical Protestants is an outgrowth of premillennialism.

Everybody Said Amen

Another word for millennial is *chiliasm*. It's normally found in references to the works of the early church fathers like Irenaeus and Cyprian, many of whom were premillennialists. So chiliasm or chiliastic often refers to groups that expect the Second Coming to happen soon, followed by the thousand-year reign of Christ. The root word means "thousand" in Latin.

Amillennial

Then there's the amillennial view. Christians who hold this position tend to read the text of Revelation metaphorically. They think the pre- and postmillennialists misunderstand the intent of the author in their effort to work out all the numbers in Daniel and Revelation, and plot all the steps that are supposed to lead to Jesus' Second Coming. Chapter 20 of Revelation speaks of a thousand-year reign, or a millennium, which amillennialists consider a metaphor for the power Jesus supplies to his church through his death and resurrection, not an actual 1,000-year reign of Christ on Earth.

Organizing the Apocalypse

Conversation about the end times has also produced several distinct, and in fact quite unusual, denominations. The Adventist churches and Jehovah's Witnesses got started when their founders established future dates for Christ's Second Coming, only to be disappointed. Although they have this common beginning point, you'll see they're quite a bit different today.

Seventh-Day Adventists

The roots of the Seventh-Day Adventist denomination lay with a date-setting premillennialist named William Miller (1782–1849). An ordinary farmer, Miller converted to the faith through a Baptist church in Vermont and thereupon began an intensive study of the Bible to find out when Christ would return. He performed a series of ingenious calculations using evidence from the book of Daniel and picked 1843 as the date Jesus Christ would make his Second Advent to earth. Miller wrote up his figures into a little booklet, got ordained as a Baptist minister, and hit the lecture circuit in 1840. Thousands who heard or read Miller waited anxiously for 1843 to arrive, but then nothing happened. Miller quickly refigured his dates and pinpointed October 22, 1844, as the new date of Armageddon. Again, disappointment.

> **Lo and Behold** _____
>
> The Seventh-Day Adventist Church is considered by experts to be a mainstream, Protestant-style denomination. But it became linked to the extremist Branch Davidian cult in Waco, Texas, in 1993, where a botched FBI raid on the compound resulted in a fire and the deaths of nearly 80 people. Koresh was an ex-SDA member who was influenced by Ellen White's prophecies and Adventist eschatology, although he identified Jesus' Second Coming with himself, and believed his war with the federal government would trigger the Apocalypse.

Millerites scattered in a hundred directions following the final embarrassment. But some hung on and formed a church out of the remnant. They remained convinced that Christ's Advent was imminent even though the precise date could not be known, and they decided that since Christ worshipped on the Jewish Sabbath (Saturday), so should they. The denomination took its present name in 1860 and moved its headquarters from New York to Battle Creek, Michigan. A leading figure at this point was Ellen White, an early convert who experienced and recorded over 2,000 visions, eventually published as a nine-volume collection titled *Testimonies*. White's visions confirmed much of Miller's doctrines regarding the end times, except for the predictions of 1843 and 1844, of course, and seventh-day Sabbath observance.

> ### Edifications
>
> One of the unique features of Adventism is its commitment to promoting good health and vegetarianism, a legacy of Adventists Ellen White and cereal maker Dr. John Kellogg. The church owns health food manufacturing concerns in a number of countries, like Australia's Sanitarium Health Food Company, Sweden's Svenska Nutana, and Korea's Sahmyook. Adventist brands like So Good and Weet-Bix dominate the soy milk and breakfast cereal markets in Australia. Overall, Adventist health food companies produced $529 million worth of products in 2002.

Following White's teaching, Seventh-Day Adventists are concerned with issues of health and avoid alcohol, tobacco, drugs, and what's described as "unclean foods." Of course, they still have a lot to say about the Second Coming of Jesus Christ: "The almost complete fulfillment of all the various lines of prophecy indicates that 'he is near, even at the doors.'" But they don't set dates anymore. Aside from these unique features, Adventists share lots in common with conservative Protestant churches like the Southern Baptists: They stress human sinfulness and need for conversion through faith in Jesus, they consider the two Protestant sacraments of baptism and communion to be merely symbolic events, and they believe the Bible is divinely inspired and infallible. In the last few years the international governing body has condemned the practice of homosexuality and voted down policies to encourage women in the ministry.

Jehovah's Witnesses

Thinking about the end times brought Jehovah's Witnesses into being in the 1870s. The founder, Charles Taze Russell (1852–1916), worked out a complicated system for ordering the events foretold in Daniel and Revelation, and picked 1914 as the end of the world. In fact, he claimed that Jesus had already come (in 1874) and was preparing for Armageddon. World War I might have appeared to be a world-ending death struggle, but in the end the Russellites were disappointed, as were the Millerites some 70 years earlier.

> ### Everybody Said Amen
>
> You should know about Anglican Bishop James Ussher from England. In 1650, he published *The Annals of the Old Testament, Deduced from the First Origin of the World*. This odd book declared that human history began in 4000 B.C.E. and would end with the Second Coming in 2000 C.E. This prediction was based on the assumption that one day is a thousand years to God; since God created the world in six days and a day is a thousand years, then all creation must span 6,000 years. His intricate chronology has inspired date-setters of every stripe ever since.

A leading figure in the movement, Joseph F. Rutherford, reinterpreted Russell's prophecies to mean that Christ entered the throne of Jehovah in the heavens and kept the millennial trumpet sounding. He and other inspired leaders made the Jehovah's Witnesses one of the fastest-growing movements through the twentieth century. Their main publication, *The Watchtower*, reached a circulation of more than 16 million copies in recent years and they claim to have distributed more than a billion Bibles. Jehovah's Witnesses believe, based on their reading of Scripture and the interpretations of it authorized by the movement's leadership, that nobody will be eternally punished for sins committed on earth. God has punished and will punish the wicked during their lifetimes. If the wicked do not repent, they die and enter into nonbeing. However, if you follow God into righteousness, you can live forever on earth once Christ has returned to claim victory in the Battle of Armageddon.

Witnesses envision believers as eternal but nevertheless physical inhabitants of an earthly paradise, restored to Edenic perfection by Jesus Christ. If you have been especially faithful and obedient, and have proceeded to *baptism into Christ* during your lifetime, you are included in a special group of 144,000 (mentioned in Revelation chapters 7 and 14) that are given entry to heaven to live with Christ. This is thought to be a spiritual rather than a physical existence.

Some observers note that Jehovah's Witnesses hold to a view of Jesus that the church fathers at the Council of Nicaea considered to be unorthodox. That's the notion that Jesus was created by God, rather than part of the Trinity since before the beginning of time. Jehovah's Witnesses also refuse blood transfusions because they believe they violate the sacredness and integrity of life, and they refuse military service to keep themselves pure from contamination by the power of Satan. These principles

Steeple Talk

Baptism into Christ is the practice among Jehovah's Witnesses of signifying a member's inclusion in the select group of 144,000 who get to go to heaven for eternity. If heaven is exclusive, paradise is not. All the faithful in Christ who persist to eternity live in an earthly paradise, while the wicked pass into nonbeing.

have brought the Witnesses into conflict with the U.S. government numerous times, but they won key Supreme Court cases that advanced the cause of religious liberty in the twentieth century.

Pop Endism: Hal Lindsay, Tim LaHaye

Prophecy belief has a tight grip on Christians in the United States today. Prophetic literature like Hal Lindsay's *Late Great Planet Earth* or Tim LaHaye and Jerry B. Jenkins's more recent *Left Behind* series (with 50 million copies sold) flies off the bookshelves, to be devoured by believers seeking hope, comfort, and certainty about where events are taking us. What the publishing success of the LaHaye-Jenkins books tells us is that their popular brand of premillennialism, with its literal reading of the Bible's prophetic passages, has become something close to an American creed.

> **CAUTION**
> **Lo and Behold** _____
>
> Don't assume that all Christians believe that Jesus Christ will return to earth to fight the Battle of Armageddon, eventually initiating a thousand-year reign. Most of those who hold this position are conservative Protestants. When Catholics were asked in a recent poll if they believed the world would end with the Battle of Armageddon as described in the Book of Revelation, only 18 percent said yes.

A Pew Research Center Poll in 1999 found that popular endism of the LaHaye-Jenkins variety, or perhaps serious study and reflection in Scripture, has had its effect. It reported that some two thirds of Americans surveyed believe that the Second Coming will occur sometime in the next 50 years. This belief has political and cultural consequences. A recent *New York Times* article noted that premillennial belief complicates efforts to find a negotiated settlement between Israelis and Palestinians: Many evangelical Christians have a highly particular notion of what Jewish control of this land will mean for the future; for them, it is a signal of the imminent Second Coming of Jesus Christ.

The Least You Need to Know

- ◆ Eschatology matters to Christians because it represents their greatest hopes and expectations.

- ◆ Christians await the Second Coming of Jesus Christ, but disagree about when and under what circumstances it will occur.

- ◆ Guesses about the date of Jesus' imminent return are scattered throughout Christian history, but have intensified with the modern rediscovery of an ancient school of Christian eschatology called premillennialism.

- ◆ The Adventists and Jehovah's Witnesses got their start when their founders became convinced that they could locate Jesus' Second Coming in time.

Chapter 20

Christian Scientists

In This Chapter

- ◆ Find out why Christian Scientists believe they can find healing through the power of the mind

- ◆ Consider the ways that Christian Scientists think about the problem of sin and the possibility of salvation

- ◆ Learn about the founder of Christian Science, Mary Baker Eddy, one of the key figures in the history of American Christianity

- ◆ Discover what it takes to be a Christian Science practitioner

In different ways, the American-made denominations like Mormons, Adventists, and Jehovah's Witnesses give special emphasis to issues of health and the body. The Mormons forego coffee and tea, the Adventists promote vegetarianism, and the Jehovah's Witnesses reject blood transfusions. But these groups have nothing on the last major U.S. denomination, the Church of Christ, Scientist (or Christian Science). Belief and practice among Christian Scientists is built around the metaphysics of healing. Members of the denomination explore the relationship between mind and body in their quest to put divine power to therapeutic use.

Divine healing in the Christian tradition goes all the way back to Jesus Christ, who went around healing the sick, restoring sight to the blind, and raising the dead. In our own time, many Christians believe that healing is one of the signs of the Holy Spirit. Massive healing conventions move from city to city, featuring faith healers and cure seekers who pray for divine power to overcome disease and infirmity.

But Christian Scientists are quite a bit different from your garden-variety faith healers. Following the lead of their founder, Mary Baker Eddy, Christian Scientists adhere to a scientific system of divine healing, designed to unite Christian principles of divine immanence and spiritual purity with techniques for overcoming sin, corruption, and disease. Nowhere can you find a group operating under the umbrella of Christianity that's more committed to exploring the relationship between spirituality and health.

Mary Baker Eddy

In order to become a member of the Church of Christ, Scientist, you have to express belief in the doctrines of Christian Science as taught in Mary Baker Eddy's book *Science and Health with Key to the Scriptures* (1875). This book and the Bible are Christian Science's authoritative texts.

The American-made denominations bear the imprint of their founders, which in the case of the Church of Christ, Scientist is Mary Baker Eddy.

(Permission for use from the Library of Congress)

Mary Baker Eddy's (1821–1910) story begins in New Hampshire in the 1830s. As a young girl, she read the Bible constantly and reportedly prayed seven times a day. Once, at the age of 12, she prayed to overcome a fever and soon mended. Later she would give this experience the classic Christian Science interpretation: God poured his love into her mind during her prayer and thereby eliminated her fears; since the fever was a physical manifestation of her fears, it left along with them.

Lo and Behold

Don't confuse Christian Science with Scientology, the movement started by L. Ron Hubbard's book *Dianetics: The Modern Science of Mental Health* (1950), and made popular by Hollywood actors Tom Cruise and John Travolta. They are vastly different movements. Christian Science grew out of Christianity and has many Christian elements, including faith in Jesus Christ. On the other hand, Scientology explains pain and suffering as memory imprints, or "engrams" on cells, that must be eliminated in order to achieve mental and physical health.

During this period of her life, Eddy found herself at a meeting point between spiritualism, occult healing, and early cognitive science. Various health cults and medical fads coursed through antebellum New England, sparking interest in mesmerism (a kind of hypnosis), hydropathy (water therapy), faradism (electroshock therapy), and a variety of other—what we now call alternative—approaches to healing. Keep in mind that she lived at a time when medical professionals were still balancing the internal humors of their patients through forced purging and blood-sucking leeches.

At this point, Phineas P. Quimby entered the story. Quimby was a clockmaker from Maine who embarked on a second career as a lecturer and mind healer after he discovered the secret behind magnetic therapy. The magnets worked, he believed, because the patients *thought* they actually had healing power. We think of this today as the placebo effect. The key to health, Quimby taught, is the mind. Eddy met Quimby during the darkest days of the Civil War and put his ideas to the test in 1866. Eddy suffered a terrible fall on the ice and wound up with a concussion and a serious spinal injury. Apparently close to death, Eddy read Matthew 9:2 regarding Jesus' healing of the palsied man, and received a visitation from God. She wrote later, "The divine hand led me into a new world of light and Life, a fresh universe." She was miraculously healed.

Edifications

Massachusetts was an incubator for mind-power movements in the late nineteenth century. Another of Phineas P. Quimby's disciples, Warren Felt Evans, published well-received works like *The New Age and Its Messenger* (1864), *The Mental Cure* (1869), and *Mental Medicine* (1872), ultimately opening a mind-cure sanitarium in Salisbury. In the 1880s, mind-power advocates opened the Church of the Higher Life in Boston, along with various reading clubs, associations, and conventions.

Eddy then searched for an explanation for her deathbed experience. She studied and prayed for the next 10 years, during which time she also began to practice the arts of healing. In 1875, she produced *Science and Health with Key to the Scriptures*, the product of her long spiritual journey, prayerful reflection, and experience in delivering friends and acquaintances from horrible diseases and illnesses. This tract provided the basic set of beliefs of the eventual Christian Science movement.

Mind and Body

Science and Health with Key to the Scriptures is a manual for healing, but also a study in metaphysics that plays off of Christian theology. At the risk of forcing an awkward comparison, Eddy's ideas about God and nature sound a little like the premise of the *Matrix* films, in which a character named Neo awakes from a computer-generated dream world to find out that everything he thought was real was actually an illusion. Of course there are some important variations between Eddy's theology and the film, but keep an open mind.

To the Christian Scientist, what's real is God, and God is Spirit, which means God is invisible to our senses, but otherwise real in every sense. And God is also infinite and all-knowing, which makes God the one and only Mind in the universe. Since we're made in the image of God, we're mental and spiritual creatures. The things that we can see with our eyes and touch with our hands are not real. They *appear* to be real in the same way that objects and people who show up in our dreams appear to be real. To Eddy, everything that exists is the product of mental activity.

Sound like *The Matrix* yet? Let's push the comparison a little further. Eddy's book *Science and Health* teaches that we shouldn't trust our senses. Remember, we are mental and spiritual beings, and the physical stuff of which we are made is really an illusion. Eddy wants us to look beyond the illusions before

> **Everybody Said Amen**
>
> Among the most-quoted passages from Eddy's book *Science and Health* is this passage about the nature of God and sickness: "All real being is in God, the divine Mind, and that Life, Truth, and Love are all-powerful and ever-present; that the opposite of Truth—called error, sin, sickness, disease, death—is the false testimony of false material sense, of mind in matter."

> **Steeple Talk**
>
> **Mind** is the most important concept in Christian Science metaphysics. In *Science and Health*, Eddy reasoned that "Mind is All and matter is naught," and further, that "Mind is All-in-all, that the only realities are the divine Mind and idea." Experts consider Eddy's philosophy to be a form of idealism, a philosophical school that considers externally perceived things to be expressions of transcendent ideas.

our eyes and see things that are true and godly. If we dedicate our thoughts to God through prayer and contemplation, we'll be rewarded with spiritual insights into things that are true, things that actually lie behind the illusions that beguile our senses.

Faith and Healing

If you understand the relationship between mind and body, Eddy's Science of Christianity is pretty straightforward. You have to allow the only Mind (God) to penetrate your thoughts, and in so doing, eliminate false ideas and erroneous thinking. These false ideas enter into our minds from our bodily senses to tell us things like "you're sick" or "you're feeling depressed." As one of their publications puts it: "As our thoughts become more and more God-like, we shall depend less and less on matter, and consequently believe less in it." (E. Mary Ramsey, *Christian Science and Its Discoverer*, 1963) Eddy thought that you could think your way to health (but only through the power of the one Mind).

Here's a representative statement direct from the source: "Mind, not matter, is causation …. You embrace your body in your thought, and you should delineate upon it thoughts of health, not of sickness." So sin, illness, and suffering are not real in the cosmic sense, they are the bodily responses to disordered thoughts. The way to health lies in identifying the falsehoods in your mind and replacing them with the truths of God. Christian Scientists like to use verses in the Bible such as "Let this mind be in you which was also in Christ Jesus" (Philippians 2:5, King James Version) and "Be ye transformed by the renewing of your mind." (Romans 12:2, KJV)

Lots of critics attacked Eddy and her new gospel of healing through the power of Mind. They asked, doesn't death negate the whole system? Death is pretty real, isn't it? Again, think of the film *The Matrix*. Christian Scientists follow Eddy's claim that there's only one kind of reality, a spiritual reality. What makes physical death seem real is nothing more than our *belief* that it's real. Since God is immortal, and we're created to be immortal, what happens at death is actually a replacement of the false material consciousness we have during our lifetimes with a real spiritual consciousness that we gain through union with the one true Mind.

CAUTION
Lo and Behold

Although Mary Baker Eddy was an associate of the famous mesmeriser Phineas P. Quimby, she soon disassociated herself and Christian Science from the practice. The *Manual of the Mother Church* warns against theosophy, hypnotism, and spiritualism (clairvoyance), and declares in no uncertain terms that "members of this Church shall not learn hypnotism on penalty of being excommunicated from this Church."

Alternative Medicine

Eddy's ideas about mind and body developed alongside her practice of actually healing people through prayer and mental conditioning. One of her patients, Asa Gilbert Eddy, actually became her third husband in 1877. A few years later, the little congregation she had gathered, calling itself the Christian Scientist's Home, was chartered as the Church of Christ (Scientist). In 1881 and 1882, Eddy hatched plans for the Massachusetts Metaphysical College in Boston, designed to train health-care workers to practice Eddy's unique brand of spiritual healing. This plan didn't outlast a series of internal squabbles and lawsuits in the 1880s, but it started the ball rolling.

> **Edifications**
>
> Another early influence on Mary Baker Eddy's unconventional ideas about spirituality and health is homoeopathy. This involves prescribing medications that produce effects similar to the disease being treated, typically in very small quantities with no other medications. Eddy practiced homoeopathic medicine as a young woman, experimenting with weaker and weaker doses until she concluded that it was the mental activity of the patient that produced good therapeutic outcomes, not the medicine.

From these beginnings the Christian Science movement sprouted, and today counts some 2,400 congregations in the United States and perhaps 475,000 adult members (though membership numbers are kept secret). Its distinctive feature is, of course, healing through prayer. Every member prays for healing, or declarations of truth leveled against the falsehoods thought to cause illness. Some members work full-time as *Christian Science practitioners*. The movement's literature says these individuals "possess a demonstrated ability to apply spiritual understanding to the overcoming of human ills and discords." They get this ability through spiritual growth and development; as they erase false thoughts in their own minds, they begin to discern more clearly God's works and words and to become more effective tools, whereby others can be healed. Practitioners advertise in various Christian Science publications and they charge a fee for their services.

> **Steeple Talk**
>
> **Christian Science practitioners** are officially sanctioned, full-time professionals who assist patients who seek out spiritualized therapies for their diseases, disabilities, or disorders. The Church of Christ, Scientist publishes a directory that lists all the practitioners who have been approved by the denomination, and holders of this title have the right to tack the initials "C. S." onto the end of their names.

In another vein, spiritual healing became an important field for defining the limits of religious freedom in the United States. An early Christian Science practitioner, Willis Vernon Cole, was prosecuted in the state of New York for practicing medicine without a license (on a person who was actually an investigator for the New York Medical Society). The case eventually wound up before the New York Supreme Court, which ruled in favor of Cole. The chief justice added, "I deny the power of the Legislature to make it a crime to treat disease by prayer." But then in 2001, the Supreme Court let stand the convictions of a Pennsylvania couple for allowing 2 of their 13 children to die of treatable illnesses—ear infection and diabetes acidosis—while attempting prayer therapy.

> **CAUTION**
>
> **Lo and Behold**
>
> Another legal victory for the Christian Science movement is the decision by the 8th U.S. Circuit Court of Appeals in 2000 to allow patients to receive treatment at Christian Science sanitariums with Medicare and Medicaid benefits. Opponents believe this blurs the line between church and state, while supporters believe it protects patients' right to choose.

Revising Christianity

Someone once said that religious freedom in the United States offers more freedom for belief than for practice. The Christian Science practice of spiritual healing is Exhibit A (and the practice of polygamy among early Mormons would be Exhibit B). But their ideas about God and Jesus Christ have been officially tolerated like any other strand of Christianity that developed on American soil.

Regarding Jesus

Probably the first question that gets asked about new groups that form in the name of Christianity is, what do they think about Jesus? *Science and Health* describes Jesus as "the highest human corporeal concept of the divine idea, rebuking and destroying error and bringing to light man's immortality." Jesus was Mind itself, embodied in human form to remind humanity of the spiritual nature of matter. Jesus clued in his disciples, who invited the Light into their minds and eliminated all sin and error from their lives. Some Scientists describe this as an awakening. So empowered, they were able to confront falsehoods and errors in others, and the truths they imparted regarding Jesus chased away the illness, infirmity, and madness that were the signs of these falsehoods. The disciples were the first to use their knowledge about God to heal.

Everybody Said Amen

Mary Baker Eddy gave this interpretation of the Lord's Prayer in *Science and Health:*

Our Father-Mother God, all-harmonious,

Adorable One.

Thy Kingdom is come; Thou art ever-present.

Enable us to know—as in heaven, so on earth—God is omnipotent, supreme.

Give us grace for today; feed the famished affections;

And Love is reflected in love;

And God leadeth us not into temptation, but delivereth us from sin, disease, and death.

For God is infinite, all-power, all Life, Truth, Love, over all, and All.

Sin and Salvation

To the Christian Scientist, sin is a form of deception that requires knowledge of God to overcome. Sins aren't punished in hell, they bear consequences in the form of present-day suffering, isolation, and sickness. These effects of sin melt away in proportion to the amount of truth a believer acquires through prayer, Scripture reading, and contemplation. In this way, they don't view the death and resurrection of Jesus Christ as a sacrifice and atonement for sin as do most Catholics, Orthodox, and Protestants.

Steeple Talk

The **Mother Church** is the First Church of Christ, Scientist church in Boston. It is the international headquarters of the denomination and the meeting place for its self-perpetuating Board of Directors. Eddy wrote special services for the Mother Church into the *Manual,* gave it its own form of government, and forbade the practice of communion in the facility.

Manner of Worship

What about Sunday services? Religious observances are outlined in the *Manual of the Mother Church* (1910), which Eddy wrote for the Church of Christ, Scientist organization when it moved its headquarters to Boston. Eddy taught that sacraments give the wrong message to Christians about the spiritual nature of matter, so baptism is left out. Communion is provided for in the *Manual,* but only in a highly spiritualized form, and only in branch churches outside Boston. No wafers or juice, only prayer. There are no pastors, either, only authorized "readers" of Eddy's *Science and Health,* which is featured in services.

The order of worship in Christian Science churches draws from conventional Protestant worship services, though with the obvious difference of readings from Eddy's book. Eddy's *Manual* dictates the order of worship for the Mother Church in Boston:

1. Hymn.

2. Reading a Scriptural Selection.

3. Silent Prayer, followed by the audible repetition of the Lord's Prayer with its spiritual interpretation.

4. Hymn.

5. Announcing necessary notices.

6. Solo.

7. Reading the explanatory note on the first leaf of *Quarterly*.

8. Announcing the subject of the Lesson Sermon, and reading the Golden Text (*a selection from the Bible*).

9. Reading the Scriptural selection, entitled "Responsive Reading," alternately by the First Reader and the congregation.

10. Reading the Lesson-Sermon. (After the Second Reader reads the Bible references of the first Section of the Lesson, the First Reader makes the following announcement: "As announced in the explanatory note, I shall now read correlative passages from the Christian Science textbook, *Science and Health with Key to the Scriptures*, by Mary Baker Eddy.")

11. Collection.

12. Hymn.

13. Reading the scientific statement of being (a selection from *Science and Health*), and the correlative Scripture according to I John 3:1–3.

14. Pronouncing Benediction.

Church of Christ, Scientist churches have organs, altars, and pews like other Christian churches. Some have sayings from Mary Baker Eddy and verses from the Bible inscribed on the walls or pillars of the church to remind

> **Everybody Said Amen**
>
> Another unique feature of the Mother Church of Christian Science in Boston is that special Easter observances are disallowed. Eddy's *Manual* reasons that Christians should be grateful for God's work every day of the year, and that when Jesus said, "Let the dead bury their dead," he meant that we should focus our attention on the Christ who lives today, not the person who lived 2,000 years ago.

worshippers of the importance of the key texts in acquiring truth. But on the whole, efforts are made to keep the minds of believers on the spiritual, rather than the physical, aspects of faith. During Wednesday evening services, this is accomplished through testimonials, in which members speak about spiritual healings they have experienced themselves or through loved ones.

Getting Out of Boston

In its early years, the Church of Christ, Scientist was very much a New England, and even more narrowly Bostonian, denomination. It absorbed the spiritualism and transcendentalism circulating around the region and took on some of the qualities of middle-class Victorian society in New England. It stressed orderliness—reflected in the Romanesque and neoclassical design of many of its early churches—and it stressed education. These qualities gave Christian Science its initial shape and character, though the denomination became more global over the twentieth century, and thereby became a lot more diverse.

Some of this globalization is sustained through a network of publications, like *Christian Science Journal, Christian Science Sentinel, Christian Science Quarterly, Herald of Christian Science,* and the seven-time Pulitzer Prize-winning newspaper, *Christian Science Monitor.* Eddy's book *Science and Health* is required reading, so it is translated into 14 different languages to meet the needs of churches in 72 countries.

The Eighth Church of Christ, Scientist in Chicago represents the spread of Christian Science outside of Boston, and beyond its middle-class white roots; most of the members of this South Side congregation are African American.

(Photo courtesy of City of Chicago Landmarks)

In a recent issue of the *Christian Science Journal,* a woman in Denmark claimed to have achieved remarkable weight-loss through prayer with a Christian Science practitioner, reading *Science and Health,* and reflecting on Jesus' Sermon on the Mount (the part about taking no thought about what you eat). The message? She came to understand that her food cravings were falsehoods that weren't part of God's creation, and in order to overcome them, her consciousness had to become more and more spiritual. If the story is not a testimony to the Lord's work, then certainly it is a testimony to the endurance of Mary Baker Eddy's vision for how to activate the power of God.

The Least You Need to Know

♦ Mary Baker Eddy started the Christian Science movement when she discovered a unique way of thinking about sickness and disease.

♦ To Christian Scientists, sickness and disease are the physical signs of bad thoughts, and can be cured by turning bad thoughts into good through the power of God.

♦ Worship services in Church of Christ, Scientist churches feature selections from Mary Baker Eddy's *Science and Healing*, delivered by specially chosen readers.

♦ Historically, Christian Science developed in Boston, but today it can be found in most of the larger cities and towns in the United States and more than 70 countries worldwide.

Part **6**

Christianity Outside the Lines

Tens of millions of Christians in the United States belong to churches affiliated with particular denominations, but may never use their denominational label to identify themselves. Instead, they use words like fundamentalist, evangelical, or charismatic. These are movements, not churches or denominations, and you can be, say, an evangelical and belong to one of a few dozen different denominations.

In this part, you'll see that these movements are among the most important shapers of Christianity in the United States and the world today. Rest assured that no education on the subject of contemporary Christianity is complete without knowledge of the fundamentalist, evangelical, and charismatic movements.

Chapter 21

Fundamentalism

In This Chapter

♦ Discover the differences between Protestant fundamentalism and Islamic fundamentalism

♦ Learn about the long history of fundamentalism in the United States

♦ Find out what fundamentalists mean when they talk about dispensationalism

♦ Consider the factors that keep fundamentalism alive and kicking today

Few questions stir up debate among the experts as much as this one: What's fundamentalism? Hard to say. It's not a church or a denomination. And it's not a creed, a style of worship, or a way of observing the sacraments. These are the sorts of things that make a Lutheran different from a Pentecostal or a Methodist, but fundamentalism doesn't observe denominational boundaries. You can find people who describe themselves as fundamentalists in Baptist, Presbyterian, Pentecostal, and Methodist churches, among others, and you can find them in thousands of unaffiliated independent churches as well. It's easy to talk about what fundamentalism isn't—although that'll still leave you wondering how you're going to know a fundamentalist when you see one.

Unfortunately, we're left dealing with a lot of intangibles. But we can narrow things down a bit: The fundamentalist movement is confined to Protestants. More than that, they are very conservative Protestants who believe that cultural standards and personal morality are in decline. In order to save Christianity and Christian civilization, they've gathered behind a set of loosely defined principles and compelling personalities. Fundamentalists participate in a decentralized, but nevertheless distinct, network of religious institutions. And at the end of the day, if you want to be a fundamentalist you'll find no barriers to entry. Just adopt the label, align with their cause.

Darwin in America

Jerry Falwell, pastor of Thomas Road Baptist Church in Lynchburg, Virginia, spoke for many fundamentalists when he appeared on Pat Robertson's cable television program, *The 700 Club*, and offered this analysis of the September 11, 2001, terrorist attacks:

> I really believe that the pagans, and the abortionists, and the feminists, and the gays and the lesbians who are actively trying to make that an alternative lifestyle, the ACLU, People for the American Way, all of them who have tried to secularize America. I point the finger in their face and say, 'You helped this happen.'

Falwell apologized soon after, but left a clear message. He and other fundamentalists believe that America was once a Christian nation, and has since become more and more secular. In a book published 20 years earlier, Falwell taught that America must "get back to basics, back to values, back to biblical morality, back to sensibility, and back to patriotism." (*Listen, America!*, Doubleday, 1980)

That's the fundamentalist program: Turn back the clock on social, cultural, and political change in America, to perhaps 1950, 1870, or 1750. Their list of things to blame for America's godlessness is long: *scientific naturalism* and evolution in public school curricula; exclusion of prayer and Bible reading in public schools; feminism and the campaign to protect legalized abortion; decriminalization of gay sex and legal recognition of gay unions; sexual, violent, and profane content in television programming, popular music, and film; wider availability of pornography and the growth of the adult industry; widespread narcotic drug use … and the list goes on. A generation earlier, fundamentalists added school desegregation, school bussing, welfare dependency, and other Great Society initiatives to the list.

Steeple Talk

To understand fundamentalism you have to understand its main enemy, **scientific naturalism,** a philosophy that holds that no supernatural force created the universe or continues to sustain its operation.

"IT FELL NOT, FOR IT WAS FOUNDED UPON A ROCK." MATT. 7:25

WORLDLY CONFORMITY CHURCH

BUILT ON THE SAND OF HUMAN CREEDS AND TRADITIONS

DR. COMPROMISE DR. FORMALITY
DR. CULTURE DR. FEARFUL

Fundamentalists chide fellow Protestants for compromising with paganism and rationalism. This early graphic makes the point clear. Drowning in front of the crumbling "Worldly Conformity Church" are Drs. Compromise, Formality, Culture, and Fearful; the message is pretty clear—if you get book learning and culture, you're doomed.

(Image credit M. W. Knapp)

Edifications

Scholars like Alexander Hodge and J. Gresham Machen illustrate the point that early fundamentalists were not fundamentalists in the mold of anti-intellectual revivalist Billy Sunday, but conservative Protestants who worried that the New Theology would undermine orthodox Protestant belief as expressed in the Reformation-era confessions of faith. Their high-caliber scholarship was aimed at supposedly heretical ideas about the nature of God and Jesus' divinity. In 1929, Machen left Princeton to start Westminster Theological Seminary, and later helped organize the Orthodox Presbyterian Church.

Fundamentalists first offered this analysis of American cultural decay toward the end of the nineteenth century. At that time, what worried them most was the advent of new ways of interpreting the Bible, and new ways to think about the origins of living things. Indeed, fundamentalism developed as a strong reaction to scientists like Charles Darwin and Alfred Russell Wallace who popularized the theory of natural selection. According to this theory, the present state of the earth and all its plant and animal life are the end result of a very long process of adaptation governed by the law of survival of the fittest. Those who win the struggle to survive get to pass their genes—mutations and all—along to the next generation, and the species gradually

Lo and Behold

Today, only 10 percent of Americans surveyed by the Gallup organization said they believed that humans developed over millions of years from less developed forms of life and that God had no part in guiding this process.

evolve. This theory troubled Christians who were used to thinking that God created everything in its present form at a particular moment in time.

In another debate in the 1870s, scholars argued over how to approach the Bible. European scholars began to use scientific methods to verify biblical claims about Hebrew civilization and the person of Jesus Christ. Newly discovered ancient texts enabled them to cross-examine the biblical record. Scholars in the United States followed the development of these fads with keen interest, and some began to believe that this growing skepticism and rationalism weakened religious commitment and led straight to apostasy.

The Fundamentals of Fundamentalism

To many American Protestants, Darwinism and biblical criticism were worrisome, but so were the spiritualists and transcendentalists, Christian Scientists and Mormons, and newly arrived Catholics and Jews, all of whom couldn't be counted on to preserve Christian truth and Christian values as Protestant church leaders understood them to be. So a few key Protestant leaders devised a set of props to shore up a faith that they believed to be in grave danger. These props became the theological and doctrinal components of fundamentalism.

> **Lo and Behold**
>
> Fundamentalist minister Billy Sunday once said in an oft-quoted line, "When the word of God says one thing and scholarship says another, scholarship can go to hell!" This brought about the popular view that fundamentalists automatically oppose any new scientific discovery that conflicts with a literal reading of the Bible.

> **Everybody Said Amen**
>
> The vast majority of fundamentalists use the King James Version of the Bible. Newer translations rely on archeological findings and newly discovered texts from the period, and are therefore thought to bear the corruptions of modern science.

Biblical Inerrancy

In the nineteenth century, Bible conferences sprouted around the United States, fueled by the Methodist camp meetings and evangelical revivals in other denominations. Leaders of these conferences assumed that the Bible was a truthful historical record of ancient civilizations in the Middle East and God's supernatural intervention into human history, especially in the person of Jesus Christ. As the revealed word of God, it was necessary to take it at face value, or to read it in its most *literal* sense.

With the advent of biblical scholarship, this preferred approach to the Bible was threatened. Many Protestants were further shocked when professors like Charles A. Briggs of Union Theological Seminary in New York began to approve of the

European approach. At this point, Alexander Hodge, along with fellow Princeton theologian Benjamin B. Warfield, developed the doctrine of biblical inerrancy.

It works like this. The Bible as we have it today is the result of transcriptions of ancient texts that have been translated into modern languages. Through the process of transcription and translation, human errors crept into the book. These aren't merely spelling errors, but errors in historical detail, numerical calculation, and so on. But Hodge and Warfield argued that in the original manuscripts—the ones Moses, Isaiah, David, Matthew, Paul, and John actually wrote—there are no errors. The original autographs, the doctrine reads, are inerrant. So the Bible we have today may contain a few human errors of transcription and translation, but it is nevertheless inspired by the Holy Spirit and infallible in what it teaches.

Core Doctrines: The Fundamentals

Hodge, Warfield, and other concerned Protestants became convinced that European ideas were sealing America's doom. Their chief index was America's seminaries. In pages of liberal journals like *Progressive Orthodoxy*, seminarians Theodore Munger, A. C. Knudson, Eugene Lyman, and others were writing about God's love and the goodness of humankind instead of the old themes like God's supernatural power and God's justice awaiting sinners.

In the minds of concerned Protestants, progressive theology paralleled the unorthodox ideas about Jesus coming out of the Jehovah's Witness, Mormon, and Christian Science churches. In response, those within the Presbyterian Church pushed the General Assembly in 1910 to adopt five core doctrines that nobody who held high office in the denomination, including seminary professors, could deny: inerrancy of Scripture, virgin birth of Christ, the substitutionary atonement of Jesus (the idea that God required a sacrifice for our sins, and Jesus provided a substitute), and his miracles and bodily resurrection. These core doctrines formed much of the content of a series of 12 books published between 1910 and 1915 under the name *The Fundamentals*. Now the conservative counterinsurgency had a doctrinal program— and a name.

The Fundamentals' subtitle says it all: *Testimony to the Truth*. In these volumes, which eventually

Lo and Behold

Heresy trials are on the rise in the Presbyterian Church (U.S.A.), echoing the famous trials of Charles Briggs and Henry Smith in the 1890s. In the summer of 2003, the PCUSA had heresy charges pending against 28 of its 21,000 ordained ministers, mostly for violating the denomination's restrictions on performing same-sex unions, but in one case for denying the bodily resurrection of Jesus.

totaled 3 million circulated copies, conservatives wrote about the five core doctrines adopted by Presbyterians, and added testimonies from converts as to how Jesus Christ miraculously transformed their hearts. These were things scientists and skeptics couldn't explain with their naturalistic theories and fancy methods of scholarship.

The Fundamentals found an audience in a number of different, but nevertheless over-lapping, circles. Holiness and Pentecostal churches stressed Spirit-filled living and demonstrations of God's divine power. Bible conferences and institutes were teaching about the importance of the Bible to the Christian faith. Seminary critics of the new theological fads staked themselves to a conception of God's sovereignty and divine will in human affairs. For all these groups, *The Fundamentals* spoke their language. In this way, these books helped to build alliances among a network of intersecting per-sonalities and institutions.

Dispensationalism

There's one more prop to fundamentalism that you should bear in mind, and that's dispensationalism. Basically, dispensationalism is a way of reading the Bible that draws together all the stories, all the events, and all the people into a general pattern. Dispensationalists like to generate grids and overlay them onto the Old and New Testaments. The grids offer a tidy way of showing progression in the relationship between God and humanity from Adam to Noah to Abraham to Moses and finally to Jesus Christ, culminating in a final dispensation at the end of time that leads to eter-nity. Within each dispensation, God is thought to have a particular agreement with humanity, which gives way to another, and another, and so on.

> ### Everybody Said Amen
>
> Fundamentalism is forever linked to the Scopes Monkey Trial of 1925 in Dayton, Tennessee. John Scopes, a biology teacher in Dayton, violated a new law passed by the Tennessee legislature banning evolution from science classrooms. The ensuing trial, which pitted celebrity defense counsel Clarence Darrow against four-time Democratic Party presidential candidate William Jennings Bryan for the prosecution, produced a guilty verdict that was later reversed on a technicality. The trial gave the newly formed ACLU, which supplied Darrow for Scopes's defense, a great deal of national exposure, and it went on to lock horns with fundamentalists in high-profile church-state cases like prayer in the public schools.

There are several major dispensational systems, but one of the more popular ones argues for seven dispensations, which includes the Edenic, Antediluvian, Postdiluvian,

Patriarchal, Legal, and Ecclesiastical Dispensations, capped off with a future Tribulation. We're currently living during the time of the Ecclesiastical Dispensation,
according to this scheme. Take note here that the first five dispensations end with the
expulsion of Adam and Eve, the flood, the Tower of Babel, the exodus, and the birth
of Christ, and the final two with the rapture of the church and Second Coming of
Jesus. All of these are supernatural events in which God works outside of the natural
laws that govern the universe.

By the way, this example rests on the assumption of a premillennial return of Jesus
Christ to Earth, as do most other dispensational systems. This gives us one of the
more important strains of fundamentalist theology: premillennial dispensationalism.
Those who accept this teaching believe Jesus will withdraw Christians from the world
any day now, in an event they call the rapture.

Premillennial dispensationalism quickly dominated the lesson plans of Bible conference lecturers and Bible institute professors within the emerging fundamentalist network. Today, dispensational schemes are still taught at 200 institutions of higher
learning like Dallas Theological Seminary, Southern Baptist Theological Seminary,
and Moody Bible Institute. And they are written into the notes of several popular
study Bibles used by fundamentalists, including the *Schofield Reference Bible* and the
Ryrie Study Bible.

Edifications

The *Schofield Reference Bible* has been cited as one of the reasons why Protestant
fundamentalists in the United States are pro-Israeli. Its notations, developed by C. I.
Schofield (a Congregational minister), presented a clear premillennial dispensationalist account of human and sacred history. It made a strong distinction between God's
dealings with Christians and with Jews who didn't convert, arguing that the organization of Jews into a nation signaled the imminent end of the current dispensation and
the coming of Armageddon. A recent poll indicates that 36 percent of all Americans
believe the modern state of Israel fulfills Biblical prophecy about Jesus' imminent Second
Coming.

Separatist Tendencies

But fundamentalism is not just a doctrinal movement promoting biblical inerrancy
and dispensationalism. Fundamentalists also believe that a personal commitment to
Jesus Christ should result in higher moral living. They despair over the decline of
public morality, measured in visible iniquities like adult bookstores, casinos, rock

music concerts, and other sin-laden venues. And above all, they preach the importance of separation from institutions that compromise with the world. Fundamentalists have been heard criticizing solid conservative Christian icons like the YMCA, Billy Graham, and the Promise Keepers (a large convention for Christian men) for promoting the evil of interdenominational cooperation.

In the early years, this put fundamentalists in the Presbyterian, Baptist, and Congregational churches in the same camp as the Holiness and Pentecostal denominations like the Christian and Missionary Alliance, the Wesleyan Methodist Church (now just the Wesleyan Church), and the Church of God. Holiness Methodists believed in the idea of entire sanctification, or eventually becoming sin-free. Now holy living took on a new meaning, which is to say fighting an increasingly decadent culture, starting with the Roaring Twenties and continuing through today.

Many Holiness and Pentecostals already had their own denominations, but fundamentalists in some of the Presbyterian, Baptist, and Congregational churches did not. Conflict among clergy and seminary professors in these denominations over biblical inerrancy, premillennialism, and other antimodern doctrines led to division. Today's Orthodox Presbyterian Church and the General Association of Regular Baptist Churches got started in this way. This impulse toward separation extended in lots of directions, like the creation of new mission boards and seminaries like Westminster Theological Seminary in Philadelphia. Separate *Bible colleges* began to sprout up in large numbers between 1920 and 1940, using intensive study of the Bible as the focal point of the curriculum, with little or no instruction directed toward modern scientific theories. Today more than 400 still maintain this vision, while others have become traditional four-year liberal arts colleges with a Christian emphasis.

> **Steeple Talk**
>
> **Bible colleges** number about 400 across the United States. The first Bible institutes, D. L. Moody's Moody Bible Institute and A. B. Simpson's Missionary Training Institute (presently Nyack College), grew out of revivals in the 1880s and the Niagara Bible Conferences, which gave vacationing laypersons a chance to learn more about the Bible.

Just to give one example of separatism in practice, Bible colleges like Maranatha Baptist Bible College in Wisconsin forbid male students to have tattoos, body piercings, mustaches, beards, or dyed/highlighted hair. Women must wear dresses at all times (although they may wear loose-fitting slacks at certain preapproved events). Necklines may not plunge below three fingers from the collarbone. Worldly music is not allowed, nor is contemporary Christian music from artists like Amy Grant, Steve Green, DC Talk, or Jars of Clay.

What's New in Fundamentalism?

Fundamentalism continues to operate as a loose array of personalities and institutions, and today uses sophisticated broadcast and electronic media to pursue its religious, cultural, and political goals. Fundamentalists have always utilized broadcast media, as with Charles E. Fuller's radio program, *Old Fashioned Revival Hour*, in the 1940s. These early efforts have more advanced parallels in Jerry Falwell's *Old Time Gospel Hour* and programs of other fundamentalist ministers on cable television.

> **Edifications**
>
> In 1999, the Kansas state Board of Education voted 6–4 to approve new educational standards for grades kindergarten through 12 that left out evolution as one of the explanations for why new species appear. Members of the Creation Science Association helped to write the guidelines, and the board's approval was interpreted as a victory for conservative and fundamentalist Protestants in the state. But in 2000, three of the board members were voted out of office, and in 2001, the board reversed its initial decision.

Their primary objective is evangelism. Fundamentalist sermons and revivalist campaigns seek conversions, but they also give fundamentalists a visible point of connection and common language with which to oppose the liberalization and secularization of American society. Fundamentalists don't speak of modernism anymore, but instead speak of secular humanism as the chief enemy of the Gospel and of the church. Secular humanism is a phrase used to describe the intellectual currents in modern academia, like feminism, postmodernism, queer theory, and of course scientific theories that presume that life began accidentally and evolves by chance. A few books with this sort of analysis gained a wide readership in fundamentalist circles, like Francis Shaeffer's *How Should We Then Live?: The Rise and Decline of Western Thought and Culture* (Good News, 1983) and Charles Colson and Nancy Pearcey's *How Now Shall We Live?* (Tyndale House, 1999).

Pentecostals and charismatics have a similar analysis of culture and a similar tendency to practice separatism. But in very recent years, fundamentalists have distanced themselves from these other conservative Protestants, mainly in areas of theology and doctrine. Fundamentalists complain that the charismatics don't give enough attention to the Bible when they speak of being filled with the Spirit. And fundamentalists do not speak in tongues. Most dispensationalist schemes hold that speaking in tongues ended when the apostles passed from the scene. Where they come back together is in the political arena. Since fundamentalists, Pentecostals, and charismatics can be classified as conservative Protestants, they form the core of the Christian Right in contemporary politics.

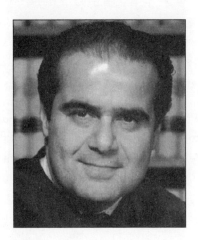

Although Justice Scalia is a Roman Catholic, fundamentalists pray that the Supreme Court will soon have more justices who hold Scalia's prolife and antigay rights positions.

(Permission for use from the Supreme Court Historical Society)

Fundamentalists, in partnership with Pentecostals, charismatics, and Evangelicals, contributed to the spectacular rise of the Christian Coalition to a position of influence in national and state-level politics in the 1990s. Voter registration and turnout drives in fundamentalist churches are thought to have been instrumental in the biggest change in U.S. politics in our generation: the conversion of the South from Democrat to Republican. In the north, fundamentalists are credited with helping conservatives like Sen. Rick Santorum of Pennsylvania find their way to Washington. Santorum, the number-three Republican in the Senate, compared gay sex to incest, bigamy, and polygamy, and has been a staunch supporter of the pro-life cause in Congress. Fundamentalist political activism in recent years is thought to be one of the key reasons why U.S. politics has drifted toward the conservative end of the political spectrum.

On a different note, it's perhaps natural to ask, in light of recent events, what the relationship is between Protestant fundamentalism in the United States and Islamic fundamentalism in the North Africa, the Middle East, and Southeast Asia. This is a complicated question, but scholars have noted both similarities and differences. Both religions object to the secularization of public life and perceive a decline in personal morality. Both seek to implement governmental policies that square with their respective sacred texts, the Bible and the Koran. Both function through informal networks of influential clerics and independent schools of religious instruction, using the Bible and Koran as the basis of the curricula.

But there are some differences, too. Muslim fundamentalists seek to create Taliban-like theocracies in the Middle East, while fundamentalists, despite their dislike for democratic outcomes, are nevertheless committed to retaining democracy. And the different setting matters: The democratic nature of the United States gives Protestant fundamentalists an outlet to pursue their aims, while the authoritarian regimes of the Middle East leave Islamic extremists with few options short of terrorism and violence.

The Least You Need to Know

- Fundamentalism is not a creed, confession, church, or denomination, but a loosely aligned network of personalities and institutions.

- Fundamentalism is chiefly a movement to protect the Bible against secular scholars and liberal theologians who wish to subject it to rigorous methods of examination and analysis.

- An important element of fundamentalism is maintaining purity through separatism, including the formation of separate denominations and Bible colleges, and refusal to join interdenominational organizations like the National and World Council of Churches.

- Experts believe that fundamentalism has been a decisive factor in the swing of U.S. politics toward conservatism and the Republican Party.

22

Evangelicalism

In This Chapter

- ◆ Consider the difficulties of defining evangelicalism
- ◆ Learn about the evangelical network of like-minded personalities and similar institutions
- ◆ Find out how VeggieTales and Bibleman fit into the evangelical picture
- ◆ Understand the political differences between fundamentalists and evangelicals

Evangelicalism tops the list of terms in Christianity that can't be defined with precision. It would be easier if all the people who use the word "evangelical" to describe themselves had the same exact thing in mind, but they don't. Some think of a set of theological positions, others think of a specific way of practicing Christianity in the home, church, and community. Still others speak of evangelicalism as a tradition going back to the time of Christ. So who's right? Well, to some degree they're all right, since nobody owns the word "evangelical," and there's no authorized organization entrusted to preserve and protect its meaning.

At the same time, experts can point to a few key things that distinguish evangelical Christians from nonevangelicals. And a few organizations actually claim to represent the entire evangelical community. With a little reflection on these matters, you'll come to terms with one of the most important trends in Christianity today.

Problems of Definition

What makes evangelical Christians different from other Christians? Ask 10 self-described evangelicals and you'll get 10 different answers. They're not trying to be evasive or cause you grief; they just lack an agreed-upon definition. And to add to the confusion, they might belong to a variety of different denominations, like the Southern Baptist Convention, the United Methodist Church, or the Evangelical Lutheran Church of America. Or they might attend a nondenominational evangelical church, which number in the thousands across the United States.

The experts have come up with a couple of different ways to approach the problem. One approach is to look for a central hub, or a place where people who describe themselves as evangelicals come together to give expression to their version of the faith. One of the candidates is the National Association of Evangelicals (NAE), an umbrella organization founded in 1942 comprised of 50 denominations and 15 million people. It has a statement of faith that lists seven doctrinal points, as follows:

♦ The Bible is the inspired and only infallible and authoritative Word of God.

♦ God is one in three persons: Father, Son, Holy Spirit.

Steeple Talk

Evangelical comes from the Greek word for "good news," *evangelion,* which is also the origin of the word "gospel." So by taking the name, evangelicals embrace Jesus' command to the disciples to go and spread the good news to all creation. (Mark 16:15)

♦ Jesus Christ is God, as seen in the Virgin Birth, but also Jesus' sinlessness, miracles, bodily resurrection, ascension, and eventual return to earth.

♦ In order to be saved, you have to experience regeneration by the Holy Spirit.

♦ The Holy Spirit dwells within the hearts and souls of believers and helps them to live godly lives.

♦ Everyone will be resurrected—some to salvation, and others to damnation.

♦ Believers are spiritually united with Jesus Christ.

With this list in hand, could you go around and test the denominations or even individual Christians to see if they're evangelical? Well, no, since the NAE doctrines cover only part of the ground we're interested in mapping. It deals with beliefs but not practices. Any expert will tell you that religion is partly a matter of theology and doctrine, and partly a matter of behavior, whether it's rubbing beads, speaking in tongues, or sprinkling babies with water. Then, too, only a fraction of the people that experts think should fall under the evangelical umbrella have membership in the NAE.

Another approach is to see evangelicalism as a tradition, a more-or-less consistent set of theological commitments and religious practices passed from generation to generation. Those who see evangelicalism in this light stress the legacies of the Reformation, which argues that the Bible is the sole source of authority (not the pope or bishops), puts Jesus Christ at the center of the plan of salvation, practices some form of baptism and communion, and expects new believers to demonstrate a transformed life (usually seen in a higher standard of morality). Later developments like revivalism and biblical inerrancy are included in the tradition as extensions of these basic beliefs and practices.

Among the acknowledged leaders of the evangelical movement in the twentieth century is Billy Graham; conservative Protestants who think he's a hero are evangelicals, while conservative Protestants who think he compromises too much with the world are fundamentalists.

(Permission for use from the Billy Graham Evangelistic Association)

But traditions can be curious and wonderful things. There's a bit of selectivity involved: Why bring Martin Luther's views about Scripture onboard, but leave behind his ideas for organizing the church? Also, traditions can make strange bedfellows. People who use the label "evangelical" can identify with either John Calvin or

John Wesley—or both—and yet their views on precisely how grace works to bring believers to Jesus Christ are incompatible. So traditions can be, if you'll excuse the word, *contested*.

Since evangelical probably meant something different to Martin Luther, Jonathan Edwards, Francis Asbury, and Billy Graham, we should try a third approach. Remember our discussion of fundamentalism in the previous chapter? We described that movement as a network of personalities and institutions that works to advance a particular cause, which is a useful way to think about evangelicalism, too. So if you think Billy Graham is great, James Dobson's radio program *Focus on the Family* is worth listening to, Amy Grant sings like an angel (well, before the crossover *Unguarded* album), and even *heard* of Phillip Yancey or Os Guinness, then odds are good that you're an evangelical.

> **Steeple Talk**
>
> **Liberal theology** is a movement in the late nineteenth century that tended to stress mankind's capacity for goodness and reject the idea of universal sin. Today, evangelicals criticize liberal theologians like Richard Rorty and Cornell West because they believe the liberals deny moral absolutes and advocate human-centered ethics.

Today's evangelicals can also be identified by their patterns of *dis*-association. They insist they are not fundamentalists even though they have a number of beliefs in common. Both are theologically conservative, but evangelicals aren't sure that the fundamentalists have the right answer to liberalism. As such, today's evangelicals consider themselves to be stewards of a classical Protestant orthodoxy that they believe is endangered by fundamentalists to their right, and liberals to their left.

Evangelicalism 101

If evangelicals can be identified by the company they keep, then perhaps we ought to take a closer look at how the evangelical network of associations developed in recent years.

Building a Network

The turning point came in 1925, when most Americans left the Scopes Monkey Trial with an unfavorable view of the conservative defenders of Protestant orthodoxy. Fundamentalists retreated to their Bible schools and their newly separated denominations. They deepened their isolation by forming the American Council of Christian Churches (ACCC) in 1941, intended as a counterweight to the supposedly communist-leaning Federal Council of Churches (founded in 1908). Its architect, fundamentalist Presbyterian minister Carl McIntire, considered the FCC's denominations to be apostate churches smitten with secular liberalism, and called for strict separation in order to preserve a godly remnant of true Christians.

A group of younger, fundamentalist-bred ministers grew concerned about this policy of isolation. At the center of this group was Harold Ockenga, and from his connections sprang the modern evangelical movement. Ockenga worried about the liberal drift of the FCC, but thought that the theological hairsplitting of his fundamentalist mentors in the ACCC was misguided. So he helped to organize a conference in 1942 to create a union of denominations, eventually called the National Association of Evangelicals, to occupy the middle ground between these rival camps.

> **Lo and Behold**
>
> The leaders of the post-World War II evangelical movement all had deep roots in fundamentalism, as their education attests. Billy Graham went to Bob Jones University and finished at Florida Bible Institute, Harold Ockenga went to Westminster Theological Seminary, and Charles Fuller attended the Bible Institute of Los Angeles, where he studied under dispensationalist theologian Reuben Torrey.

Everybody Said Amen

Christian History asked its readers—mostly self-described evangelicals—to identify the most influential Christians of the twentieth century. These figures were included on the greatest number of lists, in order of frequency:

1. Billy Graham (evangelist)
2. C. S. Lewis (scholar, apologist)
3. Mother Teresa (founder, Missionaries of Charity)
4. Martin Luther King Jr. (minister, rights advocate)
5. John XXIII (pope, convened Vatican II)
6. James Dobson (founder, *Focus on the Family*)
7. Karl Barth (German theologian)
8. Francis Schaeffer (writer, apologist)
9. John Paul II (current pope)
10. Dietrich Bonhoeffer (minister martyred by Nazis)

Source: *Christian History* (Winter 2000)

Watch closely here and you'll see the network take shape. Ockenga served as the first president of the NAE, but also as first president of Fuller Theological Seminary (founded in 1947). Ockenga worked closely with the seminary's co-founder, radio evangelist Charles Fuller of the *Old Fashioned Revival Hour.* Both believed that the interests of the Gospel were better served if conservative Protestantism maintained a less contentious public profile. The network grew when Ockenga partnered with the young Baptist minister and evangelist, Billy Graham, to carry out a series of soul-winning revivals in New England in 1950. In 1956, Graham and Ockenga got some funds from Graham's father-in-law to start the magazine *Christianity Today*, which became the standard-bearer for the evangelical movement.

Escaping Denominations

The spirit of the post-World War II evangelical community that formed around the Ockenga-Fuller-Graham network was nondenominational. In fact, Ockenga graduated from a Methodist college (Taylor University), proceeded to a fundamentalist Reformed seminary (Westminster), and then earned a Ph.D. in philosophy from the University of Pittsburgh (1939), a scholarly turn that put him at odds with avowed anti-intellectual leaders of fundamentalism like Billy Sunday and Billy James Hargis. To top it off, he took a ministerial appointment at Park Street Congregational Church in Boston.

Perhaps Ockenga's career suited the nondenominational mood of the age; President Eisenhower once said, "I am the most intensely religious man I know. Nobody goes through six years of war without faith. That doesn't mean I adhere to any sect." But then evangelicals also claim a much longer tradition of nonsectarian revivalism. Evangelical hero John Wesley expressed much the same sentiment in the eighteenth century when he said, "I refuse to be distinguished from other men by any but the common principles of Christianity," then added, "Dost thou love and fear God? It is enough! I give thee the right hand of fellowship."

> **Edifications**
>
> Back in the early 1800s, Thomas Campbell and his son Alexander started the Restoration Movement, a distant echo of today's evangelicalism. They wanted to get rid of creeds and denominations and use the New Testament part of the Bible as their sole guide to faith and practice. They hoped to restore the early church to its primitive form, hence the name restoration. Today, the Churches of Christ, the Christian Church (Disciples of Christ), and the Christian Churches and Churches of Christ (totaling about 3.5 million members) are three distinct denominations that grew, ironically, from these antidenominational roots.

The emerging evangelical network became famous for creating new associations, organizations, and institutions that studiously avoided denominational hang-ups. The NEA tops the list, but there's also the earlier New England Fellowship, the Billy Graham Evangelistic Association, the National Religious Broadcasters, Campus

Crusade for Christ, World Relief, Operation Mobilization, Promise Keepers ... the list goes on. Today, evangelicals support scores of nondenominational organizations in the areas of foreign missions, evangelism, discipleship and spiritual growth, family support, emergency relief, and political action, among other things.

Committing to Christ

The idea behind the Ockenga-Fuller-Graham coalition of the 1940s and 1950s was first and foremost to bring lost souls into a relationship with Jesus Christ. This goal is the central preoccupation of evangelicals today, and connects the modern version of evangelicalism to early European Protestants and to the historic North American revivals of the eighteenth and nineteenth centuries. This is where evangelicalism comes closest to being a tradition that reaches back to the beginnings of the Reformation.

Today, nearly all evangelicals affirm the importance of being born again. Some describe this as "surrendering their life to Jesus." This lifetime commitment is expected to produce results in the form of a more disciplined, more orderly, and more godly life. The nation's evangelical-in-chief, President George W. Bush, said in a 1999 presidential debate that Jesus was his favorite philosopher; when asked why, he said because he "changed my heart."

> ### Everybody Said Amen
>
> Among the most influential evangelical organizations today is Campus Crusade for Christ, founded by Bill Bright in 1951. It simplified the gospel message and focused on the story of Christ, moving conservative Protestantism away from the stormy theological debates of the first half of the twentieth century. Today, its 26,000 full-time staff members work with an annual budget of $374 million.

Have you heard of the Four Spiritual Laws? If you haven't, it's a wonder. Campus Crusade for Christ says that more than 1 billion of these pamphlets have been circulated worldwide, many thousands of which helped nonbelievers tread the path toward Christian commitment.

(Permission for use from Campus Crusade for Christ)

Spreading the Word

What gives the evangelical movement its unity in contemporary America is a common desire to convert non-Christians to the Christian faith. The very name evangelical echoes Jesus' instruction in the Gospel of Mark to go out and spread the good news to all creation. To evangelicals, the heroes of the faith are missionaries who carried Christianity to China, the Congo River basin, East Africa, and New Guinea over the last 150 years, often at the cost of their own lives. News of at least six killings of evangelical missionaries in the Middle East since the terrorist attacks of September 11, 2001, have galvanized support among evangelicals for mission work among Muslims in the Middle East region.

But for the most part, evangelicals speak of lifestyle evangelism, or using one's manner of life as a witness to the transforming power of Jesus Christ, rather than overt proselytizing. They seek to influence their non-Christian relatives, co-workers and acquaintances in the direction of "accepting Jesus Christ as their personal savior," as the saying goes. Often, lifestyle evangelism opens the door to personal invitations to attend church services or evangelistic rallies designed to formally introduce nonbelievers to the Gospel message.

> **Lo and Behold**
>
> Operation Mobilization, supported by evangelicals, suffered a grave loss in 2002 when one of its missionaries in Lebanon, Bonnie Penner Witherell, was shot to death outside of the prenatal-care facility where she served as a nurse's assistant. She had worked among the Palestinian refugees in Lebanon following her 1996 graduation from Moody Bible Institute in Chicago.

> **Edifications**
>
> It's hard to imagine, but Billy Graham once possessed a kind of celebrity that is reserved for multimillion-dollar athletes and Oscar-winning actors today. After his first evangelistic crusades in the late 1940s, he appeared on the covers of *Time*, *Newsweek*, and *Life* magazines, and in 1957, some 85 percent of Americans could correctly identify his name.

Christian Media

Unlike fundamentalists, evangelicals want to participate in the broader culture of the United States in order to have the opportunity to shape that culture. They speak of being salt and light, providing the sort of seasoning and illumination that a lost world desperately needs. Evangelicals gladly pursue degrees from secular colleges and universities, collaborate with supposedly liberal religious groups, build political coalitions with Catholics, and seek inroads into popular culture.

Evangelicals have been media-savvy from the beginning. Fuller's *Old Fashioned Revival Hour* in the 1940s rivaled other popular shows like *Amos 'n' Andy* and the *Ford Symphony Hour*, apparently registering 10 million listeners for its Sunday evening broadcast on the eve of World War II. Billy Graham's televised rallies at Madison Square Garden in the late 1950s found audiences as large as 6.4 million viewers, and his Puerto Rico crusade in 1995 was telecast via satellite to 165 countries, with an estimated 1 billion viewers.

In the publishing world, apocalyptic literature has proved to be a major cash cow; Jerry B. Jenkins and Tim LaHaye have reportedly sold more than 50 million volumes in the *Left Behind* series to date. On another front, Bruce Wilkerson sold more than 5 million copies of *Prayer of Jabez* (2000), which led to spin-offs like *Prayer of Jabez for Women, Prayer of Jabez for Teens, Prayer of Jabez for Little Ones,* and *Prayer of Jabez: Music … A Worship Experience.* This success sparked an ongoing debate among evangelicals about whether Christians should pray for wealth and riches, which is not exactly the point of the book, even if many readers drew this implication.

Steeple Talk

Christian contemporary music is one of the fastest-growing musical genres, second after country music. Early pioneers like Keith Green and Phil Keaggy in the 1970s wrote songs with Christian lyrics, but with a folk-rock sound borrowed from the broader youth counter-culture.

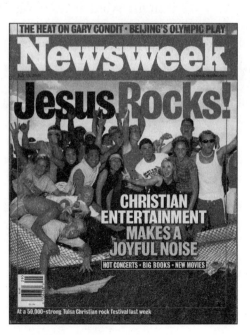

At a 50,000-strong Tulsa Christian rock festival last week

Evangelicals demonstrate more of a willingness to blend Christianity with secular forms of entertainment than their fundamentalist cousins.

(Permission for use from Newsweek)

The profile of Christian consumerism has increased right along with its economic heft. Wal-Mart's video section stocks the Veggie Tales series, a cartoon designed to teach Christian values to children. Its producer, Big Idea Productions, puts the number of copies in circulation at more than 22 million. It also carries the Bibleman videos, which feature a Batman-like superhero who quotes from Scripture while fighting sins like anger and jealousy. Wal-Mart also stocks a large selection of inspirational literature and Bibles to save you the extra trip to your local Christian bookstore.

Yet, the influence between evangelicalism and popular culture flows in both directions. *The New York Times* published a recent article about Christian grunge, indie, techno, and alternative bands that are essentially indistinguishable from their secular counterparts. One band, Anberlin, reportedly told the interviewer, "We're not a Christian band. But we are all Christians." Groups like Creed, Zao, MxPx, and P.O.D. open concerts for secular artists and seek airplay on non-Christian radio stations. And they've made headway; Christian Contemporary Music is a $3-billion-a-year industry. Some evangelicals cheer their success, while others cry foul. The Alliance of Confessing Evangelicals, for example, thinks "the church is guided, far too often, by the culture" and complains that "the beat of the entertainment world" wields more influence than the Word of God. Needless to say, the fundamentalists would agree.

> **CAUTION**
>
> **Lo and Behold**
>
> In March 2000, the National Association of Evangelicals voted to allow its member denominations to hold joint membership in the National Council of Churches, a move that fundamentalists contend signals a shift toward liberalism and compromise.

Political Mobilization

On the subject of visibility, nothing compares to the rise in political fortunes of conservative Protestants over the last generation, a trend sustained by the activism of evangelicals. Fundamentalists and evangelicals reasserted their presence in national politics in the late 1970s, starting with Jerry Falwell's successful effort to mobilize support behind Ronald Reagan's candidacy in the presidential election of 1980. Reagan opposed abortion and the Equal Rights Amendment and supported school prayer and capital punishment, which suited the tastes of fundamentalists who joined Falwell's Moral Majority. In the 1990s, the Christian Coalition picked up where the

> **Edifications**
>
> The Texas State Republican Party Platform of 2002 states: The Republican Party of Texas reaffirms the United States of America is a Christian nation, which was founded on fundamental Judeo-Christian principles based on the Holy Bible.

Moral Majority left off, handing the Republican Party a majority in Congress and propelling George W. Bush to the White House.

The political awakening of fundamentalists and evangelicals witnessed a very important, if unnoticed trend in interfaith relations in the United States: The warming of relations between evangelicals and Roman Catholics. Charles Colson, a born-again Watergate parolee and prison evangelist, organized leading evangelicals and Catholic officials and produced the political treatise "Evangelicals and Catholics Together: The Christian Mission in the Third Millennium" (1994). This is a long way from the anti-Catholicism of past evangelicals; as recently as 1962, Reformed apologist Loraine Boettner wrote that the real heretics are the Roman Catholics and the true orthodox are the evangelical Christians.

For the time being, the evangelical-Catholic embrace seeks federal support for faith-based social services, restrictions on abortions, limitation of marriage to heterosexual couples, vouchers for families with children in private schools, and suppression of sex and violence in television, film, and music. These are conservative positions, and yet evangelicals occupy a wider span of the American political spectrum than their fundamentalist cousins. Those who belong to organizations like Sojourners, Evangelicals for Social Action, and the Evangelical Environmental Network all argue that biblical principles dictate leftist politics, such as environment-friendly energy policies, expanded federal services, taxation policies that redistribute wealth from rich to poor, and increased federal aid to developing countries. There's even a governor in the South who's raising taxes because, as he says in a most evangelical sort of way, it's consistent with Scripture.

The Least You Need to Know

♦ Evangelicalism is best described as a network of personalities and institutions that place a high value on the Bible and personal commitment to Jesus Christ.

♦ The modern evangelical network formed in the 1940s when Harold Ockenga, Charles Fuller, and Billy Graham pulled away from the fundamentalists and started individual ministries and institutions.

♦ There is no central hub for evangelicals with power to dictate doctrine, though the National Association of Evangelicals offers a short statement of faith that other evangelical groups have adopted.

♦ Unlike fundamentalists, evangelicals are more willing to engage a changing culture in an effort to influence its direction, even to the point of partnering with Roman Catholics.

♦ Most evangelicals are conservative Republicans who back a pro-family, pro and pro-national-security agenda, but an important minority thinks Jesus vote left.

23

The Charismatic Movement

In This Chapter

♦ Learn how the contemporary charismatic movement grew out of Pentecostalism in the last few decades

♦ Consider the differences between the charismatic and Pentecostal views on the gifts of the Holy Spirit

♦ Find out how Catholics and Episcopalians can celebrate tradition and Episcopal authority and still experience the power of the Holy Spirit

♦ Discover the story behind the megachurch phenomenon

No question about it: The most explosive force in global Christianity today is the charismatic movement, which is an American export. Experts place the total number of charismatic/Pentecostal Christians at more than half a billion around the world. The only block of Christians that's larger is Roman Catholicism. According to the same experts, charismatic/Pentecostal Christians outnumber all other Protestants *combined*. Add to this the increased visibility of the charismatic movement—your typical television preacher is a charismatic—and you have a community of Christians that cannot be ignored.

There's a Sweet, Sweet Spirit in This Place

As a young Christian I attended a nondenominational church. One of the songs I remember well has this stanza:

> Sweet Holy Spirit, sweet heavenly dove
> Stay right here with us, filling us with your love

Now our church was not the sort you'd call Pentecostal. Nobody talked about a second blessing, or a baptism of the Holy Spirit, and we didn't prophesy, speak in tongues, or practice faith healing. But we nevertheless sang of being filled with the Holy Spirit and being revived as we worshipped together. This is Pentecostal language, or to be more precise, it's charismatic language.

What's the difference? That's a critically important question. Pentecostals emerged at the turn of the century, following the outbreaks of tongues speaking at Charles Parham's Bethel Bible School in Kansas (1898) and the Azuza Street Revival led by Parham's student William Seymour (1906). The revival promised to burst out across the denominational landscape, but in the decades to come, the gifts of the Spirit were confined to new denominations like the Assemblies of God and the different Church of God organizations.

Edifications

Experts sometimes refer to the charismatic movement of today as a **Third Wave**. This is in reference to a so-called First Wave (Holiness movement) and a so-called Second Wave (Pentecostal movement). All have in common a belief that Christians can move forward in their spiritual progress by being filled with the Holy Spirit and witnessing the Spirit's power in everyday life.

By contrast, the charismatic movement is the outbreak of speaking in tongues and other gifts of the Spirit within older denominations like the Episcopal, Mennonite, Presbyterian, and Methodist churches. Startlingly, that includes the Roman Catholic Church as well. And along with these gifts of the Spirit came informal patterns of worship, like spontaneous testimonials of faith, hand-clapping, arm-waving, and more congregational singing. Some congregations in these older denominations simply gave up their worship manuals and their formal rituals and took on all the Spirit-filled characteristics of Pentecostalism.

Charismatics Within Denominations

Believe it or not, there's actually a precise beginning point for the modern charismatic movement. It occurred in 1959, when Dennis Bennett, an Episcopalian priest in

Van Nuys, California, spoke in tongues during a long prayer session with some of his parishioners. Next year, he spoke of his experience to his congregation, which divided them bitterly. Some were receptive but others thought he was a fanatic or even demon-possessed. Bennett's spat with the anti-Pentecostal faction in his church made national news in *Time* and *Newsweek*, which seemed to inspire other tongues speakers in the Protestant mainline churches, like the Presbyterian, American Baptist, and American Lutheran Church, who now openly espoused the practices and led their congregations accordingly.

So when commentators today speak of a charismatic renewal or a charismatic movement, they are talking about speaking in tongues among Christians in the older, well-established, and more traditional denominations. One of the chief figures in promoting this experience was Larry Christiansen, a Lutheran minister. He was careful to point out the New Testament basis for the practice and warned against enthusiasm and excess. But he and others were convinced that God sent tongues to remind the world of the transcendent and miraculous nature of divine being, since society had become lax in its appreciation for the supernatural.

> **Everybody Said Amen**
>
> Want to speak in unknown tongues? One of the charismatic teachers, Larry Christiansen, tells you how:
>
> 1. Search the Scriptures for truths about gifts of the Spirit.
> 2. Clarify your reasons for wanting to speak in tongues.
> 3. Ask the Lord to send the gift.
> 4. Sit in silence and don't speak in any tongues you already know, and God will do the rest.

Denominations like the Lutheran Church in America (now the Evangelical Lutheran Church in America), the United Church of Christ, the Mennonite Church, and the Church of Christ also proved receptive to the practice. Now there's even a Charismatic Episcopal Church with about 600 parishes in the United States, blending its rich liturgical tradition with the charismatic gifts and vibrant worship. You'll have a harder time finding charismatics in the Southern Baptist Convention and the Lutheran Church—Missouri Synod. These denominations argue that the practice isn't biblical.

Catholic Charismatics

The charismatic renewal took a giant leap forward when it found fertile ground in the Roman Catholic Church. Catholics who experience the Holy Spirit through tongues, prophecy, and healing form a very important and sizable subgroup within the denomination. Some estimates place the number as high as 120 million worldwide.

As with the Episcopal Church, it all started among a small cell of believers who began to meet together in an effort to trigger the tongues-speaking event. The setting was Duquesne University in Pittsburgh, a Catholic university administered by the Fathers of the Congregation of the Holy Spirit, and the participants were deeply committed professors and seminarians. In a meeting in February 1967, the group found what it was looking for when participants experienced speaking in tongues, uncontrollable "holy laughter," ecstatic writhing, shouting, weeping, and so on. Soon, a group of Catholic theologians and students at the University of Notre Dame experienced it, too, and a movement was born.

What about the Vatican? The bishops found no reason to oppose the practice and allowed it to continue following their study of the movement in 1969, and Pope Paul VI followed suit with his approval in 1973. More recently, in 2000 Pope John Paul II sent greetings to the World Meeting of the Catholic Charismatic Renewal in Rimini, Italy. He seemed to be pleased at the "flourishing of lively communities" in which "the work of the Holy Spirit is evident."

You should keep in mind, however, that Catholic and mainline Protestant charismatics have a different spin on the gifts of the Holy Spirit than classic Pentecostals. They don't think in terms of a "baptism of the Holy Spirit" or a second and third work of grace, with signs (like speaking in tongues) following. And that is why they chose to call themselves charismatics: to avoid nettlesome theological problems that would arise if they accepted a Pentecostal-type work of grace as part of the process of sanctification.

> **Edifications**
>
> The charismatic movement within the Roman Catholic Church was a phenomenon associated with seminaries and universities in its early years. Outbreaks of glossolalia occurred at Duquesne University, University of Notre Dame, and Michigan State University in the late 1960s among professors and students seeking to deepen their spiritual experiences.

> **Lo and Behold**
>
> Charismatics in the Roman Catholic Church and the older Protestant denominations do not believe that speaking in tongues is a special sign of a so-called baptism of the Holy Spirit following conversion, as do the Pentecostal denominations.

Charismatic Empires

The Episcopalian and Catholic charismatics had some struggles to win acceptance by their fellow church members and denominational authorities. Some charismatics, or what are sometimes called neo-Pentecostals, had no such difficulty, since they just started their own churches. Charismatics are found inside the older denominations, and they're found outside denominations as well. In fact, some charismatic ministers are truly empire builders.

Some of the names should be familiar to you, like Oral Roberts and Pat Robertson. But there's also T. D. Jakes, Chuck Smith, John Wimber, and John and Carol Arnott. These inspired men and women sparked revival and brought charismatic renewal to their congregations, which then became nerve centers for multifaceted ministries, and in some cases pseudo-denominations.

Oral Roberts provides a good example. He began his empire-building career as a Pentecostal Holiness minister in Oklahoma with a particular interest in divine healing. In massive tent revivals in the late 1940s, Roberts presided over wholesale conversions and healings, and in 1954, brought his ministry to television. Ten years later, he used proceeds from mass mailings and broadcast appeals to start Oral Roberts University and later added the City of Faith medical center. During this period Roberts moderated his Pentecostalism, joined the United Methodist Church, and moved to the forefront of the new charismatic movement. At its peak, Roberts's church, university, broadcasting facilities, and other assets were valued at half a billion dollars. Roberts developed a blueprint for media-driven charismatic ministry that many others would follow in the 1980s and 1990s.

Pat Robertson offers another illustration. After getting a law degree from Yale and failing the New York bar exam, Robertson turned to the ministry. In the early 1960s, he graduated from Biblical Seminary of New York, and then took a Southern Baptist church in Norfolk, Virginia. But his sights were set on television. He bought a UHF station and canvassed his audience in an effort to secure 700 viewers willing to pledge 10 dollars a month to support his program. That's the story behind the *700 Club* and the Christian Broadcasting Network. Soon, Robertson added a graduate school, Regent University, and a political organization called the Christian Coalition. With Robertson's books, videos, and other products reaching mass audiences, you have a budding multimedia empire.

From this base Robertson launched an unsuccessful campaign for president in 1988, appealing to fundamentalists, evangelicals, and charismatics across the different

Steeple Talk

Religious Right refers to the coalition of fundamentalist, evangelical, and charismatic Protestants, along with Mormons and conservative Catholics, who favor prayer in the public schools, restrictions on abortion, school vouchers for parochial-school children, limitation of marriage to heterosexual couples, limits on pornography, stricter enforcement of drug laws, and in general, a government that's receptive to the concerns of people of faith.

Protestant denominations. Despite this failure, Robertson still commands attention, as with the coverage given to his recent calls for a national prayer campaign to trigger retirements from the Supreme Court so that justices favoring the pro-life and anti-gay-rights agenda of the *Religious Right* can be appointed. And Robertson leads conservative Republicans who oppose President George W. Bush's so-called "Road Map" to peace in the Middle East because it eventually results in a supposedly unbiblical partitioning of the state of Israel.

Robertson's charismatic empire has parallels all over the United States in varying degrees of visibility and spiritual and economic success. An interesting variation on the theme is the emerging empire of T. D. Jakes, an African American charismatic minister in Dallas whose church, the Potter's House, lists 28,000 members. He directs scores of ministries and his weekly program, *The Potter's House*, is televised on the Trinity Broadcast Network and Black Entertainment Television. He has a conference ministry, a theater production company, a music label, and T. D. Jakes Enterprises, which markets his 27 books on a for-profit basis. Jakes is giving other charismatic empire builders a serious run for their money.

Stories from the Front

You'd be mistaken if you assumed that the charismatic movement is just about speaking in tongues and building multimedia empires. There's a lot more to it than that. Here are a few stories that'll help to bring the charismatic movement to life, and explain how it has come to influence the direction of Christianity in thousands upon thousands of churches in the United States.

Edifications

One surprising development in the last 10 years is the convergence movement, comprised of charismatics who join denominations with long histories and formal worship, like the Roman Catholic, Episcopalian, and Orthodox churches. It's called convergence by its participants because they believe they are bringing together the three major strands of Christianity: the rich ceremonies of Roman Catholicism, the biblical emphasis of traditional Protestantism, and the Spirit-driven worship of the charismatic movement.

Calvary Chapel

The story of Calvary Chapel centers around Chuck and Kay Smith, who began a ministry at this tiny church in Costa Mesa, California, during the heyday of the late-1960s hippie counterculture. The Smiths took the Gospel message to the hippie hangouts and, in short order, their church became home to a growing array of converts seeking refuge from drug addiction and homelessness. In 1971, more and more so-called Jesus People converged on Calvary Chapel; Smith reportedly baptized 15,000 new converts within a few months. The church continued to grow, and numbers some 30,000 members today. It's what experts call a *megachurch*.

Chuck Smith is an important figure, since he illustrates the ways that fundamentalism, evangelicalism, and the charismatic movement sometimes overlap. He came to the ministry through the fundamentalist Foursquare Gospel Church, but grew frustrated with its doctrinal boundary making. You can see this emerging evangelical spirit in Calvary Chapel's statement of faith: "We are not a denominational church, nor are we opposed to denominations as such, only their overemphasis of doctrinal differences that have led to the division of the body of Christ." Pastor Smith preached directly from the Bible, reportedly starting at the beginning and moving through in two years, only to loop back and start again. Again, a rather evangelical way to go about the preaching task.

Evangelicals and charismatics moved quickly to respond to the youth counterculture in the 1970s, which today takes the form of sophisticated youth ministry programs in local churches with full-time staffs, multimedia technology, and copious programming efforts.

(Image credit Zondervan)

And yet Calvary Chapel is squarely in the middle of the charismatic movement as well. Its literature puts it plainly: "We remain flexible and yielded to the Holy Spirit to direct our worship." The dominant symbol of the church is a dove descending from the heavens. Smith encourages speaking in tongues, but not as evidence of the baptism of the Holy Spirit; that evidence, he says is agape-style love. Services are low-key with Pastor Smith giving the stage to church members who play music of their own making.

In fact, Calvary Chapel pioneered the praise and worship music common in many charismatic and evangelical churches today. These songs offer simple praises to God for transforming lives of believers. Calvary Chapel produced music books, records, and song sheets under the Maranatha! label, which replaced older Baptist, Wesleyan, and Lutheran hymns with simple praise music. And praise music provided the sound track to the youth-group experiences of the last few generations of Christian teenagers.

Although it disavows denominations, Calvary Chapel comes close to something like franchising by affiliating itself with 1,000 other churches. Most are called Calvary Chapel. There is no headquarters, no list of doctrines, and no national conference. But Smith operates Calvary Chapel Bible College with extension campuses, which provides a mechanism for communicating a common vision. These characteristics apply to other evangelical and charismatic franchises, like the Maranatha Christian Churches with its 65 locations throughout the world (mostly in the United States) and the International Churches of Christ with 89 churches.

Vineyard Christian Fellowship

Calvary Chapel blurs the lines between evangelical and charismatic, as does the Vineyard Christian Fellowship. This network grew out of the Calvary Chapel organization in the 1980s, and is now one of the fastest-growing pseudo-denominations around, with some 850 Vineyard Fellowships active throughout the world.

The Vineyard story begins with a group of Calvary Chapel pastors and lay leaders in the mid-1970s, who came to believe that all the gifts of the Holy Spirit are in operation today. If Calvary Chapel approved of speaking in tongues, the dissidents went further to claim that healing, prophecy, and exorcism should also be practiced. Kenn Gulliksen planted a new church in Los Angeles in 1974 (with the name of Vineyard) with Calvary Chapel–style worship and a fuller range of Spirit-led phenomena. Soon, other churches came along, and in 1982, Pastor John Wimber led his Calvary Chapel congregation into the Vineyard fold.

Edifications

The charismatic movement is one of the reasons experts consider the United States to be so deeply religious compared to other countries. During the Iraq war in 2003, Americans came to think of the British as kindred spirits when most other developed nations disagreed with the war. Yet, according to a recent Gallup Poll, only 17 percent of British citizens say that religion is "very important" in their lives, while the U.S. number is a whopping 57 percent.

Wimber brought a certain acumen for expansion and church planting to this small network of southern California churches. Earlier in his career, he taught evangelism and church growth at Fuller Theological Seminary as an adjunct instructor, and came into contact with the work of well-known evangelical church-growth expert Donald McGavaran. Wimber helped to organize Vineyard Ministries International and *First Fruits* magazine, and in 1985, formed something akin to a denominational organization with the Association of Vineyard Churches.

During a *Christianity Today* interview before he passed away in 1997, Wimber made it clear that his theology came mostly from conservative Protestant writers. He listed as his heroes Carl F. H. Henry, F. F. Bruce, J. I. Packer, and even John Wesley. But Wimber believed that the evangelicals in this list neglected the Holy Spirit in their theology, leaving little room for miraculous demonstrations of the Holy Spirit's power in congregational worship and in the lives of believers.

But when does Spirit-driven worship cross the line? Wimber and the Association of Vineyard Churches think it happened with the so-called Toronto Blessing. An outbreak of holy laughing occurred at the Toronto Airport Vineyard in 1994, which then gave rise to healing, fainting in the Spirit, and other physical demonstrations of the Spirit. In turn,

Edifications

An outbreak of holy laughing occurred in Brownsville, Texas, a few years ago, with similar claims of revival by participants and counterclaims of enthusiastic excess by critics. Like the Toronto Blessing, the Brownsville visitation made national news and sparked pilgrimages of Christians seeking to share the experience.

these experiences led to something that hadn't been seen since the old days of the Azuza Street Revival in 1906: Pentecostal tourism. Hundreds of thousands of people flocked to Toronto to witness the phenomena and perhaps take part (the church facilitates this travel by helping seekers with hotel and travel arrangements). But the Vineyard organization withdrew its endorsement because of what one critic called "bizarre phenomena" at the church. The church renamed itself Toronto Airport Christian Fellowship and followed the footsteps of Roberts, Jakes, Robertson, and other empire builders with Revival Live Network, *Spread the Fire Magazine*, and *Catch the Fire* radio ministry.

With the full communion movement of the mainline denominations, and the non-denominational tendencies of the evangelical and charismatic movements, are denominations headed for extinction?

(Photo by the author)

Setting aside the Toronto issue, are Vineyard churches the face of Christianity tomorrow? It's hard to argue against the numbers. The charismatic movement is sweeping the planet, and church after church in the United States is moving in the direction of the church-growth philosophies of Chuck Smith, John Wimber, and Willow Creek's Bill Hybels. This means the local church will get user-friendly, with dozens of niche-oriented ministries, few potentially alienating rituals or symbols, a freer style in worship, and a soft-pedaling of intellectual components of the faith. As Hybels himself has said, "Growing the church is the hope of the world." Even if that means the thunderous theological debates and hard-nosed denominational boundary making of the last few hundred years has to take a long vacation.

The Least You Need to Know

♦ Early charismatics differed from classic Pentecostals in two important ways: They tended to operate within established denominations and they tended to disagree with Pentecostals that speaking in tongues is a sign of a second blessing after salvation.

♦ The early approval of the Vatican to charismatic practices helped to give the charismatic movement a major lift in the 1970s.

♦ Protestant charismatics like Oral Roberts, Pat Robertson, and T. D. Jakes built ministry empires that played an important role in the phenomenal rise of conservative Protestant Christianity in the last decade.

♦ Modern charismatics don't keep nonbelievers away from the church to maintain purity; quite the contrary, they want the lost to come in and feel the presence of the Holy Spirit.

Appendix A

Words to Pray By

acolyte   A person who lights the candles in church.

amillennial   View of the last things that doesn't insist that the thousand-year reign of Christ on earth mentioned in Revelation chapter 20 must be taken literally.

Anabaptist   Literally, rebaptize; Protestants who believe that baptism should occur only after spiritual conversion.

Anglican   Christian who is a member of the worldwide Anglican Communion, which came from the Church of England.

apocalypse   Greek for "unveiling," in reference to the Book of Revelation, which details the events at the end of time.

apocrypha   Greek for "hidden things," and used by Protestants to refer to noncanonical books sometimes included in the Bible between the Old and New Testaments.

apostolic   In reference to Jesus' apostles, a word used by some Christians who consider their beliefs and practices to be the same as those of the first Christians.

archdiocese   A very large unit of administration in the Roman Catholic and Orthodox churches.

Arianism The belief that Jesus was made by God, and is therefore a lesser deity; this view was condemned by a large council of church leaders in 325 C.E., but still surfaces from time to time.

Armageddon The final battle between good and evil predicted in the Book of Revelation.

Arminian A person who believes that all people can be saved and therefore rejects the doctrine of predestination.

Ash Wednesday By tradition, the first day of Lent.

atonement The process by which God and man are reconciled through Jesus Christ.

autocephalous Self-governing; used in reference to Orthodox Churches in different nations.

baptism Christian rite that signifies initiation into the church.

Bible college A postsecondary institution popular among conservative Protestants that prepares students for full-time Christian service.

biblical inerrancy Doctrine that the Bible is without error in the original autographs, or manuscripts.

bishop A clerical official who oversees a number of priests and parishes.

Book of Common Prayer Manual used by Anglican Communion churches to guide congregations and direct worship.

Book of Mormon Sacred text of the Church of Jesus Christ of Latter-Day Saints, translated by Joseph Smith Jr. in the 1830s.

born again Term used to describe the experience of spiritual crisis and sudden conversion, followed by profound inner transformation.

bruderhof Communal farm of the Hutterites.

caesaropapism Belief that civil rulers should administer religious affairs.

canon Books of the Bible accepted as sacred by ecumenical councils of the church. Also refers to church law in several denominations.

capital sins Fundamental sins that lead to other sins in Roman Catholic usage, like envy and pride.

cardinal One of a body of powerful advisers to the Roman Catholic pope; also head of a very large diocese outside Rome.

catechism   Formal period of religious instruction prior to initiation in the church.

cathedral   By tradition, the seat of a bishop who administers a large diocese.

catholic   A member of the Roman Catholic Church; sometimes used to refer to the Christian church in its universal sense, pertaining to things held in common by all Christians.

charismatic   One who believes in demonstrations of *charisma*, Greek for gifts, in reference to gifts of the Holy Spirit.

chiliasm   From the Latin root for "thousand," used in reference to expectation of the imminent return of Jesus to earth.

Christian contemporary music   Gospel music produced since the 1970s with rock and folk-rock influences.

communion   Protestant term for Eucharist, or the sacrament of bread and wine taken in remembrance of Christ.

confession   Practice of admitting sins, believed to be necessary for reconciliation with God.

confession of faith   Written documents used in the Protestant family to express and defend core doctrines.

confirmation   Ceremonial rite in Roman Catholicism and liturgical Protestant denominations that denotes membership in the church.

congregational   A form of denominational organization that gives congregations a high degree of local control.

consecration   Act of separating something from the secular or profane, used in reference to the Eucharist and ordination.

convincement   Refers to a believer's conscious decision to listen to the Inner Light and follow its leadings in the Quaker tradition.

covenant theology   A system of changing relationships between God and man identified by students of John Calvin in the Reformed tradition.

creed   From the Latin word *credo* ("I believe"), a short statement of authorized beliefs.

crismation   Orthodox rite of confirmation, administered along with baptism at infancy.

deacon   In the Roman Catholic Church, an individual ordained to assist the parish priest during mass; in Protestant churches, an officer who typically organizes help for the needy.

denomination   An array of individual churches that are organized into a formal association.

diocese   A midrange unit of administration in the Roman Catholic, Orthodox, and Episcopal churches composed of a number of local parishes.

disestablishment   The act of rendering all churches and sects officially equal within a sovereign state.

disownment   Practice in the Quaker tradition of publicly severing ties to an apostate member.

dispensationalism   A system for understanding the sequence of different arrangements between God and man revealed in the Bible.

doctrine   A principle taught as the official belief of a church or sect.

ecumenical council   Meetings of church leaders representing the entire Christian faith.

ecumenical patriarch   Spiritual leader of the Orthodox Church.

ecumenism   An effort to build unity among Christian denominations.

elder   Local church officials with supervisory duties in discipline and teaching.

entire sanctification   Wesleyan Methodist view of God's grace, which eradicates sin and empowers believers to live without sinning.

episcopal   A form of denominational organization in which bishops administer large districts composed of numerous individual churches.

eschatology   The area of Christian theology that addresses the end of time and eternity.

establishment   A church that is the official church for a nation.

eucharist   The sacrament of bread and wine taken in remembrance of Christ.

evangelical   Greek for "good news," typically used in relation to churches that stress preaching the gospel of Jesus to the unsaved.

excommunication   The practice of excluding a believer from membership in the church.

extreme unction   Roman Catholic sacrament of anointing the sick.

filioque clause   Portion of Nicene Creed added in the seventh century that said the Holy Spirit proceeded from both the Father and the Son.

free church   A church that refuses to recognize the authority of an officially sponsored church hierarchy.

full communion   Policy among mainline Protestant denominations of recognizing one another's confessions, ministerial ordination, and membership standards.

full gospel   Pentecostal belief in Spirit baptism with signs of speaking in tongues and faith healing.

fundamentalism   Traditionalist Protestant movement that stressed deity of Christ, inerrancy of the Bible, and purity of the church.

gathered church   A belief that the church membership should be limited to those who've made a personal commitment to Jesus.

General Baptists   Baptists who hold the Arminian position, that all people can be saved.

gifts of the Spirit   Pentecostal and charismatic idea that the Holy Spirit empowers believers to heal, speak in unknown tongues, and perform other miracles.

glossolalia   The phenomenon of speaking in an unknown language by means of divine power or inspiration.

Great Awakening   One of two major periods of church growth and innovation in the United States, one in the 1730s and 1740s, and the other in the 1830s and 1840s.

Hail Mary   A traditional Catholic prayer often performed as penance.

heresy   Belief that contradicts established doctrine.

holiness   Nineteenth-century movement that stressed complete moral perfection of the individual.

icon   An image of Christ or revered figure, commonly used in Orthodox churches.

indulgence   A declaration by priests in the Roman Catholic Church that the penalties for sins have been erased.

Inner Light   In Quaker usage, the element of God's spirit that is found in every human soul.

intercession   An act taken on one's behalf by another.

invisible church   A set of humans and spiritual beings that are included in God's spiritual kingdom.

Jesuits   Order of Roman Catholic priests founded after the Reformation to defend and spread the Catholic faith.

just war   A war that some Christians believe is justified, so long as it meets certain criteria.

layperson   An individual who is not set apart from others in the church by special rites of ordination.

Lent   A 40-day period of fasting and prayer before Easter.

liberal theology   Movement that revised doctrines of original sin, predestination, and the meaning of Christ's death and resurrection.

liturgy   The arrangement of the elements of worship for church services.

mainline   Protestant churches with the longest histories in the United States.

mass   Roman Catholic religious service built around the observance of the Eucharist.

Maundy Thursday—Last Thursday before Easter, which commemorates the Last Supper.

meetinghouse—In Quaker usage, term used to identify place where religious services are held.

megachurch   Churches that number in the thousands and are designed to appeal to a broad spectrum of believers.

metropolitan   Orthodox priest who serves as a bishop in a major city or provincial capital.

millenarian   Literal belief in a coming thousand-year reign of Christ on earth.

Missionary Baptist   Baptists who organized denominational mission agencies.

Mother Church   First Church of Christ, Scientist in Boston, Massachusetts.

mysticism   The practice of intensive prayer and meditation to obtain an intimate experience of God.

national convention   Policy-making assembly in denominations with a representative form of government.

nonconformist   Religious dissenter in nations that have an official version of Christianity.

ordination   Special rite that sets apart a member of the clergy from the remainder of the church body.

Ordnung   German for "discipline," used in Amish practice in reference to rules for correct living.

orthodoxy   Combination of Greek words for "right" (or "true") and "opinion," in reference to established belief or doctrine.

pacifism   Belief that war cannot be justified by Christian principles.

papal infallibility   Roman Catholic doctrine that the pope cannot err when determining policy or doctrine for the church.

parish   A single congregation in Roman Catholic and Episcopal usage.

parochial school   From the Latin, *parochia*, meaning parish, in reference to a local school operated by a church.

penance   Contrition and penitence as part of forgiving sins in Roman Catholic practice.

Pentecostal   Conservative Protestants who stress immediate experience of the divine through baptism of the Holy Spirit.

perfection   Methodist belief in freedom from sins committed through conscious choice.

Pietism   Protestant movement that stressed the Bible, conversion, holy living, and avoidance of doctrinal wrangling.

postmillennial   A belief that places the Second Coming of Jesus after his thousand-year reign on earth.

predestination   Calvinist belief that it's God's will that some will be saved, and some will not.

premillennial   A belief that places the Second Coming of Jesus before his thousand-year reign on earth.

presbyterian   A form of denominational organization with ascending levels of representative government.

priest   A clergyman set apart from the body of laity through special rites of ordination and consecration.

priesthood of all believers   Protestant belief that each Christian is responsible for dealing with God on his or her own.

Primitive Baptists   Baptists who believed that denominational agencies threatened local church autonomy.

primitivism   A reaction against formal rituals and ceremonies that attempts to recreate the original practices of the church.

prophecy   In Pentecostal usage, the Spirit-given ability to see the unseen.

purgatory   In Roman Catholicism, a place of temporary punishment for sins that haven't been fully absolved during one's lifetime.

rapture   Event predicted by conservative Protestants in which the living saints are snatched away just prior to the coming tribulation.

rector   Parish priest in the Episcopal Church.

reformed   Theological tradition that traces its roots to John Calvin.

Regular Baptist   Baptists who believe in the Calvinist notion of predestination.

religious orders   Special groups of consecrated men and women who serve the Roman Catholic Church.

religious priests   Roman Catholic clergy who take special vows of poverty, chastity, and abstinence and who belong to one of the religious orders.

revival   A type of meeting common among Protestants designed to present the Gospel to nonbelievers and secure conversions.

rite   A religious observance in Catholicism, Orthodoxy, and Episcopal churches.

rosary   A set of prayers in use among Roman Catholics to encourage meditation on the life, death, and resurrection of Jesus Christ and the work of his mother, Mary.

sacrament   Observances and practices that are thought to convey God's grace to believers.

saints   Venerated heroes of the faith in heaven capable of interceding for believers, according to Roman Catholic usage.

sanctification   Doctrine of complete purification of oneself from sin.

schism   A formal separation of a church or denomination into two or more groups.

sect   In Christian usage, a group of believers who practice a version of Christianity other than the established version.

seminary   An institution of higher learning designed to train candidates for ministry.

session   The basic unit of government for each local church in the Reformed denominations, composed of active elders.

shunning The practice of complete social ostracism of apostates in Amish congregations.

social gospel A late-nineteenth-century movement among clergy to apply Christian principles to social problems.

solas Reformation-era belief that the faith rested in Scripture alone, faith alone, and grace alone.

stake A district-level body in Mormon usage, responsible for administering an array of local congregations.

synod A region-level unit of ecclesiastical governance in Lutheran and Reformed denominations.

theotokos The Mother of God, in reference to veneration of Mary in Roman Catholicism and Orthodoxy.

toleration The extension of religious freedom to religious sects in countries with established churches.

tractarians Anglicans who made favorable comparisons between the Church of England and the Roman Catholic Church.

transubstantiation Roman Catholic teaching that Eucharistic elements transform into the body and blood of Christ.

Trinity The ancient doctrine of the church that God is one in three persons, Father, Son, and Holy Spirit.

Unitarian A doctrine that rejects the Trinity and denies the divinity of Jesus Christ.

Universalism The view that all human beings will be saved.

vespers Evening religious observances in Roman Catholic, Orthodox, and liturgical Protestant churches.

vestry The basic unit of government for each local congregation in the Episcopal Church.

vicar In Anglican usage, a priest who performs service to a local parish.

visible church Those who attend religious services or maintain good standing in the church, in Protestant usage.

ward A local congregation in the Mormon denomination.

Further Readings

Christianity has a simple message of forgiveness of sin and reconciliation with God, and yet Christian practices can vary over time and across cultural boundaries. The large number of internal divisions within the Christian faith can seem terribly complicated to outsiders (and many insiders too!). Here you'll find books that explain the differences among the various Christian denominations. If you follow your interests through these readings, you'll come to a better understanding of the richness and vitality of the world's largest religion.

General

You can find dozens of general guides, reference works, and encyclopedias that provide one-stop shopping for information about the Christian faith, and here is a sampling:

Askew, Thomas A., and Peter W. Spellman. *The Churches and the American Experience: Ideals and Institutions.* Grand Rapids, Michigan: Baker Book House, 1984.

Barrett, David B. *World Christian Encyclopedia.* Oxford: Oxford University Press, 1982.

Jenkins, Peter. *Next Christendom: The Coming of Global Christianity.* New York: Oxford University Press, 2002.

Losch, Richard R. *The Many Faces of Faith: A Guide to World Religions and Christian Traditions.* Grand Rapids, Michigan: Wm. B. Eerdmans Publishing Co., 2001.

Mead, Frank. *Handbook of Denominations in the United States,* 11th ed. Nashville: Abingdon Press, 2001.

Stott, John R. W. *Basic Christianity,* rev. ed. Grand Rapids, Michigan: Wm. B. Eerdmans Publishing Co., 1986.

Catholics

Here are a few books that will get you started on the Roman Catholic Church, including a few that address developments within the last two or three years:

Dues, Greg. *Catholic Customs & Traditions: A Popular Guide.* Mystic, Connecticut: Twenty-Third Publications, 1989.

Dulles, Avery. *The Catholicity of the Church.* New York: Oxford University Press, 1988.

———. *What is Catholicism?: Hard Questions—Straight Answers.* Huntington, Indiana: Our Sunday Visitor, 1999.

Gibson, David. *The Coming Catholic Church: How the Faithful are Shaping a New American Catholicism.* San Francisco: HarperSanFrancisco, 2003.

Hastings, Adrian, ed. *Modern Catholicism: Vatican II and After.* New York: Oxford University Press, 1991.

Keating, Karl. *What Catholics Really Believe.* San Francisco: Ignatius Press, 1995.

Kreeft, Peter. *Catholic Christianity: A Complete Catechism of Catholic Beliefs Based on the Catechism of the Catholic Church.* San Francisco: Ignatius Press, 2001.

Steinfels, Peter. *A People Adrift: The Crisis of the Roman Catholic Church in America.* New York: Simon and Schuster, 2003.

Sullivan, Francis. *The Church We Believe In: One, Holy, Catholic, and Apostolic.* Mahwah, New Jersey: Paulist Press, 1999.

Orthodox

The Orthodox tradition goes all the way back to the first century after Christ, so here's a selection of books that will help you navigate its long and storied history:

August, Colleen Carroll. *The New Faithful: Why Young Adults Are Embracing Christian Orthodoxy*. Chicago: Loyola Press, 2002.

Bria, Ion. *Martyria and Mission*. Geneva: World Council of Churches, 1980.

Hakaras, Stanley S. *Let Mercy Abound: Social Concern in the Orthodox Church*. Brookline, Massachusetts: Holy Cross Orthodox Press, 1982.

Losch, Richard R. *The Many Faces of Orthodoxy*. Chicago: Loyola Press, 2002.

Ugolnik, Anthony, and Richard J. Mouw. *The Illuminating Icon*. Grand Rapids, Michigan: Wm. B. Eerdmans Publishing Co., 1989.

Ware, Timothy. *The Orthodox Church*. New York: Penguin Books, 1993.

Zizioulas, John D. *Eucharist, Bishop, Church: The Unity of the Church in the Divine Eucharist and the Bishop During the First Three Centuries*. Brookline, Massachusetts: Holy Cross Orthodox Press, 2001.

Episcopalians

In many ways, the Episcopal Church has been a bellwether of social, cultural, and political change in the United States, and these books will help you to understand why:

Bernardin, Joseph B. *Introduction to the Episcopal Church*. Harrisburg, Pennsylvania: Morehouse Publishing, 1992.

Crew, Louie. *101 Reasons to Be an Episcopalian*. Harrisburg, Pennsylvania: Morehouse Publishing, 2003.

McConnell, S. D. *History of the American Episcopal Church*. London: A. R. Mowbray & Co., 1891.

Rowell, Geoffrey, et al. *Love's Redeeming Work: The Anglican Quest for Holiness*. New York: Oxford University Press, 2001.

Schmidt, Richard H. *Glorious Companions: Five Centuries of Anglican Spirituality.* Grand Rapids, Michigan: Wm. B. Eerdmans Publishing Co., 2002.

Webber, Christopher L. and Frank T. Griswold III. *Welcome to the Episcopal Church: An Introduction to Its History, Faith, and Worship.* Harrisburg, Pennsylvania: Morehouse Publishing, 1999.

Unitarians

This selection of readings will help you to understand the relationship between Unitarianism and other branches of the Christian faith:

Buehrens, John A. *A Chosen Faith: An Introduction to Unitarian Universalism.* Boston: Beacon Press, 1998.

Bumbaugh, David E. *Unitarian Universalism: A Narrative History.* Chicago: Meadville Lombard Press, 2001.

Williams, George Huntston. American Universalism, 4th ed. Boston: Skinner House Books, 2002.

Lutherans

Scholars use Lutheranism as a case study of how European religious groups adapted to the new American setting, which is detailed in these books:

Baepler, Walter A. A Century of Grace: A History of the Missouri Synod (1847–1947). St. Louis: Concordia Publishing House, 1947.

Braaten, Carl E. *Principles of Lutheran Theology.* Minneapolis: Fortress Press, 1983.

Gritsch, Eric W. *Fortress Introduction to Lutheranism.* Minneapolis: Fortress Press, 1994.

Jensen, J. M. *The United Evangelical Lutheran Church: An Interpretation.* Minneapolis: Augsburg Fortress Publishers, 1964.

Knudsen, Johannes. *The Formation of the Lutheran Church in America.* Minneapolis: Fortress Press, 1978.

Lutz, Charles P. *Church Roots: Stories of Nine Immigrant Groups That Became the American Lutheran Church.* Minneapolis: Augsburg Fortress Publishers, 1985.

Nichol, Todd W. *All These Lutherans: Three Paths Toward a New Lutheran Church.* Minneapolis: Augsburg Fortress Publishers, 1986.

Reformed Denominations

If you want to learn more about the United Church of Christ, the Christian Reformed Church, and the several Presbyterian denominations, start here:

Gunnemann, Louis H., and Charles Shelby Rooks. *The Shaping of the United Church of Christ: An Essay in the History of American Christianity.* New York: Pilgrim Press, 1999.

Hart, D. G. *Recovering Mother Kirk: The Case for Liturgy in the Reformed Tradition.* Grand Rapids, Michigan: Baker Books, 2003.

Lingle, Walter Lee, and John W. Kuykendall. *Presbyterians, Their History and Beliefs.* Louisville: John Knox Press, 1988.

McKim, Donald K. *Introducing the Reformed Faith: Biblical Revelation, Christian Tradition, Contemporary Significance.* Louisville: Westminster John Knox Press, 2001.

Smylie, James H. *A Brief History of the Presbyterians.* Louisville: Geneva Press, 1996.

Von Rohr, John. *The Shaping of American Congregationalism: 1620–1957.* New York: Pilgrim Press, 1992.

Wells, David F. *Reformed Theology in America: A History of Its Modern Development.* Grand Rapids, Michigan: Wm. B. Eerdmans Publishing Co., 1985.

Mennonites, Amish, Brethren

Few stories are as compelling as the story of the Anabaptist movement that gave birth to the Mennonite, Amish, and Brethren denominations; read all about it in these books:

Bender, Harold S. *Anabaptist Vision.* Scottsdale, Pennsylvania: Herald Press, 1994.

Fetters, Paul R. *Trials and Triumphs: History of the Church of the United Brethren in Christ.* Huntington, Indiana: Church of the United Brethren in Christ, 1984.

Hostetler, John A. *Amish Society.* Baltimore: Johns Hopkins University Press, 1993.

Kraybill, Donald B. *The Riddle of Amish Culture.* Baltimore: Johns Hopkins University Press, 1989.

Kraybill, Donald B., and Carl F. Bowman. *On the Backroad to Heaven: Old Order Hutterites, Mennonites, Amish, and Brethren.* Baltimore: Johns Hopkins University Press, 2001.

Schlabach, Theron F. *Peace, Faith, Nation: Mennonites and Amish in Nineteenth-Century America.* Scottsdale, Pennsylvania: Herald Press, 1988.

Wenger, J. C. *What Mennonites Believe.* Scottsdale, Pennsylvania: Herald Press, 1991.

Williams, George Huntston. *The Radical Reformation.* Philadelphia: Westminster Press, 1962.

Baptists

Everywhere you look you'll find Baptists, and if you want to learn more about their beliefs and practices, these should get you started:

Allen, C., and L. Mays, eds. *Encyclopedia of Southern Baptists.* Nashville: Baptist Sunday School Board, 1984.

Ammerman, Nancy T. *Baptist Battles: Social Change and Religious Conflict in the Southern Baptist Convention.* New Brunswick, New Jersey: Rutgers University Press, 1990.

Brackney, W. H. *The Baptists.* Oxford: Greenwood Press, 1988.

George, Timothy, and David S. Dockery, eds. *Theologians of the Baptist Tradition.* Nashville: Broadman and Holman Publishers, 2001.

Hankins, Barry. *Uneasy in Babylon: Southern Baptist Conservatives and American Culture.* Tuscaloosa, Alabama: University of Alabama Press, 2002.

Lumpkin, W. H., ed. *Baptist Confessions of Faith*. Valley Forge, Pennsylvania: Judson Press, 1981.

McBeth, Leon H. *The Baptist Heritage: Four Centuries of Baptist Witness*. Nashville: Broadman Press, 1986.

McKinney, Lora-Ellen, and H. Beecher Hicks. *Total Praise: An Orientation to Black Baptist Belief and Worship*. Valley Forge, Pennsylvania: Judson Press, 2003.

Methodists

Numerous denominations got their start in the Methodist Church, so if you know more about Methodism, you'll have mapped a large region of the religious landscape! Here are a few starting points:

Allen, Charles Livingstone. *Meet the Methodists: An Introduction to the United Methodist Church*. Nashville: Abingdon Press, 1998.

Campbell, Dennis M., William Lawrence, and Russell E. Richey, eds. *Doctrines and Discipline: Methodist Theology and Practice*. Nashville: Abingdon Press, 2001.

Campbell, James T. *Songs of Zion: The African Methodist Episcopal Church in the United States and South Africa*. Chapel Hill, North Carolina: University of North Carolina Press, 1998.

Campbell, Ted A. *Methodist Doctrine: The Essentials*. Nashville: Abingdon Press, 1999.

Ferguson, Charles W. *Organizing to Beat the Devil*. Garden City, New Jersey: Doubleday Publishing, 1971.

Heitzenrater, Richard P. *Wesley and the People Called Methodists*. Nashville: Abingdon Press, 1994.

Langford, T. A. *Wesleyan Theology: a Sourcebook*. Durham, North Carolina: Labyrinth Press, 1984.

McAnally, Thomas S. *Questions and Answers About the United Methodist Church*. Nashville; Abingdon Press, 1995.

Quakers

Find out what the Quakers believe about silence, peace, and simplicity in these books:

Bainton, Roland H. *Christian Attitudes Toward War and Peace: A Historical Survey and Critical Re-Evaluation.* Nashville: Abingdon Press, 1979.

Bill, J. Brent, ed. *Imagination and Spirit.* Richmond, Indiana: Friends United Press, 2002.

Punshon, John. *Reasons for Hope: The Faith and Future of the Friends Church.* Richmond, Indiana: Friends United Press, 2001.

Punshon, John, and Matthew Fox. *Encounter with Silence: Reflections from the Quaker Tradition.* Richmond, Indiana: Friends United Press, 1997.

Pym, John. *Listening to the Light: How to Bring Quaker Simplicity and Integrity into Our Lives.* London: Rider, 2000.

Steere, Douglas, ed. *Quaker Spirituality: Selected Writing.* Mahwah, New Jersey: Paulist Press, 1984.

Trueblood, D. Elton. *The People Called Quakers.* Richmond, Indiana: Friends United Press, 1980.

Whitmire, Catherine. *Plain Living: A Quaker Path to Simplicity.* Notre Dame, Indiana: Sorin Books, 2001.

Holiness and Pentecostal Churches

Make no mistake about it: Few denominations are as important to Christianity in the United States as the family of denominations in the Holiness and Pentecostal tradition. Find out why in this selection of readings:

Anderson, Robert M. *Vision of the Disinherited: The Making of American Pentecostalism.* Peabody, Massachusetts: Hendrickson Publishers, 1979.

Bartleman, F. *Azusa Street.* South Plainfield, New Jersey: Bridge Publishing, 1980.

Blumhofer, Edith L. *Restoring the Faith: The Assemblies of God, Pentecostalism, and American Culture.* Urbana and Chicago: University of Illinois Press, 1993.

Burgess, Stanley M., and Gary B. McGee, eds. *Dictionary of Pentecostal and Charismatic Movements*. Grand Rapids, Michigan: Zondervan Publishing, 1988.

Chavda, Mahesh. The Hidden Power of Speaking in Tongues. Shippensburg, Pennsylvania: Destiny Image, 2003.

Cox, Harvey. *Fire from Heaven: The Rise of Pentecostal Spirituality and the Reshaping of Religion in the 21st Century*. Cambridge: DeCapo Press, 2001.

Dayton, Donald W. *Theological Roots of Pentecostalism*. Peabody, Massachusetts: Hendrickson Publishers, 1987.

Hollenweger, Walter J. *Pentecostalism: The Origins and Developments Worldwide*. Peabody, Massachusetts: Hendrickson Publishers, 1997.

Synan, Vinson. *The Holiness-Pentecostal Movement in the United States*. Grand Rapids, Michigan: Wm. B. Eerdmans Publishing Co., 1971.

Wacker, Grant. *Heaven Below: Early Pentecostals and American Culture*. Cambridge: Harvard University Press, 2001.

Mormons

Among the fastest growing faiths in the world is Mormonism, so you'll be ahead of the curve if you read about their beliefs and practices in these books:

Arrington, Leonard J. *The Mormon Experience: A History of the Latter-Day Saints*. Urbana and Chicago: University of Illinois Press, 1992.

Bushman, Richard L. *Joseph Smith and the Beginnings of Mormonism*. Urbana and Chicago: University of Illinois Press, 1984.

Givens, Terryl. *By the Hand of Mormon: The American Scripture That Launched a New World Religion*. New York: Oxford University Press, 2002.

Lee, Rex E. *What Do Mormons Believe?* Salt Lake City: Deseret Books, 1992.

McConkie, Bruce R. *Mormon Doctrine*. Salt Lake City: Bookcraft Publishers, 1966.

Ostling, Richard N. *Mormon America: The Power and the Promise*. San Francisco: HarperSanFrancisco, 1999.

Shipps, Jan. *Mormonism: The Story of a New Religious Tradition*. Urbana and Chicago: University of Illinois Press, 1985.

Millenarian Churches

These denominations specialize in apocalyptic thinking, which is on the rise today—learn more about them in the following books:

Francis, Richard. *Ann the Word: The Story of Ann Lee, Female Messiah, Mother of the Shakers, the Woman Clothed with the Sun*. New York: Penguin, 2002.

Gerstner, John H. *Teachings of Seventh-Day Adventism*. Grand Rapids, Michigan: Baker Book House, 1983.

Knight, George R. *Millenial Fever and the End of the World: A Study of Millerite Adventism*. Oakland: Pacific Press Publishing Association, 1994.

Land, Gary. *Adventism in America*. Berrian Springs, Michigan: Andrews University Press, 1998.

Penton, James M. *Apocalypse Delayed: The Story of the Jehovah's Witnesses*. Toronto: University of Toronto Press, 1988.

Christian Science

Millions of people are interested in the relationship between spirituality and health, and so are Christian Scientists! Find out what they have to say in these readings:

Gill, Gillian. *Mary Baker Eddy*. New York: Perseus Publishing, 1999.

Gottschalk, Stephen. *The Emergence of Christian Science in American Religious Life*. Berkeley, California: University of California Press, 1974.

Schult, Kenneth E. *God's Zion*. Overland Park, Kansas: Leathers Publishing, 1998.

Fundamentalism

Here you'll get a good start in understanding the most important, but most misunderstood, movements in American Christianity in the last century:

Ammermann, Nancy T. *Bible Believers: Fundamentalists in the Modern World*. New Brunswick, New Jersey: Rutgers University Press, 1987.

Capps, Walter H. *The New Religious Right: Piety, Patriotism, and Politics*. Columbia, South Carolina: University of South Carolina Press, 1990.

Carpenter, Joel A. *Revive Us Again: The Reawakening of American Fundamentalism*. New York: Oxford University Press, 1999.

Heyrman, Christian Leigh. *Southern Cross: The Beginnings of the Bible Belt*. Chapel Hill, North Carolina: University of North Carolina Press, 1998.

Marsden, George M. *Fundamentalism and American Culture: The Shaping of Twentieth-Century Evangelicalism, 1870–1925*. New York: Oxford University Press, 1993.

Martin, William. *With God on Our Side: The Rise of the Religious Right in America*. New York: Broadway Books, 1997.

Evangelicalism

Experts agree that evangelical Christianity is a potent force in American politics and culture, and you can find out more about this nondenominational movement in the following books:

Graham, Billy. *Just As I Am*. New York: HarperCollins, 1997.

Hart, D. G. *That Old Time Religion: Evangelical Protestantism in the Twentieth Century*. Chicago: Ivan R. Dee, Inc., 2002.

Marsden, George M. *Understanding Fundamentalism and Evangelicalism*. Grand Rapids, Michigan: Wm. B. Eerdmans Publishing Co., 1991.

Noll, Mark A. *American Evangelical Christianity: An Introduction*. Oxford: Blackwell Publishers, 2000.

Smith, Christian. *American Evangelicalism: Embattled and Thriving*. Chicago: University of Chicago Press, 1998.

Webber, Robert E. *The Younger Evangelicals: Facing the Challenges of the New World*. Grand Rapids, Michigan: Baker Book House, 2002.

Charismatic Movement

After Catholicism, the charismatic fellowship is the largest body of Christians in the world; get some insight into what may become the world's dominant variant of Christianity in these readings:

Beverley, James A. *Holy Laughter and the Toronto Blessing*. Grand Rapids, Michigan: Zondervan, 1995.

Cordes, Paul Josef. *Call to Holiness: Reflections on the Catholic Charismatic Renewal*. Collegeville, Minnesota: Liturgical Press, 1997.

Harrell, David Edwin. *Oral Roberts: An American Life*. Bloomington, Indiana: Indiana University Press, 1985.

Herzog, Davis. *Mysteries of the Glory Unveiled: A New Wave of Signs and Wonders*. Hagerstown, Maryland: McDougal Publishing Company, 2000.

Poewe, Karala. *Charismatic Christianity as a Global Culture*. Columbia, South Carolina: University of South Carolina Press, 1994.

Synan, Vinson. *Century of the Holy Spirit: 100 Years of Pentecostal and Charismatic Renewal, 1901–2001*. Nashville: Nelson Reference, 2001.

Websites of Christian Denominations

Finding Christianity-related information on the web is easy! Any search engine can direct you to thousands of sites that can help you learn about Christian history, beliefs, symbols, and practices. But you can also find official sites for numerous Christian denominations that operate in the United States. They'll inform you about their background, doctrines, programs, and contact information. Here are more than fifty web addresses to help you get started.

Catholics

- ◆ National Council of Catholic Bishops—www.nccbuscc.org

- ◆ The Vatican—www.vatican.va

Orthodox

- ◆ Orthodox Church in America—www.oca.org

- ◆ Greek Orthodox Archdiocese of America—www.goarch.org

- ◆ Armenian Church in America—www.armenianchurch.org

Episcopalians

- Church of England—www.cofe.anglican.org
- Episcopal Church in the U.S.A.—www.episcopalchurch.org

Lutherans

- Evangelical Lutheran Church in America—www.ecla.org
- Lutheran Church—Missouri Synod—www.lcms.org
- Wisconsin Evangelical Lutheran Synod—www.wels.org

Reformed Denominations

- Presbyterian Church in America—www.pca.net
- Presbyterian Church (U.S.A.)—www.pcusa.org
- Free Reformed Churches of North America—www.frcna.org
- Reformed Church in America—www.rca.org
- Christian Reformed Church—www.crcna.org

Mennonites, Amish, Brethren

- Mennonite Church—www.mennonites.org
- Fellowship of Grace Brethren Churches—www.fgbc.org
- General Conference of Mennonite Brethren—www.usmb.org
- Brethren in Christ—www.bic-church.org
- Evangelical Free Church of America—www.efca.org
- Moravian Church—www.moravian.org

Baptists

- American Baptist Churches in the U.S.A.—www.abc-usa.org
- National Baptist Convention, U.S.A., Inc.—www.nationalbaptist.com

- General Association of Regular Baptist Churches—www.garbc.org
- Southern Baptist Convention—www.sbc.net
- National Missionary Baptist Convention of America—www.nmbca.com
- National Primitive Baptist Convention—www.natlprimbaptconv.org

Methodists

- United Methodist Church—www.umc.org
- African Episcopal Methodist Church—www.aemcnet.org
- Christian Methodist Episcopal Church—www.c-m-e.org
- Congregational Methodist Church—www.congregationalmethodist.net
- Evangelical Congregational Church—www.eccenter.com
- Evangelical Methodist Church—www.emchurch.org
- Primitive Methodist Church—www.primitivemethodistchurch.org
- Southern Methodist Church—www.southernmethodistchurch.org

Quakers

- Evangelical Friends International—www.evangelical-friends.org
- Religious Society of Friends (Conservative)—www.quaker.org
- Friends General Conference—www.fgcquaker.org
- Friends United Meeting—www.fum.org

Holiness-Pentecostal Churches

- Assemblies of God—www.ag.org
- Church of God in Christ—www.cogic.org
- New Apostolic Church—www.newapostolicchurch.com
- Apostolic Christian Church—www.accfoundation.org
- Apostolic Faith Church—www.apostolicfaith.org

- Church of the Nazarene—www.nazarene.org

- Church of God (Holiness)—www.cogn.net

- Wesleyan Church—www.wesleyan.org

- Church of God of Prophesy—www.cogop.org

- Church of the Living God—www.cotlg.net

- Congregational Holiness Church—www.chchurch.com

- International Church of the Foursquare Gospel—www.foursquare.com

- United Pentecostal Church International—www.upci.org

- International Pentecostal Holiness Church—www.iphc.org

- Open Bible Standard Churches, Inc.—www.openbible.org

- Pentecostal Church of God—www.pcg.org

- Pentecostal Free Will Baptist—www.pfwb.org

Mormons

- Church of Jesus Christ of Latter-day Saints—www.lds.org

- www.morman.org (official site for nonmembers)

- Church of Christ (Temple Lot)—www.cofchrist.org

Millenarian Churches

- Seventh-Day Adventist—www.adventist.org

- Jehovah's Witnesses—www.watchtower.org

Christian Science

- Christian Scientists—www.tfccs.org

Index

S

T

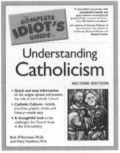

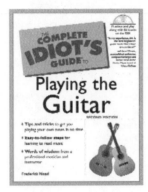

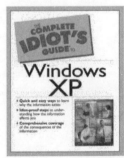